AEPS

**_Assessment, Evaluation, and
Programming System for
Infants and Children_**

Edited by **Diane Bricker, Ph.D.**

VOLUME 4

AEPS Curriculum
for Three to Six Years

D1608807

AEPS

Assessment, Evaluation, and Programming System for Infants and Children

VOLUME 4

AEPS Curriculum
for Three to Six Years

Edited by

Diane Bricker, Ph.D.

and

Misti Waddell, M.S.

College of Education
University of Oregon

Content developed by

**Liz Twombly, M.A., Kristine Slentz, Ph.D.,
Vicki Swanson, M.S., Val Oldham, M.A.,
and Younghee Kim, M.A.**

·P A U L·H·
BROOKES
PUBLISHING CO.

Baltimore • London • Toronto • Sydney

Paul H. Brookes Publishing Co.
Post Office Box 10624
Baltimore, Maryland 21285-0624

Typeset by Signature Typesetting & Design, Baltimore, Maryland.
Manufactured in the United States of America by
BookCrafters, Chelsea, Michigan.

The following AEPS lforms can be purchased separately; these separate packages are printed in different colors.

AEPS Data Recording Forms, Three to Six Years (printed in black; sold in packages of 10)

AEPS Family Report, Three to Six Years (printed in brown; sold in packages of 10)

AEPS Family Interest Survey (printed in blue; sold in packages of 30)

AEPS Child Progress Record, Three to Six Years (printed in green; sold in packages of 30)

To order, contact Paul H. Brookes Publishing Co., Post Office Box 10624, Baltimore, Maryland 21285-0624 (1-800-638-3775).

Please see page ii for information about other volumes in the AEPS series, all available from Paul H. Brookes Publishing Co.

The Assessment, Evaluation, and Programming System for Infants and Children was developed in part with support from Grants #G008400661 and #H024C80001 from the U.S. Office of Education and Grant #09DD0019 from the Department of Health and Human Services to the Center on Human Development, University of Oregon. The content, however, does not necessarily reflect the position or policy of DOE or the University of Oregon, and no official endorsement of these materials should be inferred.

Library of Congress Cataloging-in-Publication Data

Assessment, evaluation, and programming system for infants and children / Diane
   Bricker, editor.
     p.   cm.
   Includes bibliographical references and index.
   Contents: v. 1. AEPS measurement for birth to three years.
   ISBN 1-55766-095-6 (v. 1)
   1. Assessment, Evaluation, and Programming System   2. Child development—
Testing.   3. Child development deviations—Diagnosis.   I. Bricker, Diane D.
RJ51.D48A87   1992
155.4'028'7—dc20
                                             92-6690
                                               CIP

ISBN 1-55766-188-X   Vol. 4
British Library Cataloguing-in-Publication data are available from the British Library.

CONTENTS

CONTRIBUTORS

THE EDITORS

Diane Bricker, Ph.D., Early Intervention Area, 5253 University of Oregon, Eugene, Oregon 97403-5253. Dr. Bricker is Professor of Special Education and a highly respected, well-known authority in the field of early intervention. She has directed a number of national demonstration projects and research efforts focused on examining the efficacy of early intervention; the development of a linked assessment, intervention, and evaluation system; and the study of a comprehensive, parent-focused screening tool. She presently directs the Early Intervention Area, and is Associate Dean for Academic Programs, College of Education, University of Oregon.

Misti Waddell, M.S., Research Assistant and Project Coordinator, Early Intervention Area, 5253 University of Oregon, Eugene, Oregon 97403-5253. Ms. Waddell is a research assistant with the University of Oregon's Early Intervention Area and has contributed to the development, research, and training of the AEPS since the early 1980s. She has used the AEPS in classroom settings and has coordinated several federally funded, field-initiated research projects and outreach training projects. She is the project coordinator for the field-initiated research project titled "A Study of the Psychometric Properties of the Assessment, Evaluation, and Programming Test for Three to Six Years."

CONTENT DEVELOPED BY

Liz Twombly, M.A., Research Assistant, Early Intervention Area, 5253 University of Oregon, Eugene, 97403-5253

Kristine Slentz, Ph.D., Assistant Professor, Western Washington University, Mail Stop 9090, Bellingham, Washington 98225

Vicki Swanson, M.S., Consultant, PACE Options, 5255 University of Oregon, Eugene, Oregon 97403-5255

Val Oldham, M.A., Research Assistant, BASE Program, 5253 University of Oregon, Eugene, Oregon 97403-5253

Younghee Kim, M.A., Doctoral Candidate, Early Intervention Area, 5253 University of Oregon, Eugene, Oregon 97403-5253

ACKNOWLEDGMENTS

While immersed in the development of the *Assessment Evaluation and Programming System (AEPS) for Infants and Children Measurement* and *Curriculum for Birth to Three Years* (Volumes 1 and 2), requests began to appear for similar materials for the developmental range from 3 to 6 years. Although we were reluctant to expand our measurement- and curriculum-development activities, it became increasingly difficult to ignore requests for similar materials for children whose developmental level exceeded 3 years. Taking a deep breath, we plunged into the extension of the AEPS system for children 3–6 years. The *AEPS Measurement* and *Curriculum for Three to Six Years* (Volumes 3 and 4) are the result.

As with the *AEPS Curriculum for Birth to Three Years* (Volume 2), the present volume is a collaborative effort. The many individuals who assisted in the creation of this curriculum are committed to the development of content, activities, and strategies to assist interventionists in delivering quality services to young children and their families.

A number of people who contributed to the development of this curriculum deserve special mention. Juliann Cripe provided the initiative and motivation to begin work on the curriculum. Sheryl Norstad edited early versions of curriculum items, and the final format reflects some of her ideas. Kimberly Megrath contributed substantially to the initial development of the Fine Motor and Gross Motor Domains. Megrath's extensive knowledge in the area of motor development and her practical experience working with young children provided useful ideas and suggestions for integrating children with a wide range of motor abilities into a variety of group activities. Elizabeth LaCroix edited later versions of the curriculum, made substantial contributions to reorganizing the content, and added to the sections on working with children with motor disabilities. A special thanks is due to Debra Hamilton for her suggestions about working with children with visual impairments. Lorraine Duke provided the concurrent goals listed for each curriculum item as well as many examples included in the goals section. Sue Taylor and Susan Petterson contributed to the development of group and individual activity plans and schedules based on their classroom experience. Katherine Sariego was responsible for conducting the many telephone interviews with individuals who had piloted earlier versions of the curriculum. The efforts of Sariego's work and the information provided by all pilot users are reflected in this version of the curriculum. Many thanks to Elena Marshall and Karen Lawrence, who so willingly worked on many rounds of revisions.

The editors extend special thanks to the many students, children, and caregivers who have used the curriculum items and provided feedback on their clarity, usefulness, and effectiveness. We sincerely hope that the material contained in this volume will enhance intervention efforts with a broad range of children who are at risk for or have disabilities and their families.

PREFACE

Development of the *Assessment, Evaluation, and Programming System (AEPS) for Infants and Children* began in the mid-1970s and has continued to the mid-1990s. The original work focused on the developmental range from birth to 3 years and included the creation of a measurement system (*AEPS Measurement for Birth to Three Years;* Volume 1) and an associated curriculum (*AEPS Curriculum for Birth to Three Years;* Volume 2). The success of the AEPS system for infants and toddlers led to the extension of the system to cover the developmental range from 3 to 6 years. Work began on the test and associated curriculum for the developmental range from 3 to 6 years in the late 1980s and continued to the present. As with Volumes 1 and 2, the development and testing of the *AEPS Measurement for Three to Six Years* (Volume 3) and the *AEPS Curriculum for Three to Six Years* (Volume 4) have taken considerably longer to complete than was anticipated. The development of Volumes 3 and 4 has not proceeded along a singular path. In particular, the *AEPS Curriculum for Three to Six Years* has, like its predecessor, Volume 2, evolved through a series of stages and changes to its present content and form.

The format used for Volume 3 replicates that for Volume 1. The major changes are a shift in the content from items appropriate for the birth to 3 years developmental range to items for the 3–6 years developmental range. The domains remain the same, and structuring of the strands, goals, and objectives is consistent from Volume 1 to Volume 3.

Although the format for the measurement volume has remained consistent, both format and content in the associated curricula vary. Volume 2 provides introductory material designed to help the reader use the curricular materials contained in the volume. Introductory information is followed by curricular domains. The domains contain descriptions of the goals and objectives taken from Volume 1. For each goal/objective, an associated developmental programming step is listed.

Volume 4 begins with introductory material similar to that contained in Volume 2; however, the section on using the curriculum provides an array of information on the use of recommended intervention practices not contained in Volume 2. In addition, the domains are structured differently. Goals and objectives are described, accompanied by a variety of intervention suggestions; however, developmental programming steps are not included. Volume 4 offers the user suggestions for planned activities and provides information on other preschool curricula that target a particular goal or objective. This change was deemed appropriate for two reasons.

First, as children's development progresses, their repertoires become more varied, requiring the formulation of an unwieldy number of programming steps. Second, a variety of curricula of demonstrated usefulness already exist for the preschool child. Rather than ignore these valuable resources, the AEPS curriculum was designed to help interventionists use a variety of preschool curricular materials to develop effective intervention activities for children.

As with Volumes 1 and 2, the profits from the sale of Volumes 3 and 4 will be directed to a fund to provide support for the continued study and refinement of both the test and the curriculum. Future work will be directed to improving the content and format to better meet the needs of young children who are at risk for or have disabilities and their families.

Diane Bricker
August 1996

AEPS

Assessment, Evaluation, and Programming System for Infants and Children

Edited by **Diane Bricker, Ph.D.**

VOLUME 4

AEPS Curriculum for Three to Six Years

Introduction

The importance of early experience for young children has long been recognized and has been the foundation for early intervention programs designed for young children who have or who are at risk for disabilities. Early intervention programs have evolved into comprehensive approaches that produce positive change in the lives of participating children and their families. In large measure, the increasingly positive outcomes engendered by early intervention programs have occurred because of the growing sophistication of personnel, curricular materials, and assessment/evaluation tools. The assessment, intervention, and evaluation system described in this volume is an example of this growing sophistication, which will enhance future intervention efforts with young children in need of services.

Accompanying the growth in the number of early intervention programs is the improvement in the quality of personnel and tools. This growth has been systematically spurred on by the passage of important federal legislation, beginning with the Education for All Handicapped Children Act (PL 94-142), which was signed into law in 1975. This landmark legislation required public schools to accept all school-age children, no matter how severe their disability, and it introduced the concept of the individualized education program (IEP). In 1990, PL 101-476 reauthorized the Education for All Handicapped Children Act and changed the name to the Individuals with Disabilities Education Act (IDEA). Eleven years after the original enactment of PL 94-142, the Education of the Handicapped Act Amendments of 1986 (PL 99-457) extended the mandate for public school programs to 3-, 4-, and 5-year-old children with disabilities and offered states incentives to serve infants and toddlers. PL 99-457 strongly urged the inclusion of families as partners in the development of intervention plans, known as individualized family service plans (IFSPs), and in the delivery of services to their children. A further amendment, the Individuals with Disabilities Education Act Amendments of 1991 (PL 102-119) further encourages family participation, permits states to move away from the use of categorical labels for preschoolers, and permits the inclusion of children at risk for disabilities in intervention programs. A growing number of state mandates to provide services to infants and young children who have disabilities and to their families has accompanied this series of important federal enactments.

As noted, increased sophistication in the delivery of services has paralleled the growth of early intervention programs. Personnel are better prepared, curricular content is improved, intervention techniques are more effective, and assessment and evaluation approaches are more appropriate and useful. It is important to note that there has been a move to develop approaches that are cohesive, coordinated, and comprehensive. Approaches that treat program components as isolated and unrelated units are being replaced by approaches that systematically link the major components of assessment, intervention, and evaluation. The Assessment, Evaluation, and Programming System (AEPS) is one such linked approach.

1

WHAT IS THE ASSESSMENT, EVALUATION, AND PROGRAMMING SYSTEM?

The AEPS offers a variety of related materials that enhance the direct linkage among assessment outcomes, intervention activities, and evaluation strategies. The AEPS is referred to as a system because its components work together to assist interventionists and caregivers in developing functional and coordinated assessment, intervention, and evaluation activities for young children who have or are at risk for disabilities. The AEPS is a comprehensive and linked system that includes assessment/evaluation, curricular, and family participation components for the developmental range from birth to 6 years. The AEPS is divided into two developmental levels: birth to 3 years and 3–6 years, as shown in Figure 1. As indicated, the materials designed for the developmental range from birth to 3 years are contained in Volumes 1 and 2 while the materials designed for the developmental level from 3–6 years are contained in Volumes 3 and 4.

Volume 1 contains the measurement materials including the child test items divided by areas (e.g., fine motor, cognitive), associated Data Recording Forms, AEPS Family Report, and tools to assist caregivers in selecting intervention targets and in monitoring child progress. Volume 2 contains associated curricular materials designed to link directly to the child's performance on the AEPS Test.

As shown in Figure 2, the Assessment, Evaluation, and Programming System for Three to Six Years mirrors the materials developed for the developmental range from birth to 3 years and has a measurement component (Volume 3) and a curricular component (Volume 4). The *AEPS Measurement for Three to Six Years* (Volume 3) includes the AEPS Test and Data Recording Forms, which are the assessment and evaluation portion of the system; the AEPS Family Report, which is an assessment/evaluation measure to be completed by the child's caregivers; the AEPS Child Progress Record, which is a measure to assist families in monitoring their child's progress; and the AEPS Family Interest Survey, which details the family's priorities, concerns, and resources. The *AEPS Curriculum for Three to Six Years* (Volume 4) is described in the next section.

Volume 3, *AEPS Measurement for Three to Six Years,* is divided into three sections. Section I provides a comprehensive description of the Assessment, Evaluation, and Programming System. Section II presents the AEPS Test items, composed of the six domains that cover the developmental period from 3 to 6 years. Section III describes how to involve families in the assessment and evaluation process as well as providing specific strategies and forms for doing so.

The AEPS Test includes skills from across all domains of development that are important to independent functioning in the home, community, and school environ-

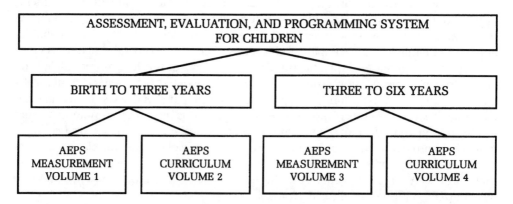

Figure 1.   Components of the Assessment, Evaluation, and Programming System.

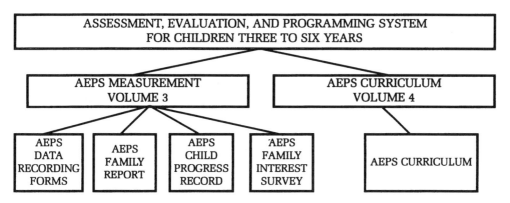

Figure 2.   Components of the Assessment, Evaluation, and Programming System for Three to Six Years.

ments of young children. The AEPS Test for Three to Six Years contains a series of test items that are appropriate intervention targets in the areas of Fine Motor, Gross Motor, Adaptive, Cognitive, Social-Communication, and Social skills for children functioning developmentally between 3 and 6 years of age. Each goal and objective represents a class of behaviors rather than a specific skill. Skills are grouped in related areas (strands) and are sequenced in a logical teaching order. For example, rather than teaching the child to cut out a certain number of specific shapes, AEPS Test goals and objectives are sequenced from cutting paper to cutting straight lines to cutting curved lines.

AEPS Test results provide a comprehensive summary of a youngster's strengths and weaknesses, as a point of departure for caregivers and interventionists to make decisions about IEP/IFSP goals and objectives. Accurate assessment results, family input from the AEPS Family Report, and family resources and priorities obtained from the AEPS Family Interest Survey are essential elements for developing accurate, functional, individualized goals and objectives and then moving to intervention activities with the AEPS Curriculum.

Volume 3 also contains summarized psychometric information on the AEPS Test, a series of IEP/IFSP goals and objectives specifically related to each item on the AEPS Test, and a set of Assessment Activity Plans.

The AEPS Test and Curriculum, when used together, will provide a systematic link between programmatic assessment, IEP/IFSP development, intervention activities, and evaluation.

INTRODUCTION TO VOLUME 4

Volume 4, *AEPS Curriculum for Three to Six Years,* is the curricular component of the second level of the Assessment, Evaluation, and Programming System and was developed for two purposes. First, the AEPS Curriculum provides interventionists (e.g., teachers, child development specialists, occupational therapists, physical therapists, psychologists, communication specialists) and caregivers with a range of activities that can be used to facilitate children's acquisition of functional and generalizable skills. Second, the AEPS Curriculum provides a direct link among assessment, intervention, and evaluation. The AEPS Test and AEPS Curriculum were developed to provide a direct and ongoing correspondence among initial assessment, IEP/IFSP development, program planning, intervention activities, and subsequent evaluation.

Target Population

The children for whom the AEPS Test and Curriculum for Three to Six Years are appropriate present a broad range of intervention needs. Some will be children with identified developmental disabilities such as Down syndrome, spina bifida, or cerebral palsy. Others will exhibit delays attributed to chronic health conditions or unknown causes. The AEPS is appropriate for children who live in high-risk conditions such as poverty and parental addiction. Whatever the cause, the resultant impairments in early skill development require systematic intervention. The content of the AEPS Test for Three to Six Years includes functional skills for children whose development is in the 3- to 6-year range. This test is appropriate for children who have or are at risk for a wide range of disabilities. Use of the AEPS Test and Curriculum with children whose chronological age exceeds 8 years may require modification of content.

Children with severe disabilities will likely have a team (e.g., occupational therapist, physical therapist, communication specialist, physician, special educator, service coordinator) who will be involved in developing strategies for intervention. The *AEPS Curriculum for Three to Six Years* lends itself well to a team approach because it presents a variety of formats for embedding individualized objectives, cues, prompts, and correction procedures within activities that are fun and interesting to children.

Overview of the AEPS Curriculum Content

Volume 4, *AEPS Curriculum for Three to Six Years,* contains five sections. Section I describes the linked systems approach to assessment, intervention, and evaluation using the AEPS systems. Section II, the Curriculum Administration Guide, explains in detail how to use the AEPS Curriculum in conjunction with the AEPS Test. The direct link between the AEPS Curriculum and Test permits efficient movement between the two. Section III describes how to plan and implement the curriculum using an activity-based approach to early intervention. This section includes information about classroom design and strategies for working with children of varying developmental levels. Section IV presents specific intervention strategies for each goal in the Fine Motor, Gross Motor, Adaptive, Cognitive, Social-Communication, and Social domains of the AEPS Test. Finally, Section V introduces a variety of activities that can be used for embedding children's goals during intervention programming.

The content of the AEPS Test for Three to Six Years is less hierarchical than the AEPS Test for Birth to Three Years. This change reflects an increase in the influence of individual experience and environmental factors on the preschool child's development. As children approach school age, they show more individuality and variability in learning new skills. The AEPS Curriculum for Three to Six Years reflects the diverse sequences through which preschool-age children acquire and combine new skills. The AEPS Curriculum for Three to Six Years differs from the objective-by-objective format characteristic of the AEPS Curriculum for Birth to Three Years. The curriculum for older children includes a more general and flexible set of considerations, strategies, and activities. The AEPS Curriculum for Three to Six Years relies on the interventionist to individualize each child's program and encourages the interventionist to explore other available preschool curricula for additional ideas and suggestions.

The AEPS Curriculum for Three to Six Years emphasizes an activity-based approach to enhance the behavioral repertoires of young children. Child-initiated activities, daily routines, environmental arrangements, and planned activities are adopted as the contexts for intervention. Focusing on functional skills and motivating activities is ideal for program settings that integrate children with developmental delays and disabilities and those without. Because the AEPS Curriculum capitalizes on child-initiated activities, daily routines, environmental arrangements, and planned activities rather than direct instruction of specific skills, it is well suited for use in community-based preschools or child care settings.

Although intervention services for preschool children are often classroom based, some children may receive intervention at home, in hospitals, and in community child care settings. The AEPS Curriculum for Three to Six Years has been designed to accommodate a wide range of service delivery locations and models.

A wealth of curricular material exists for preschool and kindergarten children. General suggestions to develop curricula for young children are readily available, as well as suggestions for teaching specific skills. The AEPS Curriculum for Three to Six Years is designed to complement, rather than replace, the many useful curricula that exist for preschool and kindergarten populations.

REFERENCES

Education for All Handicapped Children Act of 1975, PL 94-142. (August 23, 1977). 20 U.S.C. §1400 *et seq.*
Education of the Handicapped Act Amendments of 1986, PL 99-457. (October 8, 1986). 20 U.S.C. §1400 *et seq.*
Individuals with Disabilities Education Act of 1990, PL 101-476. (October 30, 1990). 20 U.S.C. §1400 *et seq.*
Individuals with Disabilities Education Act Amendments of 1991, PL 102-119. (October 7, 1991). 20 U.S.C. §1400 *et seq.*

Understanding the AEPS Curriculum

AN ACTIVITY-BASED APPROACH

The AEPS Curriculum was designed to accommodate an approach to early intervention known as activity-based intervention. The AEPS Curriculum provides information to the interventionist that encourages integration of goals and objectives into a child's daily activities and life experiences. The format of the AEPS Curriculum emphasizes child-initiated, routine, and planned activities as vehicles for addressing a child's selected goals and objectives.

The activity-based intervention approach was designed to take advantage, in an objective and measurable way, of natural instruction that parents and other caregivers use with their young children:

> Activity-based intervention is a child-directed, transactional approach that embeds intervention on children's individual goals and objectives in routine, planned, or child-initiated activities, and uses logically occurring antecedents and consequences to develop functional and generative skills. (Bricker & Cripe, 1992, p. 40)

Two features of this approach should be emphasized. First, multiple targets (e.g., motor, communication, social, cognitive, adaptive) can be addressed in single activities. For example, an art activity in which children are assembling materials can be used to promote communication ("Where is the paper?"), social skills (distributing materials to other children), adaptive skills (gathering the materials), motor skills (reaching and grasping), and cognitive skills (deciding what materials are missing). In the Planned Activities section of the AEPS Curriculum (located in the Domain Goals section of each domain), activities are included that illustrate how opportunities to embed each goal and its associated objectives may occur in a planned activity. The section entitled Concurrent Goals (also located in the Domain Goals section of each domain) helps identify the goals that can be targeted during a single activity. Incorporating multiple goals into one activity is preferable to developing a separate activity for each goal.

A second feature of activity-based intervention is the inherent reward for children when they participate in fun and interesting activities. If the activities are child selected, they should provide ample motivation for the child and artificial contingencies may be eliminated. Section V of the AEPS Curriculum provides a description of a variety of activities that preschool-age children will likely find fun.

The advantages of using an activity-based format with young children are many. First, the notion of providing relevant antecedents and consequences within an activity is incorporated into teaching functional skills in the child's usual environment. When the antecedents and consequences are relevant and are part of an activity, motivation and attention problems tend to be less frequent. Second, activity-based intervention addresses the issues of generalization and maintenance. Teaching a particular skill is not limited to just one activity; rather, the skill can be taught by a variety of interventionists and family members across different materials and settings. Third, an activity-based approach helps keep targeted objectives functional for the child. If the skills selected for intervention are targeted in daily activities, they are likely to be useful to the child in coping with environmental demands. A fourth advantage is that, when skill training is embedded in daily activities, other people, such as caregivers and peers, can be used as change agents and teaching resources. Fifth, activity-based intervention can be used with a heterogeneous group of young children. Children can act as peer models for one another and can be involved in presenting antecedents and consequences. For example, in a store activity, children can play different roles (e.g., clerk, customer). Joan can select a variety of objects from the shelves and Bill can ask her to pay for them. Other children can model Joan's and Bill's behavior or engage in other activities such as placing cans on the shelves, counting pennies, or naming foods to be purchased. Such activities promote children's participation and independence.

An activity-based approach teaches skills by embedding children's targeted goals and objectives into functional, routine activities of interest to children. For example, rather than establish special sessions to teach labeling of objects, items are named in the context of a relevant activity. Naming body parts might occur naturally during bath time, items of clothing can be named when dressing or during doll play, and labeling foods and eating utensils can be easily worked into snack or mealtimes. The child can practice the target skill of cutting out shapes with curved lines during an art activity.

AEPS Curriculum users who would like more information on how to employ activity-based intervention are referred to *An Activity-Based Approach to Early Intervention* (Bricker & Cripe, 1992).

LINKING ASSESSMENT, INTERVENTION, AND EVALUATION[1]

The AEPS Curriculum provides a direct link among assessment, intervention, and evaluation. Assessment refers to the process of establishing a baseline or entry-level measurement of the child's skills and desired family outcomes. The assessment process should produce the necessary information to select appropriate and relevant intervention goals and objectives and desired family outcomes. Figure I.1 illustrates the relationship of these three processes as well as the desired participation of professionals and family members in each. The assessment-intervention-evaluation system can be divided into six phases:

[1]Adapted from Bricker, D., Janko, S., Cripe, J., Bailey, E., & Kaminski, R. (1989). *Evaluation and programming system: For infants and young children.* Eugene: University of Oregon, Center on Human Development.

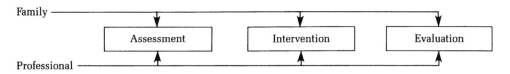

Figure I.1. Schematic of a linked assessment-intervention-evaluation approach that includes professional and family participation.

Phase One:	Initial assessment
Phase Two:	Formulation of IEPs or IFSPs
Phase Three:	Intervention
Phase Four:	Ongoing monitoring for immediate feedback on individualized intervention procedures
Phase Five:	Quarterly evaluation of children and families
Phase Six:	Annual or semiannual evaluation of individual child and family progress and program effectiveness for total groups and subgroups of children such as those at risk for or with disabilities

These phases are discussed briefly in the following sections. A more detailed description is presented in Bricker (1993) and Cripe, Slentz, and Bricker (1993).

Phase One: Initial Assessment

The link among assessment, intervention, and evaluation begins with the entry of children into an intervention program. The major objective of the initial assessment is to formulate a useful and appropriate IEP/IFSP.

In the initial assessment, a program-relevant (e.g., curriculum-based) assessment is administered to determine the content of the IEP/IFSP. This content provides the road map for moving children from their beginning skill repertoires to the acquisition of skills specified as annual goals in their IEP/IFSP. For the family, this initial assessment should help determine priority interests to be developed into family outcomes. An accurate assessment of a child's beginning skill level is crucial to the formulation of a useful IEP/IFSP, so that an intervention plan can be developed to improve problem areas. An assessment that measures functional skills and is sensitive to the conditions in which a child is most likely to perform a skill will facilitate the development of appropriate and useful IEPs/IFSPs. For this reason, the authors developed the AEPS Test for Three to Six Years.

Formulation of an IFSP allows opportunities for family outcomes as well as child goals. Family assessment should yield program-relevant information that will aid in developing functional outcome statements, but the process and tools should not be intrusive to family members. A family interest checklist, such as the Family Interest Survey in Volume 3 (*AEPS Measurement for Three to Six Years)*, and an interview are recommended to assist families in developing outcomes they consider relevant and important to their child and family.

Phase Two: Formulation of the IEP/IFSP

The IEP/IFSP will be based primarily on information accumulated during the initial assessment period. (Results from this testing should be validated at the first quarterly evaluation.) Relevant information is obtained from caregivers' knowledge of their children as well as from professional observation and testing. This initial information is used to develop a plan of action for the interventionists and caregivers to identify specific content areas that the IEP/IFSP will address. The IEP/IFSP should be straightforward so that it can be used as a guide for interventionists and caregivers. It can also be used as a criterion against which success of the intervention is evaluated.

The child's portion of the IEP/IFSP itemizes goals, objectives, and a time frame for meeting the selected goals. The family's portion of the IFSP contains a statement of family resources, concerns, and priorities related to enhancing the child's development, based on the family's identification of their interests and needs. Collaborative discussion with appropriate family members establishes priorities. A set of outcome statements evolves from these priorities, and activities, resources, and a timeline for reaching outcomes are all specified. Further information on the development of IEPs/IFSPs can be found in Chapter 5 of Bricker (1993).

Phase Three: Intervention

Once the IEP/IFSP has been formulated by caregivers and interventionists, the actual intervention activities can be initiated. The child's performance on the program assessment indicates where intervention should begin, and items the child is unable to perform become the intervention goals and objectives. Goals and objectives often require prioritization, and, if the assessment tool links directly to a curriculum, such as the AEPS, interventionists can efficiently locate the activities developed to facilitate acquisition of specific goals and objectives. The AEPS provides a direct correspondence between the assessment items (skills) identified as goals or objectives and the intervention content and strategies specified in the associated curriculum. (See Section II for an example of how to link assessment outcomes from the AEPS Test to training activities in the AEPS Curriculum.)

Phase Four: Ongoing Monitoring

A useful IEP/IFSP specifies both the tasks to be conducted and the manner in which success is to be evaluated. A variety of strategies may be used for daily or weekly monitoring of child progress (e.g., trial by trial, brief probes during or after intervention activities). Specific goals or objectives, program resources, and the need for daily or weekly monitoring to keep intervention efforts on track will all determine the strategies selected.

Phase Five: Quarterly Evaluation

Quarterly evaluations should focus on determining the effect of intervention efforts on objectives specified in the IEP/IFSP. This can be done by using the initial assessment measures (e.g., readministration of the AEPS Test) in conjunction with the weekly data collection. Quarterly evaluations should be used to compare the child's progress with some standard or expectation for progress. Without assigning expected completion dates for objectives and goals, it is difficult to determine if the progress made by the child is acceptable.

Phase Six: Annual or Semiannual Evaluation

Annual or semiannual evaluations are used to evaluate the progress of individual children and families as well as the overall effectiveness of the program (i.e., group or subgroup analysis). Without subgroup comparisons, it is difficult to know how to improve intervention strategies for subpopulations of children and families. Methodological design and measurement problems that face the field of early intervention make subgroup evaluations difficult; however, analyses of subgroups may yield important findings on generalization of outcomes for selected groups of children and families.

SUMMARY

The AEPS Curriculum is designed to be used with an activity-based intervention approach. The curriculum emphasizes the use of routine and planned activities to develop children's targeted IEP/IFSP goals and objectives. An understanding of activity-based intervention serves as an excellent foundation for curriculum users.

The six phases of the linked system emphasize the importance of directly relating the processes of assessment, intervention, and evaluation. Employing this system allows efficient effort and use of resources, accountability in terms of program impact over time, and individualization through the design of programs specific to the needs of children and their families. Fundamental to such a system is an appropriate assessment/evaluation tool and an associated curriculum, such as the AEPS Test and AEPS Curriculum.

REFERENCES

Bricker, D. (Ed.). (1993). *Assessment, evaluation, and programming system for infants and children: Vol. 1. AEPS measurement for birth to three years.* Baltimore: Paul H. Brookes Publishing Co.

Bricker, D., & Cripe, J.J. (1992). *An activity-based approach to early intervention.* Baltimore: Paul H. Brookes Publishing Co.

Cripe, J., Slentz, K., & Bricker, D. (Eds.). (1993). *Assessment, evaluation, and programming system for infants and children: Vol. 2. AEPS curriculum for birth to three years.* Baltimore: Paul H. Brookes Publishing Co.

AEPS Curriculum Administration Guide

SECTION

II

The AEPS Curriculum contains intervention activities and strategies for each of the AEPS Test goals and objectives. The numbering system used in the AEPS Test and Curriculum permits the user to move directly from assessment or evaluation outcomes or both to appropriate and relevant intervention activities. For each AEPS Test assessment/ evaluation goal and objective, the AEPS Curriculum describes relevant intervention content and a variety of intervention strategies from naturalistic to adult guided. Prior to using the AEPS Curriculum, it is essential to read the administrative procedures in this section that describe the Curriculum's format and procedures for use.

The AEPS Curriculum has important features that make it compatible with the AEPS Test. First, the AEPS Curriculum provides intervention content that is directly tied to the IEP/IFSP goals developed from the AEPS Test results. Second, program information tied directly to assessment outcomes enhances efficiency of program staff. Third, the curricular content is focused on assisting program staff to target functional and useful skills. Finally, information provided in the AEPS Curriculum assists interventionists in implementing an activity-based intervention approach, which encourages generalization of learned skills through the integration of targeted goals into daily activities.

AEPS CURRICULUM FORMAT

The AEPS Curriculum is designed to be used in conjunction with the AEPS Test. The content of this test covers the domains of behavior and specific skills considered essential to independent functioning and coping with environmental demands for young children with developmental ages of 3–6 years. Six broad areas of development, or domains, are used in the AEPS Test and Curriculum: Fine Motor, Gross Motor, Adaptive, Cognitive, Social-Communication,

13

and Social. Each domain encompasses a set of skills or behaviors traditionally seen as related developmental phenomena.

The six domains are divided into a series of strands, which organize related groups of behaviors under a common category. Every strand contains a series of items called goals, which were developed as annual goals on a child's IEP/IFSP. Associated with each goal is an accompanying set of objectives that represents more discrete skills. These objectives enable the examiner to accurately pinpoint a child's level within a specific skill sequence and can be used as short-term objectives on IEPs/IFSPs.

The identification system associated with the strands (e.g., A, B), goals (e.g., 1.0, 2.0), and objectives (e.g., 1.1, 1.2) reflects the sequential arrangement of the test items on the AEPS Test. In addition, the numbering system helps AEPS Test users locate and refer to items.

The AEPS Curriculum follows the same identification system for strands, goals, and objectives as the AEPS Test, providing a direct correspondence between the assessment and the curriculum. The cross-referencing system in the AEPS Curriculum utilizes an abbreviated term for the name of the domain (e.g., SC for Social-Communication) and then the strand, goal, and objective are listed. For example, Soc A:1.3 refers to the Social Domain, Strand A, Objective 1.3; GM B:2.0 refers to the Gross Motor Domain, Strand B, Goal 2. Goals are identified by a number followed by a period and a zero, and objectives are identified by the number of the goal, a period, and then the number of the objective. The names of each domain are abbreviated as follows:

Fine Motor Domain:	FM
Gross Motor Domain:	GM
Adaptive Domain:	Adap
Cognitive Domain:	Cog
Social-Communication Domain:	SC
Social Domain:	Soc

Section IV of this curriculum contains goals, objectives, and associated training activities. Each of the six domains is divided into four main sections: Intervention Considerations, Suggested Activities, Using Activity-Based Intervention, and Domain Goals. An introductory section provides a summary of the domain content and a brief developmental overview of the domain. The Intervention Considerations section provides a description of strategies to be adopted to help children reach their IEP/IFSP goals and objectives. The Suggested Activities section provides general information on resources that will be helpful in addressing domain goals and objectives. The section titled Using Activity-Based Intervention provides suggestions for embedding targeted goals and objectives in daily occurring activities. The final section, Domain Goals, contains information appropriate to teaching each goal contained on the AEPS Test.

The Domain Goals section begins with a brief overview followed by a list of the strands and their associated goals and objectives. Next appear individual descriptions of the curriculum for each goal in the strand. Each of these goal pages contains the letter or number and a description of the strand, the goal, and its associated objectives, as well as the following information:

- *Concurrent Goals* lists other AEPS Test items that can be targeted while the child works on the current goal or associated objectives. This section identifies targets that can be combined into activities, rather than developing a specific activity for each targeted goal. This section is particularly helpful when developing group activity plans.

- *Daily Routines* provides a list of routine home and classroom events that may be useful training times. These routines are likely to provide opportunities for the child to practice targeted goals. Because home and classroom routines vary between settings and families, it is important that this section is adapted to meet individual child and family needs. (Daily Routines in Section III provides detailed information on developing a curriculum plan for home or school settings based on daily routines.)
- *Environmental Arrangements* lists examples of environmental arrangements that may offer opportunities to embed targeted goals and associated objectives during child-initiated, routine, and planned activities. Some strategies are specific to a targeted goal (e.g., providing button-up shirts in the dramatic play area to increase opportunities for children to practice buttoning), whereas other strategies are more general (e.g., providing fewer materials than children need to increase opportunities for children to request additional items). (Environmental Arrangements in Section III provides detailed information on arranging the classroom into activity centers.)
- *Planned Activities* offers strategies and suggestions for embedding targeted goals and associated objectives in planned activities. Planned activities should be fun and interesting and should have an accompanying explicit plan of instruction for individual youngsters. Interventionists should assemble materials and plan prompts, cues, and consequences necessary to provide frequent opportunities for targeted goals to be practiced within each activity. A list of activities likely to elicit domain skills can be found in Section V. (Planned Activities in Section III provides detailed information on writing activity plans.)
- *Preschool Curricula with Similar Goals* lists other preschool curricula that contain suggested activities, strategies, and ideas potentially useful in providing children opportunities to work on their targeted goal or objectives. For each listed curriculum, the section of particular relevance to the target goal is designated. Not all curricula are listed under each goal. (A list of these curricula with reference sources is provided in the Appendix to this volume.)

LINKING THE AEPS TEST WITH THE AEPS CURRICULUM

The strength of the AEPS and similar systems that foster a direct link between assessment, intervention, and evaluation activities is the assistance they provide caregivers and professionals in moving from assessment results to IEP/IFSP development, to intervention planning and implementation, and finally to evaluation. The steps to link child/family outcomes from the AEPS Test to the selection of intervention activities in the AEPS Curriculum are described below.

Step 1: The professional team completes the AEPS Test on the child while the parent or other caregiver completes the AEPS Family Report and AEPS Family Interest Survey. Completion of these tools is dependent on the family's interest in doing so.

Step 2: Team members and family members review results from the AEPS Test, Family Report, and Family Interest Survey. IEP/IFSP goals are selected and prioritized.

Step 3: Using the AEPS Curriculum, team members locate the appropriate section for each priority goal. They read the introduction and review suggestions given for concurrent goals, daily routines, environmental arrangements, planned activities, and other preschool curricula.

Step 4:   Using the information provided by the AEPS Curriculum, team members
           develop a program plan to address each selected goal or objective. (Section III
           provides information on developing program plans.)
Step 5:   Team members develop an individual or group activity schedule to guide the
           embedding of selected goals into routine and planned activities. (Section III
           provides information on developing activity schedules.)
Step 6:   Team members develop an activity plan for embedding selected child goals
           into specific activities that can be routine, planned, or child initiated. (Sec-
           tion III contains information on the development of activity plans.)

An example is provided to illustrate this stepwise progression. Sally is a 4-year-old
child with a developmental delay of unknown origin, making her eligible for early
intervention services in her community. Step 1 requires that, upon entry into the program, the intervention team members observe Sally over a 2-week period using the

---

AEPS   Adaptive Domain

Adaptive Domain

S = Scoring Key	Q = Qualifying Notes
2 = Pass consistently	A = Assistance provided
1 = Inconsistent	B = Behavior interfered
performance	R = Reported assessment
0 = Does not pass	M = Modification/adaptation
	D = Direct test

Name: **SALLY**

		Test Period:	**1**							
		Testing Date:	**6/95**		/		/		/	
		Examiner:	**NB**							
	IFSP	S	Q	S	Q	S	Q	S	Q
A. Dining									
1. Eats and drinks a variety of foods using appropriate utensils with little or no spilling		2							
1.1 Eats a variety of food textures		2							
1.2 Selects and eats a variety of food types		2							
1.3 Eats with fork and spoon		2							
2. Prepares and serves food		0							
2.1 Prepares food for eating		0							
2.2 Uses knife to spread food		1							
2.3 Pours liquid into a variety of containers		1							
2.4 Serves food with utensil		2							

Figure II.1.   Professionally completed protocol for a portion of the Adaptive Domain of the AEPS
for Sally.

AEPS   Adaptive Domain

Adaptive Domain

	6-95				date

1. Does your child eat and drink a variety of foods using forks, spoons, and other utensils with little or no spilling? (A1)

    Y

    (*Note:* If you scored Question 1 with an "S" or an "N," please indicate if your child is able to do a–c by placing a check mark beside the item.)

    ____ a. Does your child eat and drink foods of different textures? For example, your child eats or drinks soft food such as bananas, liquids such as milk, and hard foods such as raw vegetables. (A1.1)

    ____ b. Does your child choose to eat different kinds of food, such as dairy, meats, and fruit? (A1.2)

    ____ c. Does your child eat with a fork and spoon without much spilling? (A1.3)

2. Does your child help prepare and serve food? For example, your child removes peels and wrappers, uses a knife to spread soft foods, pours liquid, or uses a fork or spoon to serve food from one container to another. (A2)

    N

    (*Note:* If you scored Question 2 with an "S" or an "N," please indicate if your child is able to do a–d by placing a check mark beside the item.)

    ✓ a. Does your child remove peels and wrappers before eating food? For example, your child peels a banana and removes a candy wrapper. (A2.1)

    ____ b. Does your child use a knife to spread soft foods such as cream cheese or peanut butter onto bread or crackers? (A2.2)

    ____ c. Does your child pour liquid from one container into another, such as juice into a cup? (A2.3)

    ____ d. Does your child serve food from one container to another with a fork or spoon? For example, your child spoons applesauce from a jar into a bowl. (A2.4)

Y = Yes; S = Sometimes; N = Not Yet.

Figure II.2.   Portion of a parent-completed Adaptive section of the AEPS Family Report for Sally.

AEPS Test to guide their observations. During the same period, Sally's parents agree to complete the AEPS Family Report and AEPS Family Interest Survey.

At the scheduled IEP/IFSP meeting, the professional team and Sally's parents share and compare their findings (Step 2). Figure II.1 (on p. 16) shows the completed protocol of the Adaptive Domain from the professionally completed AEPS Test, and Figure II.2 (on p. 17) shows the parent-completed AEPS Family Report. An examination of Sally's performance on Strand A: Dining indicates that both parents and professionals agree that she reached criteria for Goal 1.0 (Eats and drinks a variety of foods using appropriate utensils with little or no spilling) but has not reached criteria for Goal 2.0 (Prepares and serves food). After discussing these outcomes, the parents and intervention team select Goal 2.0 as the IFSP goal for the Adaptive Domain. In addition, they choose Objectives 2.1, 2.2, and 2.3 as short-term objectives.

Step 3 requires reviewing the AEPS Curriculum section that relates directly to the Adaptive Domain, Strand A, Goal 2.0. Figure II.3 (on pp. 19–21) presents the portion of the curriculum that addresses this specific goal. The information provided by the AEPS Curriculum will assist the team in developing an appropriate program plan for Sally's Goal 2.0 (Step 4), an activity schedule (Step 5), and an activity plan (Step 6).

SUMMARY

This introductory material is included to set the stage for efficient and effective use of the AEPS Curriculum in conjunction with the AEPS Test. The user is urged to carefully read this material prior to employing the curriculum. In addition, the authors recommend that the AEPS Curriculum be used in association with the AEPS Test. Without accurate, in-depth knowledge of children's behavioral repertoires, selecting appropriate intervention activities is guesswork, as is monitoring progress. The field of early intervention has become, through legal, professional, and parental interest, a legitimate enterprise that should not tolerate less-than-quality outcomes. Producing these outcomes for children and families is dependent on careful and comprehensive assessments that lead to appropriate intervention accompanied by ongoing evaluation. Use of the AEPS Test and AEPS Curriculum may help interventionists attain this quality.

GOAL 2.0 Prepares and serves food

Objective 2.1	**Prepares food for eating**
Objective 2.2	**Uses knife to spread food**
Objective 2.3	**Pours liquid into a variety of containers**
Objective 2.4	**Serves food with utensil**

CONCURRENT GOALS

FM A:1.0   Manipulates two small objects at same time
SC A   Social-Communicative Interactions (all goals)
SC B   Production of Words, Phrases, and Sentences (all goals)
Soc A:2.0   Initiates cooperative activity
Soc B   Interaction with Environment (all goals)
Soc C:1.0   Communicates personal likes and dislikes

DAILY ROUTINES

Routine events that provide opportunities for children to prepare and serve food include

Mealtime
Snack time
Unstructured play time

Example   During snack, Latifa peels a banana, spreads peanut butter on bread, and pours juice from a small pitcher into her cup. Latifa's mother sits by her, providing verbal cues and the least level of physical assistance necessary for Latifa to prepare her snack. *(Adap A:2.0)*

ENVIRONMENTAL ARRANGEMENTS

- Arrange the classroom into activity areas that include a dramatic play center. Although a dramatic play center usually uses pretend foods, as a special treat the interventionist might provide real foods for the children to serve and eat. Include forks, spoons, knives, pitchers, and cups for children to practice preparing and serving food, with or without real food.
- Present materials during snack or mealtimes that provide opportunities for children to practice the following:

  - Preparing food (e.g., wrapped crackers, foods in containers, bananas with skin, hardboiled eggs with shell, cheese with plastic wrappers, closed soft drink cans)
  - Using a knife to spread (e.g., dull knives to spread peanut butter on bread, cream cheese on crackers, jam on toast)

(continued)

Figure II.3.   Goal 2.0 from Strand A (Dining) of the Adaptive Domain of the AEPS Curriculum.

Figure II.3.   *(continued)*

– Pouring liquid into containers (e.g., juice from a child-size pitcher into a cup, milk from a small bottle into a cup)
– Serving food with a utensil (e.g., scooping applesauce or yogurt into a bowl, spearing melon with a fork and transferring to a bowl or plate)

>   *Example*   Alice uses a knife to practice spreading cream cheese on a cracker. The interventionist uses verbal cues and the least level of physical assistance to prompt Alice to stabilize the cracker with her left hand while she spreads the cheese with her right. *(Adap A:2.2)*

- Positioning is an important consideration for children with motor impairments. Make sure the child is upright and well supported during mealtimes.
- Adaptations to materials may be necessary for children with special needs. Contact a qualified specialist for adaptation needs of children with sensory and/or motor impairments. Children with motor impairments may benefit from the use of nonslip surfaces to stabilize materials (e.g., bowls, plates) or by using utensils with built-up or shortened grips.

PLANNED ACTIVITIES

Two examples of how to embed this goal and the associated objectives within activities are presented here. For a complete set of activities that address goals and objectives across domains, see Section V.

Animal Cookies

Children make cookies with a favorite sugar cookie dough and animal cookie cutters. They can actively participate in making the cookies by opening containers, transferring ingredients from containers to the bowl, pouring liquids into the bowl, and stirring ingredients together. When the cookies have been baked, children can use dull knives to spread frosting or jam on them. Close supervision during cooking activities will ensure safety.

Fruit Animals

Children practice food preparation and serving skills while making animals from fruit. The interventionist can provide canned fruit such as pineapple slices, maraschino cherries, and pear halves, as well as sliced bananas, oranges, raisins, grapes, and apricot halves. Children create animals on paper plates using the pineapple rings or pear halves as faces, cherries or raisins for eyes, wedges of oranges or apricot halves for ears, and bananas for mouths. Children practice food preparation skills as they peel bananas, remove raisins from boxes, and spoon or spear fruit while transferring it from bowls to paper plates. Children eat their creations during snack time.

PRESCHOOL CURRICULA WITH SIMILAR GOALS

The following preschool curricula provide information on this goal or similar goals. Interventionists whose programs have access to one or more of these curricula may refer to the referenced sections for additional programming strategies.

(continued)

Figure II.3.   *(continued)*

The Carolina Curriculum for Preschoolers with Special Needs
Self-Help Skills
- Eating

High Scope—Young Children in ACTION
Active Learning
- Taking care of one's own needs

Portage Guide to Early Education Activity Cards
Self-Help
- Prepares own sandwich
- Uses knife
- Pours from pitcher
- Serves self at table

Using the AEPS Curriculum

This section is designed to assist interventionists in using the AEPS Curriculum by employing a naturalistic approach that emphasizes children's involvement in child-initiated, routine, and planned activities. The purpose of this section is to address a variety of topics that will assist the user in the understanding and application of the curriculum and will help interventionists establish a coordinated and cohesive approach to curricular programming.

CREATING EFFECTIVE LEARNING ENVIRONMENTS FOR CHILDREN

The content and strategies offered in this curriculum are designed to encourage child-initiated activities, encourage self-exploration and self-control, promote communication, support problem solving, enhance social and cooperative play, and build independence. The range of disability and delay exhibited by the children in a program should be considered when selecting the curricular content, intervention strategies, and environmental arrangements. Promoting effective learning in children with disabilities requires flexibility in approach, attention to the child's needs, and engagement in meaningful activities. Adopting such an approach requires that developmentally appropriate practice is used and opportunities are available that address children's targeted goals and objectives.

Developmentally appropriate practice is predicated on three essential features. First, children are offered a variety of activities, events, and environmental arrangements appropriate to their developmental capacities. Second, these activities, events, and environmental arrangements must be meaningful to children. A final essential element is that the activities, events, and environmental arrangements provide a balance between learning to participate according to others' directions (e.g., peers, teachers, caregivers) and learning to initiate activities according to one's own desires and interests.

Daily routines at home and in developmentally appropriate preschool programs give children choices about activities, although adults do not give children complete freedom to decide what they will do. Adults create a framework by designing the environment, choosing materials and activities, and taking a facilitative role in the learning process. As children explore their environment and expand on play activities, adults capitalize on child initiations and create additional learning experiences and opportunities.

For children who have or are at risk for disabilities, it is particularly important that their activities be guided into productive endeavors. It is essential to offer children developmentally appropriate activities with multiple opportunities to work on the acquisition and maintenance of targeted goals and objectives. Being developmentally appropriate is not sufficient; activities should offer many opportunities for children to practice behaviors that enhance their communication and problem-solving skills and build their independence. Ongoing observation and evaluation are necessary to ensure that the environment offers adequate opportunity for children to practice these targeted goals. Without careful monitoring of progress, children may engage in fun and meaningful self-initiated activities but fail to improve in targeted areas.

The following sections describe naturalistic training strategies that promote developmentally appropriate practice and provide multiple opportunities for embedding children's goals. These strategies include using 1) daily routines, 2) environmental arrangements, and 3) planned activities. The remainder of the chapter addresses the role of the interventionist and caregiver and the use of the AEPS Curriculum with children who have or are at risk for disabilities.

DAILY ROUTINES

Daily routines at home or at school can be used to provide multiple opportunities for children to practice targeted goals and objectives across important developmental domains. The use of daily routines (e.g., meals, cleanup, travel, bedtime) should be encouraged for two important reasons. First, daily routines are likely to be important and meaningful to children; therefore, the interventionists or caregivers do not have to create artificial or special activities, nor do they have to find ways to make the activities relevant. Second, daily routines help people get through regular activities that need to be accomplished (e.g., bathing, eating). Because these activities occur routinely, they can be effective and efficient as training vehicles.

An analysis of the home will reveal a variety of activities or events that occur regularly and predictably. For example, upon waking, most families follow bathing, dressing, and eating routines that prepare them for the day. With thought, these routines may be usable to assist children in practicing targeted goals or objectives. For example, dressing provides preschoolers the opportunity to work on adaptive skills (e.g., pulling on pants, buttoning, zipping), communication skills (e.g., "help," "where shoes?"), or cognitive skills (e.g., finding clothes, matching socks or shoes). Breakfast, lunch, and dinner provide numerous opportunities to practice cognitive skills (e.g., help set the table with appropriate number of utensils; find salt, napkins; locate what is missing), social-communication skills (e.g., indicate food choices), and motor skills (e.g., climb into chair). Without analysis of events and consideration of the child's goals, caregivers may overlook opportunities to use daily routines as training vehicles. Not all daily routines, of course, will be appropriate training times for all families (e.g., families who have tight timelines for getting to work may find it difficult to use breakfast as a training time).

A similar analysis of daily routines in center-based programs will yield a variety of routines that can be used to target children's goals. For example, arrival at school offers opportunities to practice motor skills (e.g., running, jumping), adaptive skills (e.g., removing jacket and hanging it up), and social skills (e.g., greeting other children). Washing up for a snack gives children the opportunity to practice social skills (e.g., taking turns), adaptive skills (e.g., washing and drying hands), and social-communication skills (e.g., asking what's for snack, asking a peer to sit nearby). By observing program activities, interventionists can identify numerous opportunities for children to practice targeted goals and objectives as they engage in daily routines.

ENVIRONMENTAL ARRANGEMENTS

Children's environments can be arranged in a variety of ways to provide multiple opportunities to practice targeted goals and objectives. A useful strategy for young children in center-based programs is to arrange the environment into activity centers, equipping each area of the classroom with specific materials. Classroom space can be creatively organized to afford multiple opportunities for children to engage in activities that enhance learning. The goal is to design the environment so that multiple skills across domains can be elicited in the activity centers and that multiple opportunities to practice skills are provided.

The use of activity centers is an excellent strategy for encouraging child-initiated activities. When a child initiates an activity—begins to play with a toy, asks a question, or creates a game—the activity is likely to be of considerable interest to the child. Encouraging child initiations capitalizes on children's involvement in activities that they find motivating and fun. Self-selected activities provide little demand for artificial reinforcers or other external supports to maintain the child's interest and involvement. Section IV of this Curriculum provides additional suggestions for specific environmental arrangements for each goal in the AEPS Test for Three to Six Years.

Well-designed activity centers concentrate a child's interest and effort in multiple skill areas. An activity center with puzzles, blocks, and other manipulatives can be used to promote fine motor and cognitive skills. An obstacle course encourages the use of gross motor and social skills. A book or listening area promotes early literacy skills and may encourage labeling feelings, identification of colors, or problem solving. A sample illustration of an activity center is shown in Figure III.1.

Designing a variety of activity centers allows interventionists to target developing skills across domains. Children can make choices among activity centers, and appropriate assistance from an interventionist facilitates opportunities to learn and practice targeted skills. Activity centers can be a permanent foundation for a center-based program, and a rotation of materials is necessary to capitalize on children's ideas, expand activities, and maintain children's interest throughout the year.

Arrangement of activity centers involves the following:

1. Planning five to seven "centers" and designing space accordingly (see *The Creative Curriculum for Early Childhood* [Dodge & Colker, 1992] for useful information on designing learning centers).
2. Identifying materials, rules of access, and adult roles for each activity center.
3. Determining targeted IEP/IFSP goals and objectives to be addressed in each center.

Figure III.1.   A sample activity center.

The number and type of activity centers designed will depend on space, daily schedules, the population of children, and available resources (e.g., materials, equipment).
For example, programs that have an outdoor play space may not need to develop a
gross motor activity center. It is important to provide definition to activity centers and
to separate noisy and quiet centers as much as space allows. Shelves or commercial
dividers help divide and define spaces.

Arrangement of space to promote multiple uses is preferable. Many classrooms
have a "messy" area with tables that are easily cleaned after sand or water play, snacks,
or art activities. Another favorite is a "quiet" area of books, tapes, comfortable chairs,
and pillows. This space might be used for group storytime, independent use of books
and tapes, or even naps. A dramatic play center provides an area for children to dress
up, role play, and act out story sequences while supported by a changing array of furniture, props, decorations, and clothing. Figure III.2 shows a schematic of a classroom
with a variety of activity centers.

Once the desired activity centers have been established, each one should be outfitted with materials designed to promote overall skill development (e.g., motor, communication) and with materials that will facilitate practice on children's targeted IEP/IFSP
goals and objectives. For example, addition of a coat, cups, a stuffed cat, and plastic corn
on the cob to the dramatic play center will provide multiple opportunities for a child to
practice the "k" sound. Selection of appropriate materials should be keyed to ability levels of children, expertise and interests of interventionists, and available resources. The
most important consideration is that the children can *safely* use all materials. Regular
introduction of novel materials into an ongoing center maintains interest and expands
the practice of new skills. Figure III.3 shows an example of a block center outfitted with
materials, as well as a list of targeted IEP/IFSP objectives, intervention strategies, and
prompts for two children who will be using the center.

As children engage in the activities of a center, interventionists should evaluate the
usefulness of the activities in moving children toward their IEP/IFSP goals and objectives. Activity centers that do not consistently engage children are likely to be ineffec-
tive, whereas those that both address target areas and elicit child engagement will be
more effective.

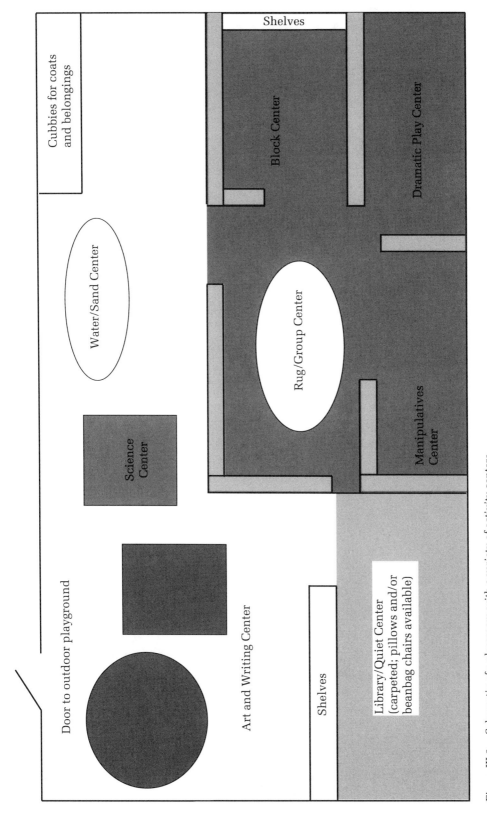

Figure III.2. Schematic of a classroom with a variety of activity centers.

27

- Block building can help children learn sizes, shapes, numbers, order, area, length, and weight as they select, build with, and clean up blocks.

- Block building can help children use large muscles to carry blocks from place to place. As they carefully place blocks together to form a bridge or an intricate design, they refine small muscles in their hands, which is important for writing skills.

- Block play can help social development. One child's idea of how to build a zoo may differ from another's, but children learn to respect different viewpoints and learn from one another. As children build together, they solve problems and learn the benefits of cooperation.

Name	Objective	What the adult can do	Current prompting level
Tama	SC B:1.6 (Uses present progressive "ing")	Comment, using "ing" (building, driving, stacking, sharing)	Model
Tama	Cog H:2.1 (Counts five objects)	Ask Tama, "How many blocks in your zoo?"	Partial physical assist to point to object one at a time
Joey	Soc A:2.1 (Joins others in cooperative activity)	"Look, Tama's building a bridge." "It looks like she needs more blocks."	Verbal cue
Joey	Matches three different shapes	Ask Joey to sort the square, rectangular, and triangular blocks into piles.	Verbal cue or partial physical assistance

Figure III.3.   Example of a block center. (Adapted with permission from Diane **Trister** Dodge and Laura J. Colker, "The Creative Curriculum® for Early Childhood, 3rd Ed." Copyright © 1992 by Teaching Strategies, Inc., P.O. Box 42243, Washington, DC 20015.)

The roles of adults will vary from center to center. A science center may require more adult interaction than a block center. Children with severe delays and disabilities may need additional assistance from adults in using activity center materials. Posting a brief description of each center and a summary of the skills targeted in that center helps adults, including assistants, volunteers, and specialists, provide consistent guidance to children.

Access to activity centers is an important consideration. Children need specific rules about when they may use activity centers, how many children may be in a center, and how to move from one center to another. Most classrooms have specified times when activity centers are used (e.g., free play, choice activity groups) and other times (e.g., circle or snack time) when centers are not available. The size of the center and the nature of the activity will determine the number of children allowed in the center. Five or six children may work well at an art table, whereas three or four children may be more appropriate for a gross motor center.

Use of a child-initiated approach will require *flexibility* in activity centers. If rules for materials and the center are too rigid, interventionists risk losing valuable learning opportunities. For example, if a child is building a house in the block center and has an idea to bring dolls from the dramatic play center to live in the house, this can be encouraged by the interventionist, facilitating independence of thought and creativity in the child. The interventionist might expand the activity to provide opportunities to practice targeted goals and objectives. If a child's idea is safe and will not cause undue disruption to the classroom, flexibility in the use of materials should be allowed.

Effective learning in activity centers requires the following criteria:

- Equipment, materials, and activities are safe for all children.
- Guidelines for the activity center are posted.
- Potential goals and objectives are listed for each child.
- Reminders are provided to encourage child initiations.

The hallmark of effective early intervention is systematic and consistent environmental arrangements that promote learning in children. In center-based programs, thoughtfully designed activity centers provide children with a set of materials and events that are developmentally appropriate and promote opportunities for practice of targeted goals and objectives.

PLANNED ACTIVITIES

Planning is necessary to successful intervention because it helps ensure that opportunities to practice targeted IEP/IFSP goals and objectives are arranged. This planning is essential at many different levels and should include all team members (e.g., caregivers, specialists) when possible. Large-scale planning may include the themes to be addressed during the year, the general arrangement of the environment to promote skill development across developmental domains, the roles and responsibilities of adults in the classroom, and adaptations necessary for children with special needs. A number of strategies assist interventionists and caregivers in planning, including development of program plans, activity schedules, and activity plans, as described below.

Program Plans

Interventionists develop individual program plans for each child with an IEP/IFSP. Program plans delineate the intervention content, outline teaching guidelines, and determine criteria for monitoring progress on priority goals and objectives. Program plans should be developed cooperatively by the intervention staff or team. Input from team members can be shared and then synthesized into a program plan to guide intervention activities and ensure a cohesive, coordinated approach to addressing the child/family goals and objectives.

As shown in Figure III.4, individual program plans specify the goal and its associated objectives when appropriate. Daily routines, environmental arrangements, and planned activities that afford potential opportunities to work on the child's goal are also listed. In addition, potentially effective antecedents/prompts/cues and consequences are provided. Finally, other considerations and child progress procedures are discussed. Program plans are much like an architect's blueprint in that they provide the specifications necessary to reach a goal. Program plans should be followed and modified as necessary so that interventionists and caregivers always have a specific plan to guide their activities.

Program Plan

Child: **ALICE HENDERSON**   Interventionist: **SANDY TOBIAS**

Initiated: **9/96**   Expected Completion: **12/96**   Completed: _____

Goal[a]   Alice will use appropriate verbal (e.g., "Come on, let's play house") or nonverbal strategies to initiate cooperative activities and encourage peers to participate.

Objective[a]   During group activities, Alice will independently share or exchange objects with peers engaged in the same activity in at least three activities in 1 day for 2 consecutive weeks.

Daily Routines

Circle time
• Share time (Alice's share day is Tuesday—remind Mom)

Unstructured play times at home and school
• Encourage sharing during free play activities

Snack time
• Serve snack family style
• Encourage Alice to pass food and drinks and share with peers

Environmental Arrangements

• Sit Alice next to peers (adult close by).
• Provide fewer materials than children during activities.
• Alice should be out of her wheelchair and in her adapted chair for any table activities, and on floor during floor activities and circle time.
• Group Alice with Joey, Maria, or Manuel during small group activities (good models of sharing).
• Remove tray on wheelchair whenever possible.

Planned Activities

Arrange any planned activities considering the above environmental arrangements:
• Dramatic play
• Big art projects
• Group games
• Outdoor play with balls, wagons
• Puppets
• Blocks
• Tent building
• Water/sand play

Antecedents/Prompts/Cues

Least assistance to most assistance—provide the least assistance necessary for Alice to share
• Provide materials to share.
• Model sharing and draw attention to peers for sharing (make a big deal out of other children sharing: "Wow! That was really nice of Timmy to share with you. What a good friend").
• Ask Alice to share with a friend.
• Ask Alice to share with a peer.
• As a last resort, physically assist Alice to share.

Consequences

(+) If Alice does share then
• Alice loves attention and praise, so reinforce her for sharing (fade use of praise over time).

(–) if Alice refuses to share then
• Use a more directive prompt.
• If Alice refuses to share (with adult) say, "Oh well, I guess you don't want to play right now," and move away to another activity.

_____
(continued)

Figure III.4.   Sample program plan for Alice for Social Domain, Strand A, Goal 2.0. (Taken from the AEPS Test for Three to Six Years [Bricker & Pretti-Frontczak, 1996].)

Figure III.4.   *(continued)*

- If Alice refuses to share (with peer), provide a model of a strategy for Alice (e.g., "Tell Jimmy, 'You can have it when I am finished'").
- If Alice still does not share, try to redirect peer; as a last resort physically assist Alice to share.

Other Considerations

- It may be helpful to give Alice some warning before asking her to share ("In a few minutes it will be Jimmy's turn") or to reassure her that she can finish what she needs to do and then she can share ("After you are finished using the glue, Jimmy would like a turn").

Child Progress Procedures

Monitor this skill once a week during snack, free play, and planned activities, noting Alice's ability to share or exchange objects given three opportunities (e.g., a friend or adult asking for an item). Note whether Alice shares (+), does not share (−), or shares only when prompted (indicate level of assistance needed: V = verbal cue, P = physical assistance).

Decision Rule

- Review progress during monthly meeting.
- If progress is not occurring at school or at home, family and team members should revise program plan and if necessary indicate specific program steps to meet objective.
- Objective will be met when Alice consistently and independently meets criterion. The behavior should be functional and generalized (occur in a variety of settings with different people and materials).
- Establish new objective when this objective is completed to the satisfaction of family and team members.

Activity Schedules

Most children are sensitive to changes in their environment and may become upset if continually unable to anticipate or predict future events. Providing a level of structure and consistency to home- and center-based environments can greatly enhance a child's independent functioning and increase a sense of security. Posting of weekly and daily activity schedules is one way to provide some of this structure. Quality preschool programs offer a balance of child-initiated and planned activities, large and small group activities, active and quiet activities, and indoor and outdoor activities. Figure III.5 displays a weekly schedule for a center-based program and Figure III.6 a daily schedule. Schedules help staff balance activities and plan opportunities to address children's targeted goals.

Center/Group Activity Schedules   Activity schedules help an interventionist or caregiver determine the best times for children to practice targeted IEP/IFSP goals and objectives. Center-based programs have a variety of daily routines that have potential as excellent training vehicles. For example, arrival can be used to practice adaptive skills (e.g., remove jacket and hat) and foster independence (e.g., select an activity prior to group time). Snack time can be used to practice and improve cognitive skills (e.g., matching chairs needed for all children eating snack), social-communication skills (e.g., request items, discuss the day's events), and adaptive skills (e.g., use a napkin to wipe hands). Cleanup is often an opportune time to promote social interactions and cooperation (e.g., children help each other pick up toys), improve fine and gross motor skills (e.g., put toys on shelves or in boxes), and practice social-communication skills (e.g., follow directions, ask questions).

Activity schedules can be developed for an individual child or groups of children. Figure III.7 illustrates an activity schedule developed for three children in a center-based program. The children's names are placed across the top of the matrix, and their

Activity schedule	Monday	Tuesday	Wednesday	Thursday	Friday
Arrival					
Activity centers 1. Art	Decorate flower pots	Paper flowers	Nature collage	Yarn "worm" art	Watercolor pain- ting with flowers
2. Dress up	Everyday: Gardening clothes				
3. Building center	Everyday: Transportation toys				
Circle	Everyday: Weather chart—Sing: Ring around the rosie, pockets full of posies, thunder, thunder, we all fall down.				
Snack	Sunflower seeds	Garden fresh vegetables	Fresh fruit chunks	Spaghetti "worms"	"Ants on a log" – stuffed celery with raisins
Outside play	Outdoor gardening	Painting with water	Nature walk	Digging for worms — sand table	Obstacle course
Activity center/ social activity	Planting seeds	Washing toys – garden	Washing toys– Spring cleaning	Cooking for snack– Spaghetti "worms"	Water play– outdoors
Cleanup					
Circle/story	Discover box– planting items Story about seeds	Garden items/ tools Gardening story	Items from hike Nature story	Worm/dirt items; worm or fish story	Child choice Cleaning story
Departure					

Figure III.5.   Weekly schedule for center-based program.

specific goals/objectives are listed below their names. On the left side of the matrix are the daily classroom activities and times. An "X" is placed in the box of each goal/objective to indicate that a training opportunity is likely to occur within the activity. For example, every classroom activity offers an opportunity for Tama to work on following three-step directions. Activity schedules will differ depending on settings and their restrictions and resources, as well as on the individual needs of children. Figure III.8 provides an example of a modified activity schedule that can also be used as a progress monitoring (i.e., data collection) system. As shown in Figure III.8, dates are written under each objective, and a child's progress is recorded below the date each time the child independently performs the skill (+), does not perform the skill (–), or performs the skill with assistance or prompting (p).

Activity	Time
Arrival	8:20–8:30
Activity Centers	8:30–9:00
Circle	9:00–9:20
Snack	9:20–9:45
Outdoor Play	9:45–10:20
Activity Centers/Special Activities	10:20–10:50
Cleanup	10:50–11:00
Circle/Story	11:00–11:30
Departure	11:30–12:00

Figure III.6.   Daily classroom schedule.

	Child's name: TAMA		Child's name: JON		Child's name: VICKI	
	Goal/Objective: Follows three-step directions	Goal/Objective: Selects activities and/or objects	Goal/Objective: Suggests acceptable solutions to problems	Goal/Objective: Alternates between speaker/listener role	Goal/Obj.: Watches, listens, and participates during small group activities	Goal/Objective: Joins others in cooperative activity
8:20–8:30 Arrival	X			X		
8:30–9:00 Activity centers	X	X	X	X	X	X
9:00–9:20 Circle	X		X	X	X	X
9:20–9:45 Snack	X	X	X	X	X	X
9:45–10:20 Outdoor play	X	X	X	X		X
10:20–10:50 Special activities	X	X	X	X	X	X
10:50–11:00 Cleanup	X		X		X	X
11:00–11:30 Circle/story	X		X	X	X	
11:30–12:00 Departure	X			X		

Figure III.7.   Group activity schedule completed for three children.

Observing each skill daily may be overwhelming; a monitoring system in which observations are staggered (i.e., by child, day, objective, or setting) may make the task more manageable. For example, a schedule that staggers the activity being monitored may be helpful (e.g., observations will be made during arrival and departure on Monday, in activity centers on Tuesday, and during outdoor play on Wednesday). Spreading the responsibility for progress monitoring across staff members is also helpful, if team members are provided with continual reminders of opportunities for children to practice targeted skills during daily activities. For example, if a staff person is unable to observe Tama following three-step directions during arrival because no three-step directions are given, the staff member should concentrate on providing that opportunity during arrival the next day.

Center/Group Activity

Activity Schedule	TAMA — Follows three-step directions (9/5)	TAMA (Date)	TAMA (Date)	TAMA — Selects activities and/or objectives (9/6)	TAMA (Date)	TAMA (Date)	JON — Suggests acceptable solutions to problems (9/5)	JON (Date)	JON (Date)	JON — Alternates between speaker/listener role (9/8)	JON (Date)	JON (Date)	VICKI — Watches, listens, and participates during small group activity (9/5)	VICKI (9/9)	VICKI (Date)	VICKI — Joins others in cooperative activity (9/7)	VICKI (9/9)	VICKI (Date)
8:20–8:30 Arrival																		
8:30–9:00 Activity centers	+ – –			p –			– p			+ + +			+	+ +		+ +	+	
9:00–9:20 Circle	+ +									– p +			+	+ +		+		
9:20–9:45 Snack	+ +			+ +			– – p +									– p +	+ +	
9:45–10:20 Outdoor play	+ +			+ +			p +			p + +			+ +	+ + +		+	–	
10:20–10:50 Special activities	+ + +									+ +			+	+ +				
10:50–11:00 Cleanup							+						– p +	+				
11:00–11:30 Circle/story	+ + + + +									– p +						+ +	+	
11:30–12:00 Departure	p +									– – p								

Figure III.8. An activity schedule modified to create a progress monitoring system (+ = independently performs skills; – = does not perform skills; p = performs skills with assistance or prompting).

Home/Individual Activity Schedules   Activity schedules can also be used effectively in the home. Caregivers are the best source of information to determine which daily routines address certain skills. Each family's schedule, values, and priorities, combined with their knowledge of the child's preferences, interests, and level of involvement in home and community activities, make them, as caregivers, critical to the development of an accurate and useful program plan and activity schedule in the home environment. Home/individual activity schedules help communicate an activity-based approach to families and provide a structure for working with children in their routine activities, without creating unnecessary "drill" sessions.

Many possibilities are available to families. Bathtime can be a time to expand vocabulary, search for missing objects, or improve adaptive skills. Traveling in the car may be an ideal time to expand the child's communication skills by pointing out people and objects. Figure III.9 provides examples of how two IFSP objectives for Raynell can be practiced within her family's typical daily routine.

The advantages of using daily routines for teaching are many. First, children are more likely to be motivated to learn a new skill if it is naturally required in the course of a routine. Second, when a skill is acquired in the course of daily activities, generalization of the skill is more likely. The skill is mastered in the setting where it is used, which eliminates the need to transfer the learned skill from a formal teaching situation. Third, caregivers and interventionists do not have to adopt "training" or "instructional" behaviors because they are already engaging children.

Considerations When Creating Activity Schedules   The development of useful and efficient activity schedules requires consideration of the following factors.

Preparation   A transition time of approximately 5 minutes will be needed for most children to move from one activity to the next. Ten minutes before the end of an activity time, it is helpful to announce that in 5 minutes it will be time to clean up and prepare for the next activity (e.g., "In 5 minutes we will clean up and wash our hands for snack"). This helps children complete their projects and prepare for the next activity. It is useful to communicate with each child, particularly those who find transitions stressful, to ensure understanding of the upcoming transition.

Time Constraints   It is important to provide adequate time for children, especially those with mobility impairments, to move independently between activities to the greatest extent possible. Interventionists need to exhibit flexibility and sensitivity to meet individual needs. Rigid adherence to a schedule will stifle opportunities to capitalize on a child's initiation, on "teachable moments," and on a child's ability to perform a task independently. For example, it may be tempting to quickly put a basket of materials away for a child with a motor delay. However, if the child is provided extra time and encouragement, an excellent opportunity is available for the child to use motor, problem-solving, communication, or social skills to complete the task.

Attention Factors   Whereas some children may require extra time to shift from one activity to another, others may need a quick transition to hold their attention. Interventionists should anticipate these situations and be prepared to offer additional options to these children. For example, children who clean up quickly, wash their hands, and are ready for snack may be given additional responsibility to help set the table.

Communication Factors   Many programs use pictures to communicate daily schedules to children who have difficulty processing auditory information, as well as children who have difficulty moving between activities. Most children appear to enjoy following picture schedules, and using a picture schedule with all the children in a center avoids singling out a child with a disability. Picture schedules in the home environ-

Home/Individual Activity Schedule

Child: **RAYNELL**   Date: **9/8**

Activity Schedule	Goal/Objective: Follows directions of three or more related steps that are not routinely given.	Goal/Objective: Alternates between speaker/listener role
Wakeup/Dressing	Ask Raynell to select clothing, get dressed, and come to breakfast.	Greet Raynell—ask about last night's dreams and wait for response. Talk about the type of day it is and have Raynell tell you what type of clothing should be worn.
Breakfast	Ask Raynell to get a bowl, get cereal, and sit at the table.	Ask Raynell about food tastes and plans for the day, and listen for response.
Playing/outing	Ask Raynell to get a jacket, put it on, and wait at the door.	
Lunch	Ask Raynell to wash her hands, set the table, and sit down.	While eating lunch, talk about afternoon plans with Raynell. Have Raynell tell you about the plans, and then ask her to listen as you talk about your plans.
Play group	Ask Raynell to choose an activity. Have her get the materials, bring them to a designated area, and begin the activity.	As Raynell plays, make comments and ask questions about the activity or game. Wait for Raynell to respond.
Dinner	Ask Raynell to wash her hands, put cups on the table, and get silverware.	Have each person at the dinner table talk about the day's events while others listen.
Watching television		Have Raynell help select the TV program to watch. Talk about the program. Listen while Raynell talks and have her listen while you talk.
Story/bath	Ask Raynell to select pajamas, select a book for after her bath, and undress for bath.	
Bedtime		Ask about Raynell's day and wait for response. Read a bedtime story. Ask questions about the story and wait for response.

Figure III.9.   Home/individual activity schedule for Raynell.

ment have been very successful for children who have trouble making transitions. Figure III.10 provides an example of a picture schedule.

Children with Significant Disability   For most children, participation in an enriched, developmentally appropriate, and child-directed program will provide adequate practice on targeted IEP/IFSP goals and objectives. However, young children with signifi-

Figure III.10. Example of a picture schedule.

cant delays or disabilities will need frequent opportunities to learn and perform targeted goals and objectives. Ongoing planning is vital to activity-based intervention to
ensure that these children are given adequate learning and practice time. Use of the
AEPS Curriculum with children with significant disabilities is discussed in detail later in
this section.

Activity Plans

Planned activities are designed to provide children multiple opportunities to learn and
use targeted skills. Planning activities involves three steps:

1. Identifying the children who will participate and noting their targeted goals and
    objectives.
2. Choosing a developmentally appropriate activity and writing an activity plan that
    serves as a guide for the general flow of the activity.
3. Determining within the sequence of the activity where opportunities to embed
    goals occur. Also, materials, environmental arrangements, prompts, cues, and
    consequences that facilitate acquisition of skills at different levels of difficulty are
    noted.

Identifying children to be involved in each activity group is important because the
range of skill levels will vary. In a storytime activity, for example, one group of children
might have a wide range of skills, from using books functionally and describing past
events to sounding out words and alternating between speaking and listening. Another
group might have more homogeneous IEP/IFSP goals and objectives such as blending
sounds and sounding out words. First identifying the children for a group and noting
their objectives provides the necessary framework for developing the scope and
sequence of an activity.

The second step involves creating a written activity plan that will engage and moti-
vate children while the adult elicits specific target behaviors. Activity plans provide a
description and sequence of the activity, including a clear opening and closing. The
plans note possible variations for the activity and list necessary materials. The "variations" section of the activity plans is helpful because variations provide a way to expand
or enhance the activity if children are initially uninterested. Children often have creative ideas for variations to activities, which should be included when possible. In addition, variations may allow the introduction of more advanced skills for some children
while providing repetition that other children need to practice targeted goals and objectives. Figure III.11 provides an example of an activity plan for a snack.

Activity plans indicate which IEP/IFSP goals are to be addressed for each child and
when the child's targeted goals can be embedded in activities. The detailed plan may
include strategies for providing multiple opportunities within activities and the
prompting levels children often need to first acquire skills or to master difficult skills.
Figure III.12 lists goals and objectives for three children; these goals and objectives are
targeted in the activity plan in Figure III.13.

An activity plan designed for one group of children can be modified for other children. For example, the shaving cream activity plan described in Figure III.13 can, with
modification, be used with most preschoolers. Programs may choose to develop a
"bank" of generic activity plans and modify them as necessary. Another activity plan
using a different format is shown in Figure III.14. This plan illustrates how children
with a wide range of skill levels can participate in the same activity as well as how skills
across developmental domains can be targeted during an activity.

Activity Plan

Snack

Activity description/sequence

- Prior to snack, children wash their hands
- Children assist in setting the table
- Serve snack family style, so that children request food and drinks from each other, pass items, serve themselves
- Encourage children to use this time to discuss the day's activities, talk about their families, talk to friends, and so forth
- When children are finished, they clean their plates, throw away garbage, put utensils in sink
- After cleanup, children read a story until three slower children are finished; then an adult can go outside with them

Variations

- Go on a picnic
- Children prepare their own snack
- Eat in a restaurant

Materials

- Cups, small pitcher
- Bowls or plates
- Napkins
- Snack items (food, drink)
- Sponges for cleanup

Figure III.11.   Example of an activity plan for a snack.

Activity plans often require modification, because an activity that seems appropriate may not be effective with a group of children or the children may choose to use the materials in ways not anticipated. Following the children's lead within the activity is advisable, as long as IEP/IFSP objectives continue to be addressed.

Considerations When Developing an Activity Plan   The development of useful and effective activity schedules requires consideration of the following factors.

Setup and Cleanup   Although many adults consider setup and cleanup their responsibility, these aspects of an activity often provide excellent opportunities to practice targeted IEP/IFSP goals and objectives. For example, a child with the cognitive objective of counting objects could count the number of smocks needed for a painting activity, a child learning to manipulate objects could be physically assisted to pass out brushes to classmates, a child working on problem solving could find a container to hold water, or two children could work together to wash off the table, promoting social interaction.

Introduction and Recap   Introduction refers to a brief preview of an activity before it begins. Recap refers to a similar review once the activity has been completed. During the introduction, the interventionist familiarizes children with the sequence of the activity (demonstration with actual objects or pictures may be necessary for some children) and covers basic rules or expectations. The recap provides an excellent opportunity to talk to children about the activity. For preverbal children, alternative methods of communication (e.g., pointing, gesturing) are encouraged.

Process versus Product   During an activity, the focus is on the exploration and learning that occurs during the process rather than on the product. For example, during an art activity the interventionist supplies the children with paper, scissors, glue, and crayons and asks if they can create butterflies. During the process of the activity, the interventionist focuses on facilitating general skill development across domains

Child's name	Goal/objective	Opportunities for embedding targeted goals and objectives in Shaving Cream Activity
Tama	Follows directions of three or more related steps that are not routinely given	"Get a smock, put it on, and sit down at the table." "Get a sponge, wipe off the table, and put the sponge in the sink."
	Sounds out words	Make simple words (e.g., cat, dog) in shaving cream and ask Tama, "Can you read this word?"
Timmy	Uses signs to make commands to and requests of others	Delay providing assistance when Timmy is putting on/taking off his smock and trying to squirt shaving cream. Prompt him with, "What do you need?" and provide a model for words if necessary (e.g., sign, "HELP ME.")
	Shares or exchanges objects	Observe Timmy's ability to share shaving cream and sponges during activity. If necessary, prompt him (e.g., "When you are done, pass it to Tama").
	Copies simple shapes	Make people in shaving cream with circle faces and stick figures. Prompt Timmy to copy.
Joey	Asks questions	Do not offer materials until Joey asks.
	Uses descriptive words	Encourage Joey to use descriptive words for his activities (e.g., "cream is cold and wet").
	Copies complex shapes	Provide model of house and animal for Joey.

Figure III.12.   List of IFSP goals for Tama, Timmy, and Joey to be targeted in a shaving cream activity (see Figure III.13).

(e.g., sharing materials) and individual children's targeted IEP/IFSP objectives (e.g., use of concepts, categorizing), rather than on children's abilities to create a recognizable "butterfly." It is useful at times to be nondirective or nonspecific. The interventionist might present materials by saying, "What can you do with these things?" Another approach is to introduce a specific problem to the children. For example, the interventionist might provide scrap wood pieces, a stick, and tape and ask "Can you make a bridge with these materials?"

ROLE OF THE INTERVENTIONIST AND CAREGIVER

When employing a naturalistic intervention approach such as activity-based intervention, the preferred strategy is to follow children's leads and to guide their behavior in desired directions. However, interventionists and caregivers usually cannot rely exclusively on child initiations to provide the necessary opportunities to practice goals and objectives. Whenever possible, it is important to observe children's behavior and introduce intervention content into activities that children initiate and choose.

The interventionist is a facilitator rather than a director of the child's learning. Through observation and interactions with the child, the interventionist provides the least level of assistance necessary for the child to practice targeted goals or solve problems. For example, an interventionist may observe a child attempting to build a tall block tower. The child uses a small block for the base, the tower continues to topple over, and the child cries. The interventionist decides to provide support but, rather than hand the child a large block, the interventionist moves a block nearby to encourage the child to try a new strategy to solve the problem.

Interventionists and caregivers who are sensitive to children's needs in an activity-based program do not stay involved in the children's play for longer than necessary.

Activity Plan
Shaving Cream

Activity Description/Sequence

Offer opportunities for children to participate in setting up the activity *(goal for Tama)*. Allow children to problem-solve what they could do to keep from getting messy during the activity, such as wearing a smock *(goal for Tama, Timmy)*. Provide fewer cans of shaving cream than number of children to encourage interactions and communication while they share *(goal for Tama, Timmy, Joey)*.

Shaving cream can be visible, but out of the children's reach, to encourage children to use communication to request a turn *(goal for Tama, Joey)*. Delay providing assistance to squirt shaving cream until the child requests it. Prompt child to use language to communicate request if he or she is getting frustrated.

Allow children to experiment with and discuss the physical properties of shaving cream *(goal for all children)*. Model drawing simple and complex shapes in the cream (e.g., crosses, circles, squares), as well as individual letters or the children's names *(goal for Tama, Timmy)*. Encourage the children to practice prewriting/fine motor skills.

Children can help with cleaning up by sponging off the table, wiping down their aprons, and washing their hands *(goal for Tama)*.

Variations

• Add chopsticks, Popsicle sticks, or unsharpened pencils to "write" in the shaving cream
• Add food coloring or tempera paint to shaving cream
• Build with soft blocks, using the shaving cream as "glue"
• Add small figurines (e.g., people, dinosaurs) to the shaving cream
• Use whipped cream, pudding, fingerpaints, or soap flakes mixed with water instead of shaving cream

Materials

Shaving cream
Table top
Aprons
Sponges

Figure III.13.   Shaving cream activity plan detailing goals to be targeted for Tama, Timmy, and Joey.

Interventionists and caregivers can use a variety of techniques to facilitate rather than direct learning in children.

Techniques for Interacting with Children

A variety of techniques and strategies that can be employed with young children are described below. First, a set of general strategies is discussed. Second, a set of strategies used with social-communication behavior is described. Finally, a set of specific procedures is presented.

General Strategies   The following are strategies that are often effective in working with young children.

Follow the Child's Lead   When participating in an activity with a child, the interventionist should follow the child's lead whenever possible and appropriate. Although children can be enticed into activities of the adult's choosing, it is often easier and more effective to subtly change or redirect an activity chosen by the child into a vehicle for practicing a targeted goal or objective. For example, if a child is playing in the sandbox, the interventionist follows the child's lead and joins in the play. If the child picks up a stick and pokes in the sand, the interventionist imitates the play and encourages peers to join in. To become effective at following a child's lead, it is critical that interventionists and caregivers be good observers of children, watching them to learn about their motivations and their actual capabilities.

Activity Plan
Play-Doh

Activity description/sequence

Introduce activity by asking children what types of things they are going to make out of Play-Doh. Provide Play-Doh in screwtop, plastic jars and delay providing assistance opening jars unless children ask for help.

Have additional materials (e.g., rolling pins) in sight but out of reach, providing opportunities for children to request materials.

Encourage children to experiment with manipulating Play-Doh, offer opportunities for trading items, and discuss children's creations.

Children can help clean up by putting away toys and Play-Doh and wiping down the table.

Variations

Make dough

Use four colors—let children mix small bits of dough to create new colors

Include cookie cutters and make a cookie factory

Use clay, let creations harden, then paint

Materials

Play-Doh

Plastic jars with lids

Rolling pins

Dull knives

Small figurines

Scissors

Objects that make impressions

Objectives

Fine Motor	Gross Motor	Adaptive	Cognitive	Social-Communication	Social
Print letters in Play-Doh (provide pencil-like sticks).	Maintains balance in walking (children play "Follow the Leader" when moving to the Play-Doh table)	Fasten fasteners on smock.	Follow three-step directions. Count 10 objects (e.g., balls, Play-Doh).	Use descriptive words (e.g., adjectives, adverbs, prepositions, articles).	Resolve conflicts by selecting effective strategy.
Cut out shapes from Play-Doh		Select smock and dress self.	Use quantitative concepts (all, more, lots, none).	Use three-word utterances. Ask questions.	Share and exchange rolling pins and cutters.
Rotate wrist on horizontal plane (opening jar with Play-Doh).	Assume balanced sitting position.	Wash hands (after activity).	Interact appropriately with materials during Play-Doh activity.	Use signs "want, more help, mine."	Initiate and maintain communicative exchange with peer.

Beginning ──▶ Advanced

Figure III.14. Activity plan displaying potential range of objectives that could be addressed during the activity.

42

Model Desired Behaviors or Draw Attention to Peer Models   Adults and peers with advanced skills can provide excellent models of desired behaviors and targeted goals and objectives throughout child-initiated, routine, and planned activities. This strategy can be used to expand on the child's initiations by taking the activity one step further. In the sandbox activity described above, the interventionist, knowing the child has an objective to copy simple shapes, might draw a circle in the sand or draw the child's attention to peers who are drawing shapes in the sand.

Provide the Least Level of Assistance   Prompts provide additional information or support to help a child perform a behavior correctly. When engaging children, adults should offer the least assistance necessary for the child to perform the target response. Providing too much support or direction may result in the child becoming overly dependent on the adult for assistance and delay the development of independent skills and problem-solving behavior. Examples of prompts follow, from the least intrusive to the most intrusive.

Verbal prompts: Adults make statements that help the child perform the behavior. For example, if the objective is to tie shoes, a verbal prompt is, "First you make a bow...."
Gestural prompts: Adults make hand, arm, or other movements that communicate information to the child about what to do. For example, if the objective is to follow a one-step direction such as "Come over here, please," a gestural prompt is waving an arm to the child to come over.
Model prompts: Adults or peers demonstrate the desired behavior.
Partial physical prompts: Adults partially physically guide a child's movements.
Full physical prompts: Adults physically guide a child's movements.

Group Children Heterogeneously   Whenever possible, children of varied ages or developmental levels should be grouped together. Heterogeneous groupings provide opportunities for children to learn new skills by observing peer models or enhance skills by assisting children who are less able.

Plan Time for Children to Complete Tasks   During busy schedules at home and school, adults often find themselves rushing children through activities to keep on schedule. When possible, adequate time should be allowed for children to complete tasks independently or with as little assistance as necessary.

Strategies Used with Social-Communication Behavior   The following strategies are often associated with social-communication goals, although they can be used across domains.

Adjust Speech Complexity   When addressing communication goals, it is important to adjust the complexity of one's speech to reflect the child's level of understanding. In addition, it is important to remember that too much adult talk may interfere with the development of the child's communication or with child-to-child interactions. Adults should monitor their talk and actions to permit children to communicate with each other.

Use Different Types of Talk   When possible, vary the strategy used with children, including the following:

Self-Talk: Talking aloud to oneself, verbalizing what one sees, hears, does, and feels. Also describing actions, objects, and events throughout the day for children (e.g., "I'm rolling out a long snake").
Parallel Talk: Using talk that focuses on what the child is seeing, hearing, doing, and feeling (e.g., "Juan is sharing with Maria").

Expansion: Expanding on what the child says. For example, if the child says "mo" after eating a cracker, expansion might be, "More crackers?"

Expatiation: Elaborating on the topic. Using the example above, the interventionist might say, "You want more crackers? You must be hungry."

Provide Choices   Offering a child choices can prompt a verbal response. For example, instead of asking a child, "Do you want more crackers?", offer a choice such as "Do you want more *crackers* or more *juice*?", with emphasis on the choices. Choices also provide an excellent strategy to less intrusively direct a child. For example, if a child consistently avoids manipulative activities and needs to practice fine motor goals, it may be appropriate to offer a limited choice such as, "The activities to choose from this morning are blocks, Tinkertoys, or Mr. Potato Head. Which would you like to play with?"

Use Open versus Closed Questions   Questions should be used sparingly when working with children, because questions put children "on the spot" to respond and may inhibit communication. However, using open questions may require children to use more complex language in response. Open questions cannot be answered in one word and typically begin with "what," "why," "how," or "could" (e.g., "What do you want to do now?", "How did you make that picture?"). Closed questions can be answered in one word and often begin with "is," "are," or "do" (e.g., "Do you want to go outside?").

Mand/Model   In the mand/model procedure, the interventionist initiates an interaction by asking a question (the "mand") that requires a response about the activity in which the child is engaged. If the child does not respond or only partially responds, the interventionist provides a "model" of the verbal response with an emphasis on a targeted word or phrase. For example, while playing with bubbles, the interventionist holds up the bubble wand and says, 'What should I do?" If the child does not respond, the interventionist models, "Say, 'Blow bubbles.'"

Specific Procedures   The following strategies should be used only when they help children meet designated goals and objectives and should be used in a thoughtful and sensitive manner. If the strategies are used sparingly, they can produce rewarding, fun experiences for the child; but, the strategies should be stopped if the child becomes unhappy or uneasy.

Forgetfulness   The interventionist fails to provide the necessary equipment or materials or omits a familiar component of a routine or activity. For example, a food is not immediately available for snack time, providing an opportunity for the children to recognize the missing element (e.g., "Where are the crackers?") and providing practice in asking questions, searching for materials, and engaging in other problem-solving behavior.

Visible but Unreachable   Objects that are desirable or necessary for the completion of activities are placed within sight of children but out of their reach. Children will need to use problem-solving skills to retrieve the items. For example, placing the playground balls on a high shelf forces the child to find a step stool to reach the balls or to go to an adult for help.

Violation of Expectations   Omitting or changing a familiar step or element in a well-practiced or routine activity violates children's expectations. Children's recognition of change will provide information about their discrimination and memory abilities and provide ideal situations for problem solving. For example, the interventionist tries to draw or write with a pencil by using the eraser. The child recognizes the problem and suggests a solution (e.g., turning the pencil so the pointed end is down).

Sabotage   This strategy involves a deliberate, usually covert action that interferes with the conduct of an activity. For example, the interventionist might unplug the record player prior to a group music activity or remove chairs from the room before snack time to stimulate problem solving among children.

Interruption   Interruption requires that the interventionist or caregiver stop the child from continuing a chain of behaviors that has become routine. For example, during hand washing, the interventionist or caregiver interrupts the child who is reaching for the soap and ask, "What do you want?" The child must then indicate what is needed to complete the task.

Assistance   This strategy involves using materials in activities that require assistance from an adult or peer to access and use. For example, placing a snack in a clear container with a lid that the child cannot remove independently prompts the child to communicate a need for assistance.

Negotiation   If slightly inadequate amounts of materials are provided for a given activity, the child must "negotiate" with his or her peers to get more materials. For example, during an art activity, several colors may be provided, each in a separate container. The children must share and communicate with each other if they want to use different colors.

THE AEPS CURRICULUM AND CHILDREN WITH SEVERE DISABILITIES

Learning to use the AEPS or any other curriculum for children with severe disabilities is a challenge for interventionists, teachers, and support staff. Enhancing learning and development in young children with severe disabilities can be successful if staff individualize assessment and intervention, accurately target areas of need, and use developmentally and age-appropriate activities.

Intervention activities should be tailored to accommodate the individual child's physical or cognitive limitations or both, as well as the environmental demands. Program staff should not have a set of intervention activities to be used with all children regardless of their needs or goals but should have available a range of intervention activities. An activity-based approach offers a structure to accommodate a wide variety of intervention activities that can be tailored to meet the needs of individual children.

Although children with severe disabilities may be 3–6 years old, it might be necessary to use the AEPS Test for Birth to Three Years to obtain an accurate assessment and the corresponding Birth to Three Curriculum for intervention activities. Some children with severe disabilities may fall between the two assessments, requiring the use of the AEPS Test for Birth to Three Years for some domains and the AEPS Test for Three to Six Years for other domains.

Program staff may find that, for some children with severe disabilities, even the AEPS Test for Birth to Three Years is too complex or advanced, requiring that objectives in this assessment be further refined through task analysis. In general, conducting a task analysis requires three steps: 1) identifying the objective, 2) dividing the objective skill into smaller steps, and 3) sequencing the steps for teaching.

An important consideration when working with children with severe disabilities, regardless of the severity of disability, is to embed targeted goals and objectives in activities appropriate to a child's chronological age. Use of the AEPS Curriculum for Three to Six Years will help in choosing activities appropriate for 3- to 6-year-olds, regardless of a child's targeted goals. For example, a 5-year-old child may have the goal of orienting to (i.e., turn, look, reach, and/or move toward) auditory, visual, and tactile events (a goal taken from the AEPS Test for Birth to Three Years). It may be appropriate to shake a rattle for a child under age 2 to provide an opportunity to turn toward the sound, but for a 5-year-old child a rattle is not appropriate. Shaking a tambourine near the child during a music activity would be more appropriate.

Considerations When Working with Children with Severe Disabilities

1. One assistant is assigned to each child; he or she should only provide assistance as needed and should fade involvement in a child's play whenever possible. One-to-one assistants should consider themselves part of the whole classroom, teachers to all children but of special assistance to one particular child when necessary.
2. Children learn how to interact with others in part from adult models, so it is vital to be conscious of the subtle messages we communicate to children (e.g., do not use "baby talk" with children). Interventionists should try to include all children in all activities, at whatever level they are able to participate.
3. Attention should be drawn to children's strengths, and all children should be allowed to take on responsibilities that affect the group (e.g., preparing snack, being line leader). Activities should be designed to capitalize on a child's strengths and abilities. For example, during a painting activity, a child with profound hearing and visual impairments may enjoy using the sense of smell or touch to explore materials. Materials can be added or adapted to an activity to provide opportunities for all children to participate to the greatest extent possible.
4. The interventionist should translate a child's behavior whenever necessary. Children with more pronounced disabilities or severe communicative impairments often have difficulties joining play activities with other children. Their peers, who are just beginning to learn to interact, may have difficulty "reading" behaviors and communicative attempts different from those they know. Adults play a crucial role in translating the child's behavior for peers. For example, during a song at circle time, Maria, who has cerebral palsy, starts to "sing," but her voice sounds almost like a cry. The children appear alarmed, and the interventionist translates for the children, "I can hear Maria singing to the music."
5. Adults may need to provide assistance to help children access and participate in different play activities. The interventionist can suggest play ideas (e.g., "I wonder if you all could build a house together?") and provide suggestions for how a child with more severe impairments might participate in an activity (e.g., "I bet Eric could hold onto the sheet while you get some chairs to make a tent"). Peers often have the best ideas for how to include classmates in activities. Simple solutions such as altering the location of activities may provide opportunities for children with disabilities to be included.
6. Children may need additional structure and guidance to practice and enhance their social skills. Activities such as rocking a boat, playing seesaw, and playing catch encourage children to play in pairs. Modeling questions such as "Can I play too?" or "Do you want to play house with me?" or using sign language with non-verbal children are effective strategies.
7. The child should be allowed to be as independent as possible with peers. For example, the interventionist can let peers know they can approach a child with a visual impairment and say, "Hi Eric, it's Joey." A child with cerebral palsy who uses a wheelchair for mobility might participate in an art project by sitting in a modified chair at a table with other children rather than in the wheelchair.
8. Straightforward, honest answers to questions posed by children will help facilitate understanding of disabling conditions. Specialized equipment may isolate a child if the equipment remains a mystery. The interventionist should be open and honest

when answering questions from the child's peers, and allow him or her to explore adaptive equipment (with the permission of the child), with the understanding that the equipment is a tool and not a toy.

9. The interventionist should assist children without disabilities in learning how to interact and play with peers with disabilities. For example, one can tell the peer that, when he or she colors with a child with a visual impairment, it is helpful to put markers back in the original place; when a peer talks to a child with a hearing impairment, it helps to face the child and speak clearly. Peers should be encouraged to address children with disabilities directly (e.g., "Can I push your wheelchair outside?").

10. It is helpful to enhance the social image of children with disabilities by selecting clothing, toys, and accessories (e.g., lunch boxes) that are age appropriate and currently popular.

SUMMARY

The material in this section is designed to set the stage for efficient and effective use of the AEPS Curriculum in conjunction with the AEPS Test. In particular, strategies for using naturally occurring environmental arrangements and activities to embed children's IEP/IFSP goals and objectives are described. In addition, the planning of interesting activities and the creation of activity centers to provide opportunities to practice targeted goals and objectives are discussed.

Although the content of this curriculum can be used with teacher-directed approaches, we believe that interventionists should begin by using an activity-based approach. The use of routine, child-initiated, and meaningful planned activities capitalizes on children's interests and motivation and therefore should produce effective and efficient learning.

REFERENCES

Bricker, D., & Pretti-Frontzcak, K. (Eds.). (1996). *Assessment, evaluation, and programming system for infants and children: Vol. 3. AEPS measurement for birth to three years.* Baltimore: Paul H. Brookes Publishing Co.

Dodge, D.T., & Colker, L.J. (1992). *The creative curriculum for early childhood.* Washington, DC: Teaching Strategies.

Assessment, Evaluation, and Programming System Curriculum

AEPS

FINE MOTOR DOMAIN

Motor development provides children a means of independence that enhances sensory stimulation and interactions with people and the physical environment, facilitating all other areas of development. Fine motor development refers to the control of arm and hand movements involved in reaching, grasping, releasing, and manipulating objects. The development of fine motor control skills typically involves stability and strength in the neck, trunk, and arms as well as eye–hand coordination, the perception of touch, accurate visual-spatial perception, the ability to organize and sequence fine motor tasks, an awareness of the body in space, and the coordination of the left and right sides of the body. Children's increasing mastery of fine motor skills contributes to their enjoyment of manipulating toys with many small pieces, their independence in dressing and undressing, and their experimentation during creative play activities with scissors, crayons, and pencils.

Infants initially have little voluntary control of their arms, hands, and fingers. In the first 6 months of life, the infant's uncontrolled prereaching movements progress to voluntary reaching patterns. The integration of the muscles in the shoulder and elbow with the muscles of the wrist and hand contributes to the development of the infant's grasp. The infant's repeated interactions with the environment and the maturation of the central nervous system are responsible for the development of eye–hand coordination. The infant learns to manipulate simple objects by mouthing, waving, shaking, and banging. Newborns will automatically close their hands when an object is placed in the middle of their palm. Typically, by 12 months of age, the infant's grasping patterns have evolved to include more precise movements. The raking finger movement used in picking up a block and the pincer grasp used in picking up a raisin are two more advanced grasping patterns.

The infant's initial gross response for releasing objects is replaced with fine motor skills required for controlled release of objects. The eye–hand coordination necessary to precisely time grasp-and-release patterns in the manipulation of objects is demonstrated in the young child's independence in eating with a spoon. The infant's ability to coordinate sight and touch is refined as the brain matures and arm movements become more controlled, contributing to the infant's sophistication in manipulating objects. Typically, by 18 months of age, the hand grasp and the random, uncontrolled release has been refined to include independent coordination of the fingers and the thumb. Toddlers experiment with the complex manipulation of two or more objects, and their play becomes more meaningful and goal directed. During play activities, toddlers are interested in stacking blocks or using a crayon to scribble spontaneously and imitate a vertical stroke.

During the preschool years, most young children become increasingly successful in using two hands together, enabling them to perform tasks such as stringing beads.

The fine motor control required in the manipulation of handheld objects becomes progressively more refined between the ages of 3 and 5. Preschool children develop the dexterity and speed necessary for writing skills. This is also the time when most children establish hand dominance in fine motor tasks, and they learn to use the preferred hand to perform a number of skills, such as unscrewing a jar, activating a wind-up toy, and buttoning a shirt. The preschool child's fine motor skills, coordination of the left and right sides of the body, and visual skills enable the child to tie his or her shoes.

The Fine Motor Domain of the AEPS Curriculum was designed to create opportunities for young children to practice reaching, grasping, releasing, and manipulating objects for the purpose of mastering the fine motor skills required for independence in activities of daily living and success in the academic environment. The preferred approach is to embed training goals into the activities and routines that typically occur throughout the child's day. The Fine Motor Domain is composed of two strands. Strand A (Manipulation of Objects) focuses on a young child's ability to coordinate two-hand activities, beginning with manipulating two objects and progressing to the fine motor control required to manipulate handheld instruments (scissors) and different types of fasteners. Strand B (Prewriting) addresses the use of each hand independently from the other. This is represented in the development of hand dominance and the continued refinement of dexterity, speed, and precision necessary for prewriting skills, beginning with copying simple shapes and moving to printing letters.

The Fine Motor Domain curriculum is divided into four sections: 1) Intervention Considerations, 2) Suggested Activities, 3) Using Activity-Based Intervention, and 4) Domain Goals. Intervention Considerations addresses important factors an interventionist may wish to consider prior to and when working with children who are at risk for or who have disabilities. Suggested Activities provides a selected list of activities that may be particularly helpful when working on fine motor skills. This section also provides suggestions for additional materials that will increase the opportunities for children to practice targeted fine motor skills. The third section provides an illustration of how to target IEP/IFSP goals in the Fine Motor Domain using an activity-based intervention approach. The final section, Domain Goals, provides suggestions for concurrent goals, daily routines, environmental arrangements, and planned activities in the home and classroom for each goal identified in the Fine Motor Domain of the AEPS Test for Three to Six Years. This section also lists other commercially available curricula that provide intervention activities for each goal.

INTERVENTION CONSIDERATIONS

General considerations when working on fine motor goals are discussed below.

■ Some preschool special education programs emphasize school skills (e.g., writing skills) in an attempt to have children look as "normal" as possible and give them an academic head start. It is important to remember that nonacademic skills, such as effective communication and social skills, following directions, attending to an activity for short periods of time without supervision, and moving easily from one activity to the next, are as important for success in public school environments as are academic skills.

■ An occupational or physical therapist or both can help assess children with motor impairments to determine if a fine motor goal is functional or realistically attainable for a child. In addition to providing information concerning the modification of motor activities, environmental arrangements, and utilization of adaptive equipment, a therapist may recommend some type of preparation, such as therapy to help normalize a child's muscle tone to enhance the child's participation in fine motor activities.

■ Children will benefit from planned activities that provide practice on fine motor goals. In addition to practicing motor skills, children with motor skill impairments may benefit from compensatory strategies such as modifications to the environment or adaptive equipment to increase their independence. Lap trays on wheelchairs provide excellent surfaces for children to write, draw, and manipulate objects. Adaptive equipment such as hand splints, adapted scissors, built-up grips for writing tools, nonslip surfaces, or Velcro fasteners can provide the support necessary for children to participate in a variety of activities. It is important to consult a qualified specialist to provide information concerning special equipment and adaptations to the environment, activities, or materials.

■ Only after it has been determined that a particular child is not likely to achieve the functional fine motor control required for fine motor skills, such as writing, should alternative methods or adaptations of that skill be considered.

■ Preschool children may intentionally avoid participation in tasks that accentuate their limited fine motor control. Sensitivity regarding interaction with peers is important when encouraging children to participate in fine motor activities at their present level of mastery.

■ Be aware of how adaptive devices may prevent children from interacting with their peers. Positioning is an important consideration for children with motor impairments. The child should be upright and well supported when participating in fine motor activities such as cutting with scissors or writing. However, adaptive equipment such as lap trays on wheelchairs creates physical barriers between a child and peers. Whenever possible, children should be seated in regular chairs or in adapted chairs (if extra support is required), or positioned on the floor with their peers.

■ Plan adequate time for children to complete tasks. Providing sufficient time for the child to practice a skill may make the difference in a child with sensory and/or motor impairments achieving independence in dressing, for example.

SUGGESTED ACTIVITIES

It may be helpful to designate an area of the classroom or home environment for fine motor activities. Store materials on low, open shelves to make them accessible and to allow children to be active participants in setup and cleanup activities. Keep the area interesting and appealing to children by rotating materials periodically, making sure the materials are clean, complete, and in good condition.

Some adaptations may be required to make activities accessible to children with sensory and/or motor impairments. Adaptations may be simple, such as using a pair of adapted "loop" scissors or a nonslip surface for puzzles, or more complicated, such as assistive devices for arms. Decisions concerning environmental arrangements or modifications of materials may make the difference between the child completing the activity independently or requiring assistance. Consult a motor specialist for adaptations.

The following list of activities and materials may be particularly helpful for eliciting skills within the Fine Motor Domain. For a complete list of activities, see Section V.

Dramatic Play Activities

Children can work on fine motor goals in a naturally occurring context in dramatic play. The following activities are particularly helpful when embedding fine motor goals: Housekeeping and Post Office.

Other Activities

- Paper Chains
- Books/Book Making
- Fall Colors
- Paper Bag Animals
- Collages
- Group Fingerpainting

- Dinosaur Eggs
- Manipulatives
- Washing Babies
- Stringing Activities
- Weaving

USING ACTIVITY-BASED INTERVENTION

An illustration of how an interventionist can incorporate activity-based strategies to enhance the development of a child's fine motor skills is provided below. The child's targeted IEP/IFSP objective is to copy simple shapes (e.g., circles, crosses, Ts).

- The interventionist observes that Timmy chooses to play in the sandbox. She *follows the child's lead* by joining the child in his play and encourages peers to join. The classroom consists of a *heterogeneous* (at varied skill levels) group of children, providing opportunities for the child to learn new skills by observing peer models or to enhance skills by assisting children who are less able. The interventionist *expands on the child's initiation* by picking up a stick and drawing simple shapes in the sand, using *self-talk* to comment on her own actions ("I'm going to draw with this stick").
- The interventionist *models* how to draw simple shapes in the sand and draws Timmy's attention to peers who are displaying more advanced skills (e.g., "Look at Latifa. She's making circles in the sand").
- The interventionist uses additional strategies to encourage *multiple opportunities* for Timmy to practice a skill, such as *parallel talk* to comment on the shapes he has drawn, or provides a new "twist" ("Can you make a big circle?") to encourage Timmy to continue practicing the skill.
- Throughout the activity, the interventionist uses the *least amount of assistance* necessary for Timmy to successfully practice targeted goals.

DOMAIN GOALS

This section provides suggestions for concurrent goals, daily routines, environmental arrangements, and planned activities for the fine motor goals listed in the AEPS Test for Three to Six Years. If an objective has been targeted, the interventionist can turn to the corresponding goal and determine which suggestions are relevant to facilitate that objective. A standard format is used for each goal: 1) Strand, 2) Goal, 3) Objective(s), 4) Concurrent Goals, 5) Daily Routines, 6) Environmental Arrangements, 7) Planned Activities, and 8) Preschool Curricula with Similar Goals. Concurrent Goals list AEPS goals that can often be addressed at the same time the child works on the target goal or associated objectives. Daily Routines present a list of routine activities that may provide opportunities to practice targeted skills. The Environmental Arrangements should be considered when designing children's programs around child-initiated, routine, and planned activities. The Planned Activities offer examples of how to embed targeted goals within the context of planned activities. Finally, Preschool Curricula with Similar Goals list other curricula that can be used to supplement the AEPS Curriculum for Three to Six Years. If a given program has one or more of these preschool curricula, the interventionist can refer to the referenced sections to find additional programming strategies for the targeted goal or objective. Additional information on daily routines, environmental arrangements, planned activities, and themes is provided in Section III.

Strand A   Manipulation of Objects
        G1.0   Manipulates two small objects at same time
              1.1   Manipulates two hand-size objects at same time
        G2.0   Cuts out shapes with curved lines
              2.1   Cuts out shapes with straight lines
              2.2   Cuts paper in two
        G3.0   Ties string-type fastener
              3.1   Fastens buttons
              3.2   Threads and zips zipper

Strand B   Prewriting
        G1.0   Copies complex shapes
              1.1   Copies simple shapes
        G2.0   Prints first name
              2.1   Prints three letters
              2.2   Copies first name
              2.3   Copies three letters

FM

Strand A   Manipulation of Objects

GOAL 1   Manipulates two small objects at same time

Objective 1.1   Manipulates two hand-size objects at same time

CONCURRENT GOALS

Adap A:1.0   Eats and drinks a variety of foods using appropriate utensils with little or no spilling
Adap A:2.0   Prepares and serves food
Adap C:1.0   Unfastens fasteners on garments
Adap C:3.0   Fastens fasteners on garments
Cog A:2.0   Watches, listens, and participates during small group activities
Cog A:3.0   Watches, listens, and participates during large group activities
Cog C:1.0   Groups objects, people, or events on the basis of specified criteria
Soc B:1.0   Meets physical needs in socially appropriate ways

DAILY ROUTINES

Routine events that provide opportunities for children to practice manipulating objects include the following:

Unstructured play times
Cleanup
Snack time

Example   After completion of an art project, Timmy's mother helps him match the colors of the markers with the caps before asking him to put the caps back on the markers. *(FM A:1.0)*

ENVIRONMENTAL ARRANGEMENTS

■ Present materials that provide opportunities for children to manipulate objects (e.g., blocks, Tinkertoys, stringing and weaving activities; see Construction/Manipulation Activities in Section V) and arrange the classroom into activity areas that include a dramatic play center. The home and classroom environment should be arranged to allow safe, purposeful exploration of hand-size objects.

Example   The interventionist assists Eric, who has a visual impairment, in choosing building materials from the shelf in the classroom. She asks Eric, "Do you want to build something with the blocks or the Tinkertoys?", as she guides his hands first to the open container of blocks and then to the Tinkertoys. After Eric selects the

blocks, the interventionist sits down to play with him at the table. Eric puts the blocks together to "build a bridge" with verbal cues and physical assistance from the interventionist. *(FM A:1.1)*
■ A discussion of adaptations necessary to successfully practice this goal and its associated objective should include the specific activity; the environmental arrangement of the activity, including the arrangement of materials and positioning of children; special equipment needs of the children (assistive devices); and the specific texture, size, shape, and weight of the objects to be manipulated.
■ Practicing manipulating objects is essential to the development of fine motor control with handheld implements (e.g., scissors, crayons, pencils).

PLANNED ACTIVITIES

Two examples of how to embed this goal and the associated objective within activities are presented here. For a complete set of activities that address goals and objectives across domains, see Section V.

Fruit Salad

Children cut soft fruits such as bananas, watermelon, pears, grapes, and strawberries into chunks with dull plastic knives. They put the fruit in a bowl and can stir in yogurt or sprinkle granola over the mixture and eat their creations for snack. Children have opportunities to manipulate objects as they get ready for (e.g., button their smocks), participate in (e.g., stabilize the fruit with one hand while cutting with the other), and clean up (e.g., put lids back on yogurt containers) the activity.

Cheerios Necklaces

Children make necklaces out of Cheerios. The interventionist ties a large knot in one end of a piece of heavy yarn or string and wraps a short piece of tape around the other end to make a firm tip. Opportunities can be provided for the children to manipulate two hand-size objects by placing the Cheerios in a plastic jar and encouraging children to take off the lid to retrieve Cheerios. Children can string Cheerios, tie the string ends, and paint the Cheerios to make a necklace.

Example When the class prepares to make a Cheerios necklace, Maria independently walks to the table using her walker. Maria sits in her chair, which is adapted with additional trunk support to maximize fine motor control. The interventionist congratulates Maria on successfully stabilizing the string with her right hand and manipulating the Cheerios with her left. A few minutes later the interventionist provides physical assistance and verbal cues so that Maria can practice stringing the Cheerios with her right hand while holding the string with her left. *(FM A:1.0)*

PRESCHOOL CURRICULA WITH SIMILAR GOALS

The following preschool curricula provide information on this goal or similar goals. Interventionists whose programs have access to one or more of these curricula may refer to the referenced sections for additional programming strategies.

The Carolina Curriculum for Preschoolers with Special Needs
Fine Motor Skills
■ Manipulation

FM A

- Bilateral skills
- Tool use

The Creative Curriculum

Blocks
Table Toys
Art
Sand and Water
Outdoors

High Scope—Young Children in ACTION

Active Learning
- Manipulating, transforming, and combining materials
- Choosing materials, activities, purposes
- Acquiring skills with tools and equipment

Peabody Developmental Motor Scales Activity Cards

Fine motor
- Winding toys
- String beads

Portage Guide to Early Education Activity Cards

Motor
- String beads
- Take-apart/put-together toys
- Nesting toys
- Threaded objects

GOAL 2.0   Cuts out shapes with curved lines

Objective 2.1   Cuts out shapes with straight lines
Objective 2.2   Cuts paper in two

CONCURRENT GOALS

Cog A   Participation (all goals)
Cog B:2.0   Demonstrates understanding of five different shapes

DAILY ROUTINES

Routine activities that provide opportunities for children to practice cutting skills include indoor play times. The use of children's scissors in the home or classroom requires close supervision to ensure a safe, enjoyable play experience.

Example: During indoor play activities at home, Joey's mother draws different sizes of circles on colored pieces of paper. Joey, his mother, brother, and sister follow the lines to cut out the circles. Together they create a funny "circle" animal by pasting the shapes on a large piece of paper. *(FM A:2.0)*

ENVIRONMENTAL ARRANGEMENTS

■ Materials that provide opportunities for children to use scissors (e.g., paper, stencils, writing tools) should be available for the children to play with during indoor play. Arrange the classroom into activity areas, including an art and dramatic play center. Many children enjoy cutting Play-Doh, which provides a stable material to practice cutting skills.

   Example: Timmy is a postal clerk in the classroom "post office." When a classmate arrives to buy "stamps," the interventionist reminds Timmy to first cut out the "stamps." Timmy independently cuts straight lines with his adapted (loop) scissors and proudly sells the "stamps" to his classmate. *(FM A:2.1, with adapted materials)*

■ Art/writing centers in the home or classroom should include an adequate space with tables and chairs, as well as a plan for setup and cleanup with adult and child responsibilities designated.

■ The design of activities for children with sensory and/or motor impairments may require consultation with a qualified motor specialist. Adaptations of fine motor activities with scissors for a child with sensory and/or motor impairments will include adequate supervision and safety procedures, the positioning of the child, the height of the surface, the special equipment needs of the child (assistive devices for the arms and hands), the variety of adapted scissors available, the child's level of participation, and the optimal combination of modeling, physical assistance, and verbal cues.

■ The fine motor control of handheld implements such as scissors requires strength and stability in the arm and hand, finger dexterity, the coordination of both sides of the body, and the ability to accurately plan and time the necessary fine motor movement pattern for cutting. Hand dominance begins to develop prior to 2 years of age and is followed by a period of apparent ambidexterity between the ages of 2½ and 3½. From 4 to 6 years of age, right- or left-hand dominance gradually increases. In general, 4-year-old children cut with scissors using the preferred hand.

PLANNED ACTIVITIES

Two examples of how to embed this goal and the associated objectives within activities are presented here. For a complete set of activities that address goals and objectives across domains, see Section V.

Dinosaur Eggs

The children make dinosaur eggs by cutting out oval shapes from paper and decorating them with crayons, markers, and glitter. Children practice cutting skills as they cut out eggs and shapes with straight or curved lines (e.g., circles, squares, triangles) to paste on their eggs for decoration; if necessary, adaptive scissors can be provided. The least level of assistance necessary for each child to complete the activity is provided by the interventionist.

Example   Eric is responsible for cutting out the various sizes of white dinosaur eggs for the class dinosaur project. His interventionist places the scissors in the regular upper right-hand location on Eric's project tray. After successfully locating the scissors, Eric follows the bold black line on the white paper (high contrast) to cut out his dinosaur eggs. His interventionist's advanced planning allowed Eric to complete his dinosaur project independently. *(FM A:2.0)*

My Stegosaurus

In this art activity, children create a stegosaurus. Depending on varying skill levels, the interventionist may provide either an outline for the children to cut out or a precut version for children to decorate with crayons, markers, and glitter. Opportunities can be provided for the children to cut out shapes with straight lines while cutting out triangles to make the plates that line the dinosaur's back. *(FM A:2 1)*

PRESCHOOL CURRICULA WITH SIMILAR GOALS

The following preschool curricula provide information on this goal or similar goals. Interventionists whose programs have access to one or more of these curricula may refer to the referenced sections for additional programming strategies.

The Carolina Curriculum for Preschoolers with Special Needs
Visual-Motor Skills
- Cutting

The Creative Curriculum
Art

High Scope—Young Children in ACTION
Active Learning
- Manipulating, transforming, and combining materials
- Choosing materials, activities, purposes

Peabody Developmental Motor Scales Activity Cards
Fine motor
- Cutting circle
- Cutting square

Portage Guide to Early Education Activity Cards
Motor
- Cut pictures
- Cut/paste shapes
- Cut circle
- Cut curve
- Snip with scissors

GOAL 3.0   Ties string-type fastener

Objective 3.1	Fastens buttons
Objective 3.2	Threads and zips zipper

CONCURRENT GOALS

Adap C:1.0   Unfastens fasteners on garments
Adap C:3.0   Fastens fasteners on garments
Cog A:2.0   Watches, listens, and participates during small group activities
Cog A:3.0   Watches, listens, and participates during large group activities
Cog G:1.0   Engages in imaginary play
Soc B:1.0   Meets physical needs in socially appropriate ways

DAILY ROUTINES

Routine activities that provide opportunities for children to practice manipulating different types of fasteners include the following:

Dressing and undressing
Arrival and departure
Indoor play activities (e.g., dramatic play, doll play)
Bath time

Example   When Alice wakes in the morning, she transfers from the bed to her wheelchair in order to complete her personal hygiene routine in the privacy of the bathroom. In the bedroom, she selects clothes from the open shelves at the appropriate height. After placing her clothes on the bed, Alice transfers from her wheelchair to the bed because it is easier to put her jeans on while lying down. Alice dresses independently, transferring back to her wheelchair. When breakfast is finished, Alice's mother reminds her to wear her sweater to school. With her mother's encouragement, Alice takes the time to button the sweater before they leave for the bus. *(FM A:3.1)*

ENVIRONMENTAL ARRANGEMENTS

- Select a large number of materials that provide opportunities for children to manipulate different types of fasteners (e.g., dolls with doll clothes with fasteners such as laces, zippers, buttons, or Velcro fasteners; dress-up clothes with different types of fasteners). Arrange the classroom into activity areas, including a dramatic play center, and store materials so that children have easy access. Children with visual impairments should be given adequate time to tactilely or visually explore what they will be manipulating. For example, have the child touch and look at all the buttons and holes before attempting to button. As the child buttons items, verbally describe his or her actions and provide hand-over-hand assistance if necessary.

Example   Latifa's mother asked the interventionist to teach Latifa how to fasten zippers, because she always needs help zipping her new winter coat. When it "rains" in the dramatic play center campground, Latifa runs to put on a raincoat. The interventionist stands behind Latifa and models threading and zipping the raincoat. With continued verbal cues, Latifa zips the raincoat independently. *(FM A:3.2)*

■ Consultation with a qualified motor specialist may assist the interventionist in designing planned activities to include children with sensory and/or motor impairments. Adaptations for manipulating fasteners to maximize a child's potential for functional independence may include a discussion of position (standing or sitting), sequence of the activity, type of fastener, modification of clothes, assistive devices for the arm or hand, and the optimal combination of modeling, physical assistance, and verbal cues.

■ Children with disabilities who have limitations in fine motor control may need the assistance of peers, family members, or classroom personnel in dressing activities. Children with fine motor impairments typically require significantly greater amounts of time to complete dressing activities. The interventionist should schedule adequate time to manipulate fasteners during dressing and play activities rather than simply offering assistance to save time.

■ Mastery of the fine motor control required to manipulate various types of fasteners involves the integration of body awareness; coordination of the left and right sides of the body; eye–hand coordination; mobility and strength of the neck, trunk, arms, and hands; accurate visual-spatial perception; perception of touch; and correct organization and sequencing of the fine motor movement pattern.

PLANNED ACTIVITIES

Two examples of how to embed this goal and the associated objectives within activities are presented here. For a complete set of activities that address goals and objectives across domains, see Section V.

Feet Painting

Children take their shoes off and paint with their feet on a big piece of paper. This is a very messy project; tubs of water, soap, and towels for cleanup, as well as an extra adult to help, will be needed. Opportunities can be provided to manipulate fasteners as children get ready for the activity (e.g., buttoning or tying on a smock) and at the end of the activity, when children should be encouraged and prompted to tie their shoes. The interventionist should provide the least level of assistance necessary for children to meet targeted goals.

Washing Babies

Children wash their "babies" (rubber dolls) in tubs of water with soap and washcloths, dry the babies with towels, and dress them in doll clothes. The children will enjoy expanding on the activity by shampooing and brushing their babies' hair or pretending to brush their babies' teeth. To keep dry, the children can wear smocks that fasten with buttons, zippers, string, or Velcro fasteners. The interventionist should provide doll clothes with different types of fasteners, as well as doll shoes that have string fasteners.

Example   Timmy is ready to give his baby doll a bath. He leaves her in the crib while he puts on his smock, independently attaching the Velcro fasteners carefully in place. He undresses her, washes her in the bath, and wraps her in a towel. After Timmy dresses his baby doll in a playsuit, the interventionist models putting the buttons through the button holes. With physical assistance and verbal cues, Timmy successfully buttons the last button. *(FM A:3.1)*

PRESCHOOL CURRICULA WITH SIMILAR GOALS

The following preschool curricula provide information on this goal or similar goals. Interventionists whose programs have access to one or more of these curricula may refer to the referenced sections for additional programming strategies.

The Carolina Curriculum for Preschoolers with Special Needs
Fine Motor Skills
- Bilateral skills
- Manipulation

Self-Help Skills
- Dressing

The Creative Curriculum
House Corner

High Scope—Young Children in ACTION
Active Learning
- Taking care of one's own needs

Peabody Developmental Motor Scales Activity Cards
Fine Motor
- Buttoning

Portage Guide to Early Education Activity Cards
Self-Help
- Ties
- Buttons
- Zips

Strand B   Prewriting

GOAL 1.0   Copies complex shapes

Objective 1.1   Copies simple shapes

CONCURRENT GOALS

Cog A:1.0   Initiates and completes age-appropriate activities
Cog A:2.0   Watches, listens, and participates during small group activities
Cog B:2.0   Demonstrates understanding of five different shapes
Cog H:3.0   Identifies printed numerals 1–10
Cog I:3.0   Sounds out words
Cog I:4.0   Reads words by sight

DAILY ROUTINES

Routine activities that provide opportunities for children to copy shapes include indoor and outdoor play times.

Example   While playing outside in the sandbox, Joey picks up a stick and starts to "write." The interventionist follows Joey's lead, picking up a stick and drawing a circle saying, "I'm making a circle. Can you make one too?" *(FM B:1.1)*

ENVIRONMENTAL ARRANGEMENTS

- Design the home and classroom to include materials that provide opportunities for children to copy shapes during indoor and outdoor play times. For example, provide writing tools such as chalk, pens, pencils, crayons, and markers, as well as materials to write and draw on, such as lined paper, construction paper, or cardboard. Blackboards, tabletops, sandboxes, and easels offer a selection of work surfaces.
- General adaptations for prewriting skills may include using contrasting surfaces such as bold pencil and dark lines on white paper, increasing finger sensitivity for children who will be using braille, or using raised-line paper or a screen board for coloring or writing.
- Provide pictures, stencils, and models of simple and complex shapes in the classroom and art center.
- Some children with motor impairments will require alternative methods of written communication. However, children should continue practicing writing skills, with adaptations as necessary, until it is determined that this will not be a functional method of communication for the individual child.

- The interventionist should consult with a qualified motor specialist in designing and implementing activities for children with sensory and/or motor impairments. Often, a process of trial and error is important to determine a child's best position; any special adapted equipment needs (e.g., assistive devices for the arms and hands, adapted writing tools); the best writing surface and writing implement; and the ideal combination of physical assistance and verbal cues to promote mastery of prewriting skills.
- Precision in prewriting skills requires not only fine motor control but body awareness; integration of the left and right sides of the body; eye–hand coordination; mobility and strength of the neck, trunk, arms, and hands; perception of touch; visual-spatial perception; and correct organization and sequencing of the fine motor pattern. Children who are 1–2 years old will hold a crayon or pencil with a gross grasp to imitate a scribble or to scribble spontaneously. As the control of handheld implements becomes more refined between the ages of 2 and 4, children will begin to imitate horizontal and vertical strokes, copy a circle, and trace a diamond. Children between the ages of 4 and 6 are able to copy a cross, square, triangle, and diamond using an adult fine motor grasp.

PLANNED ACTIVITIES

Two examples of how to embed this goal and the associated objectives within activities are presented here. For a complete set of activities that address goals and objectives across domains, see Section V.

Shaving Cream Fun

Children experiment with the sense of touch while finger painting on a surface with shaving cream. The interventionist prompts the children to copy shapes in the shaving cream by providing models of shapes while drawing pictures (e.g., drawing a circle to make a face, a rectangle to make a car) and by encouraging the children to draw shapes. Smocks, tubs of water, towels, and sponges help with cleanup.

My Face

Children look at themselves in a mirror, then draw their faces and talk about what the eyes do (see), nose does (smell), and ears do (hear). The children can either draw their picture on a piece of paper or, if enough mirror space is available, they can draw their face directly on the mirror with erasable markers. The interventionist can model drawing a circle for a face and provide opportunities for children to copy complex shapes by embellishing pictures with triangle hats, stick figure bodies, or square houses.

Example Alice uses a pencil with an adapted grip to draw her face. The interventionist models the activity by first drawing her own face and encourages Alice with verbal cues as needed to copy complex shapes. *(FM B:1.0, with adapted materials)*

Note Creating a perfect picture is not the goal of this activity. Depending on individual goals, children should be given the least level of assistance necessary to practice targeted goals.

PRESCHOOL CURRICULA WITH SIMILAR GOALS

The following preschool curricula provide information on this goal or similar goals. Interventionists whose programs have access to one or more of these curricula may refer to the referenced sections for additional programming strategies.

The Carolina Curriculum for Preschoolers with Special Needs
Visual-Motor Skills
■ Pencil control and copying

The Creative Curriculum
Art
Library

Peabody Developmental Motor Scales Activity Cards
Fine Motor
■ Copying square
■ Copying cross

Portage Guide to Early Education Activity Cards
Motor
■ Copies drawings
Cognitive
■ Copies shapes

GOAL 2.0   Prints first name

Objective 2.1	Prints three letters
Objective 2.2	Copies first name
Objective 2.3	Copies three letters

CONCURRENT GOALS

Cog A:1.0	Initiates and completes age-appropriate activities
Cog A:2.0	Watches, listens, and participates during small group activities
Cog I	Prereading (all goals)
SC A:1.0	Uses words, phrases, or sentences to inform, direct, ask questions, and express anticipation, imagination, affect, and emotions

DAILY ROUTINES

Routine activities that provide opportunities for children to copy and print letters include indoor and outdoor play times.

Example   At school Eric learned to print his name with a screen board, which uses a tactile model so he can feel the letters that have been written. He is excited about showing his mother how he can write by himself. During play time at home, Eric uses a name card that allows him to feel his name. His mother encourages his writing by saying, "I can read that. It says Eric." *(FM B:2.2, adapted)*

Example Whenever children with this goal complete art projects at school, the interventionist reminds them to write their names on their pictures. By providing the optimal combination of modeling, verbal cues, and physical assistance, the interventionist ensures that the children successfully write their names on their art projects.

ENVIRONMENTAL ARRANGEMENTS

- The classroom environment should have letters and words prominently displayed. Include examples around the classroom of the letters of the alphabet and children's names. For example, children's names can be displayed on helper charts, attendance charts (the children sign in when they come to school, with assistance if necessary), and individual cubbies. Name cards are made from cardboard to keep in the art center as models. Words for the days of the week, classroom jobs, materials, and snack items can be displayed around the classroom in appropriate locations to provide letter models. Books in the library provide letter models.

    Example The dramatic play center in the classroom is arranged as a restaurant. Latifa and Joey sit at the table during free play and practice copying letters found in the classroom that represent different menu items. During lunch, Latifa and Joey take the other children's food orders by writing the letters on a small pad of paper. *(FM B:2.1)*

- Design the home and classroom to include materials that provide opportunities for the children to copy shapes during indoor play times. Include writing tools such as chalk, pens, pencils, crayons, and markers, as well as materials to write and draw on, such as lined paper, construction paper, and cardboard. Chalkboards, tabletops, sandboxes, and easels offer a selection of work surfaces.

- As children approach school age, greater emphasis is placed on table and chair activities specifically designed to refine the adult fine motor grasp. The increased practice of this goal and its associated objectives in a context similar to the requirements of a school environment enhance the probability of a child successfully transferring prewriting skills to the academic setting.

- General adaptations for prewriting skills include using contrasting surfaces such as bold pencil and dark lines on white paper, increasing finger sensitivity for children who use braille, or using raised-line paper or a screen board for coloring or writing.

- Consult a qualified motor specialist for adaptations that facilitate a child's ability to create letters. Adaptations include the child's positioning, the height and angle of the writing surface, assistive devices for the arms and hands, and the size and weight of the writing implement.

- Some children with motor impairments will require alternative methods of written communication. However, children should continue practicing writing skills, with adaptations as necessary, until it is determined that this will not be a functional method of communication for the individual child.

PLANNED ACTIVITIES

Two examples of how to embed this goal and the associated objectives within activities are presented here. For a complete set of activities that address goals and objectives across domains, see Section V.

Pudding Painting

The interventionist makes instant pudding (food coloring can be added to vanilla pudding) and puts it on individual paper plates for the children to fingerpaint with. Children will be surprised when they realize they can lick their fingers. Children talk about how the pudding feels, tastes, and smells. The interventionist provides models of different letters and encourages children to copy or print letters in the pudding.

Example   The interventionist draws a *J* in the pudding, commenting, "I'm making a *J*, the first letter in your name, Joey." *(FM B:2.3)*

Sand Print Names

Children write their names on a piece of cardboard, tracing the letters in glue and then sprinkling sand (or cornmeal, glitter, and so forth) over the letters. The glue is allowed to dry and the excess sand is shaken off. The children can then "feel" their names and use their name cards for a model in future activities.

Note   Provide necessary level of assistance for children to produce a good model of their name.

PRESCHOOL CURRICULA WITH SIMILAR GOALS

The following preschool curricula provide information on this goal or similar goals. Interventionists whose programs have access to one or more of these curricula may refer to the referenced sections for additional programming strategies.

The Carolina Curriculum for Preschoolers with Special Needs

Visual-Motor Skills
■ Pencil control and copying

The Creative Curriculum

Art
Library

Portage Guide to Early Education Activity Cards

Motor
■ Prints letters

GROSS MOTOR DOMAIN

Children's successful negotiation of the physical environment is largely dependent on their gross motor skills. Gross motor development refers to movements involving the large muscles of the body, such as 1) assuming and maintaining postures such as sitting and standing; and 2) performing whole body movements such as crawling, walking, and jumping. The sequence of gross motor development is determined largely by the maturation of the child's central nervous system.

Infants initially have little ability to support their body against gravity and are largely dependent on caregivers to meet their fundamental needs. Involuntary primitive and postural reflexes present at birth are inhibited in the first 12 months of life. Integration of the sensory and motor systems occurs, and infants develop voluntary movement. Gross motor milestones that typically develop in the first 18 months of life include head control, rolling segmentally, sitting alone, crawling, pulling to stand, creeping, and walking independently. Individual differences in the rate of acquisition of gross motor milestones may be a result of the infant's experience with the environment.

Stability, locomotion, and manipulation movements are mastered through practice in the second 12 months of life. The child practices and refines the gross motor skills learned during the first year and becomes more adept at skills requiring balance. The "toddler" learns to assume a standing position from sitting and begins to take steps backward while pulling a toy. Running and stair climbing are basic motor patterns that emerge during the second year. These gross motor accomplishments enhance children's cognitive and social growth, providing the independence necessary to explore and interact with objects and people in their environment.

During early childhood, increased control of voluntary movement contributes to the child's interest in experimenting with movement through active exploration of the environment. Attaining stability in an upright position against the force of gravity allows children to develop the dynamic and static balance required for balancing on one foot or walking on a balance beam. Walking provides the foundation for running, jumping, hopping, and skipping. The combination of stability and movement allows early reach and grasp-and-release responses to evolve into throwing, catching, and kicking activities.

The development and refinement of gross motor movements may be facilitated through play. Encouragement as well as opportunity for practice and instruction promote children's continued learning from experiences with movement. Play in early childhood should include activities designed to enhance perceptual motor development. Gross motor movement requires body awareness, the knowledge of body parts, and the ability to organize the body to perform various movements. These skills include spatial awareness, knowledge of the body in relationship to space; directional awareness, understanding of up–down, in–out, front–back, and top–bottom; and temporal awareness, the coordination of the sensory and motor systems through rhythmic movement.

The Gross Motor Domain of the AEPS Curriculum was designed to systematically build and enhance children's gross motor movement in daily activities. The preferred approach is to embed training into the activities and routines that typically occur throughout the child's day. The Gross Motor Domain is composed of two strands. Strand A (Balance and Mobility in Standing and Walking) focuses on the refinement of stability. Strand B (Play Skills) encourages a diversity of manipulation and locomotion movements that can be used to facilitate motor development and enhance social interactions with peers. Jumping, running, skipping, riding and steering a two-wheel bicycle, bouncing, catching, throwing, and kicking are addressed in this strand.

The Gross Motor Domain curriculum is divided into four sections: 1) Intervention Considerations, 2) Suggested Activities, 3) Using Activity-Based Intervention, 4) and Domain Goals. Intervention Considerations addresses important factors an interventionist may wish to consider prior to and when working with children at risk for or who have disabilities. Suggested Activities provides a selected list of activities that may be particularly helpful when working on gross motor skills. This section also provides suggestions for additional materials that will increase the opportunities for children to practice targeted gross motor skills. The third section provides an illustration of how to target IEP/IFSP goals in the Gross Motor Domain using an activity-based intervention approach. The final section, Domain Goals, provides suggestions for concurrent goals, daily routines, environmental arrangements, and planned activities in the home and classroom for each goal identified in the Gross Motor Domain of the AEPS Test for Three to Six Years. This section also lists other commercially available curricula that provide intervention activities for each goal.

INTERVENTION CONSIDERATIONS

General considerations when working on gross motor goals are discussed below.

- Safety issues are particularly important when working on gross motor goals. Some goals (e.g., jumping forward) may be inappropriate for children with specific disabilities. Children need to be aware of the limits of indoor and outdoor areas and must develop self-protective skills before working on specific goals (e.g., a child with a visual impairment searches for a handrail before climbing stairs or clears a path before running). Be aware of children's health issues and how those issues may affect decisions concerning gross motor activities.
- An occupational therapist, physical therapist, or both can help assess children to determine if a gross motor goal is functional or realistically attainable. In addition to providing information about the modification of motor activities, arrangement of the environment, and utilization of adaptive equipment, a therapist might recommend some type of preparation, such as therapy to help normalize a child's muscle tone, to help the child participate in motor activities.
- Children with disabilities may benefit from environmental arrangements and planned activities to attain gross motor goals. For example, a child with a visual impairment may benefit from the adaptation of materials (e.g., audible balls) or from being paired with a seeing peer to encourage gross motor skills. Adaptive equipment such as wheelchairs, standers, or braces can provide the support necessary for children to participate in a variety of activities. A qualified specialist should determine

under what circumstances (e.g., daily routines, planned activities) children with motor impairments will need to utilize special equipment.

■ Children may intentionally avoid participation in tasks that accentuate their limited gross motor control. Sensitivity regarding interaction with peers is important when encouraging children to participate in gross motor activities at their present level of mastery.

■ Plan adequate time for children to complete tasks. Providing sufficient time to practice a skill may make the difference in a child with sensory and/or motor impairment achieving independence in walking, for example.

SUGGESTED ACTIVITIES

The following list of activities and materials may be particularly helpful for eliciting skills within the Gross Motor Domain. For a complete list of activities, see Section V.

■ Firefighter Play   ■ Simon Says
■ Spaceship   ■ Obstacle course
■ Follow the Leader   ■ Animal games
■ Group outdoor games   ■ Group games

USING ACTIVITY-BASED INTERVENTION

An illustration of how an interventionist can incorporate activity-based strategies to enhance the development of a child's gross motor skills is provided below. The child's targeted IEP/IFSP objective is to bounce a large ball at least twice, using the palm of one hand.

■ The interventionist *observes* Latifa kicking balls during outdoor play. She *follows the child's lead* by joining Latifa in her play and encourages peers to join in as well. The classroom consists of a *heterogeneous* (at varied skill levels) group of children, providing opportunities for children to learn new skills by observing peer models or to enhance skills by assisting children with fewer abilities.

■ The interventionist *expands on the child's initiation* with the balls by picking up a ball and bouncing it. The interventionist uses *self-talk* to comment on her own actions (e.g., "I'm going to bounce this ball") and draws attention to peers who are *modeling* the targeted skill (e.g., "Look at Manuel! He's bouncing the ball with one hand!").

■ The interventionist uses additional strategies to *encourage multiple opportunities* for the child to practice bouncing. For example, the interventionist uses *parallel talk* to comment on Latifa's attempts to bounce or provides a new twist to the activity, such as counting the number of bounces, introducing different types (sizes, colors) of balls, or trying to bounce the ball on different surfaces to encourage Latifa to keep practicing.

■ Throughout the activity, the interventionist uses the *least amount of assistance* necessary for Latifa to successfully practice targeted goals.

DOMAIN GOALS

This section provides suggestions for concurrent goals, daily routines, environmental arrangements, and planned activities for all of the gross motor goals listed in the AEPS Test for Three to Six Years. If an objective has been targeted, the interventionist can turn to the corresponding goal and determine which suggestions are relevant to facilitate that objective. A standard format is used for each goal: 1) Strand, 2) Goal, 3) Objective(s), 4) Concurrent Goals, 5) Daily Routines, 6) Environmental Arrangements, 7) Planned Activities, and 8) Preschool Curricula with Similar Goals. Concurrent Goals list the AEPS goals that can often be worked on at the same time the child works on the target goal or associated objectives. Daily Routines present a list of routine activities that may provide opportunities to practice targeted skills. The Environmental Arrangements should be considered when designing children's programs around child-initiated, routine, and planned activities. The Planned Activities offer examples of how to embed targeted goals within the context of planned activities. Finally, Preschool Curricula with Similar Goals list other curricula that can be used to supplement the AEPS Curriculum for Three to Six Years. If a given program has one or more of these preschool curricula, the interventionist can refer to the referenced sections to find additional programming strategies for the targeted goal or objective. Additional information on daily routines, environmental arrangements, planned activities, and themes is provided in Section III.

Strand A   Balance and Mobility in Standing and Walking
>   G1.0   Alternates feet walking up and down stairs
>   >   1.1   Walks up and down stairs

Strand B   Play Skills
>   G1.0   Jumps forward
>   >   1.1   Jumps in place
>   >   1.2   Jumps from platform
>   >   1.3   Maintains balance in walking
>   >   1.4   Balances on one foot
>   G2.0   Runs avoiding obstacles
>   >   2.1   Runs
>   G3.0   Bounces, catches, kicks, and throws ball
>   >   3.1   Bounces ball
>   >   3.2   Catches ball
>   >   3.3   Kicks ball
>   >   3.4   Throws ball
>   G4.0   Skips
>   >   4.1   Hops
>   G5.0   Rides and steers two-wheel bicycle
>   >   5.1   Pedals and steers two-wheel bicycle with training wheels

Strand A   Balance and Mobility in Standing and Walking

GOAL 1.0   Alternates feet walking up and down stairs

Objective 1.1   Walks up and down stairs

CONCURRENT GOALS

Cog A	Participation (all goals)
Cog D:1.0	Follows directions of three or more related steps that are not routinely given
Cog G:1.0	Engages in imaginary play
Cog G:2.0	Engages in games with rules
SC B:1.0	Uses verbs
Soc A	Interaction with Others (all goals)

DAILY ROUTINES

Routine activities that provide opportunities for children to walk up and down stairs include the following:

Indoor and outdoor play times
Transitions (e.g., moving from one activity or place to another)

Close supervision ensures safety during gross motor activities.

Example   When Timmy and his father visit the park, Timmy can practice stair climbing on the slide. His father stands at the bottom of the stairs to offer the necessary physical support and verbal encouragement. By using his arms and hands, Timmy can successfully climb the slide with a step-by-step approach. *(GM A:1.1)*

ENVIRONMENTAL ARRANGEMENTS

■ Provide climbing stairs and blocks of varying heights as well as stairs with and without handrails. When learning to climb stairs, children may initially use a handrail for support or use a step-by-step approach. Children will typically be more successful in climbing stairs lower in height. Eventually children may no longer require a handrail for support and stairs of greater height may be negotiated using a step-over-step approach.

■ The outdoor play area can include small climbing structures that do not require arms and hands for support and large slides that necessitate using the upper extremities.

■ Arrange the classroom into activity areas that include gross motor and dramatic play centers. Provide close supervision for all children engaged in physical activity, regardless of their present level of gross motor skills.

PLANNED ACTIVITIES

Two examples of how to embed this goal and the associated objective within activities are presented here. For a complete set of activities that address goals and objectives across domains, see Section V.

Firefighter Play

A fire station is created in the dramatic play center of the classroom. Children think of props to include in the station, such as fire hats, raincoats, cots, a bell, hoses, chairs, and a wheel for a "fire truck." A set of portable stairs can be provided to climb up to reach the "burning house." The interventionist should consider the height of the stairs and whether handrails should be present. Encouraging children to hold a hose while climbing stairs provides an opportunity to climb without using the railing for support.

Example   Maria uses ankle-foot orthoses (braces on both legs) and a walker when playing with her friends in the classroom. When it is Maria's turn to hold the fire hose on the "burning building," the interventionist selects the stairs that are smaller in height with the handrails closer together. Maria can climb the stairs independently using the handrails. When she has her balance at the top of the stairs, she can signal her "firefighting assistant" to hand her the fire hose. *(GM A:1.1)*

Obstacle Course

This activity can be introduced with a discussion about how community helpers (e.g., firefighters, police officers) need to exercise to do their jobs. An obstacle course can be set up with some stair-climbing activities by providing portable steps and a small slide or climbing structure. Include other gross motor activities such as jumping, crawling through tunnels, and weaving in and out of cones. A specific course may be set (the interventionist can demonstrate); and physical assistance, a combination of physical assistance and verbal cues, verbal cues alone, or modeling can be provided as required for the children to successfully practice stair climbing with the goal of achieving functional independence.

PRESCHOOL CURRICULA WITH SIMILAR GOALS

The following preschool curricula provide information on this goal or similar goals. Interventionists whose programs have access to one or more of these curricula may refer to the referenced sections for additional programming strategies.

The Carolina Curriculum for Preschoolers with Special Needs
Stairs
■ Up stairs
■ Down stairs

The Creative Curriculum
Outdoors

High Scope—Young Children in ACTION

Active Learning
- Using the large muscles

Peabody Developmental Motor Scales Activity Cards

Gross Motor
- Walking down stairs
- Walking up stairs

Portage Guide to Early Education Activity Cards

Motor
- Walks down stairs
- Walks up stairs

GM A

Strand B   Play Skills

GOAL 1.0   Jumps forward

Objective 1.1   Jumps in place
Objective 1.2   Jumps from platform
Objective 1.3   Maintains balance in walking
Objective 1.4   Balances on one foot

CONCURRENT GOALS

Cog A	Participation (all goals)
Cog B:6.0	Demonstrates understanding of 12 different spatial relations concepts
Cog D:1.0	Follows directions of three or more related steps that are not routinely given
Cog G:1.0	Engages in imaginary play
Cog G:2.0	Engages in games with rules
Cog H: 1.0	Recites numbers from 1 to 20
SC B:1.0	Uses verbs
SC B:5.0	Uses descriptive words
Soc A:1.0	Has play partners

DAILY ROUTINES

Routine activities that provide opportunities for children to practice gross motor skills involving balance and jumping include the following:

Dressing
Indoor and outdoor play times
Transitions

Close supervision ensures safety during gross motor activities.

Example   When Joey and his mother walk to school, Joey's mother stops at each curb along the way. She holds Joey's hand and jumps off the edge of the curb, encouraging Joey to jump by saying, "Jump, Joey!" *(GM B:1.2)*

Example   When the class moves from one activity to the next, as in going out to play, the interventionist makes the transition from classroom to outdoor play area more exciting by encouraging Latifa and Manuel to hop like bunnies down the hall. *(GM B:1.0, 1.1)*

ENVIRONMENTAL ARRANGEMENTS

Environmental arrangements should allow children to successfully participate in balance and jumping activities at their current skill level while promoting higher levels of mastery and independence in gross motor skills.

- Assemble equipment such as mini trampolines, mats, balance beams, short stairs, platforms, small obstacles, or materials such as ropes, sticks, tape, or chalk to mark lines to balance on or jump over. Use gross motor classroom areas for indoor themes or during inclement weather. Closely supervise all children practicing balance and jumping skills.

    Example   Joey and Latifa are excited about learning to hop on one foot. First they practice standing on one foot with and without using their arms for support. The interventionist arranges the children in a circle so all the children can have fun participating. Alice is seated in her wheelchair in the circle and offers her hand to a peer for support. Maria uses her walker for support when standing on one foot. *(GM B:1.4)*

PLANNED ACTIVITIES

Two examples of how to embed this goal and the associated objectives within activities are presented here. For a complete set of activities that address goals and objectives across domains, see Section V.

Animal Moves

Children identify and imitate the movements of animals. The activity can be introduced by reading a story about animals or looking at pictures of different animals. Opportunities can be provided for the children to practice balancing and jumping skills by choosing stories or pictures of animals that jump (e.g., kangaroos), walk (e.g., monkeys), or balance on one foot (e.g., storks).

Example   Survival in the wild also depends on "standing" absolutely still. Alice enjoys the game because she has an opportunity to practice balance by using the muscles of her trunk when sitting and when on hands and knees. Alice has a chance to play on the floor with the other children without her wheelchair, and balancing with her trunk improves her posture and gives her more endurance. (Alice's goal is taken from *AEPS Measurement for Birth to Three Years*.)

Pop Goes the Weasel

This activity involves the children reciting the rhyme "Pop Goes the Weasel" and jumping up in the air whenever the word "Pop!" comes around.

> All around the cobbler's bench, the monkey chased the weasel.
> The monkey thought that it was fun. POP! goes the weasel.
> A penny for a spool of thread. A penny for a needle.
> That's the way the money goes. POP! goes the weasel.

As the children recite the song, they walk in a circle until it is time to jump, practicing maintaining balance while walking.

GM B

PRESCHOOL CURRICULA WITH SIMILAR GOALS

The following preschool curricula provide information on this goal or similar goals. Interventionists whose programs have access to one or more of these curricula may refer to the referenced sections for additional programming strategies.

The Carolina Curriculum for Preschoolers with Special Needs

Jumping
- Broad jumping
- Jumping up
- Jumping down

Locomotion
- Walking

Balance
- Static balance

The Creative Curriculum

Outdoors

High Scope—Young Children in ACTION

Active Learning
- Using the large muscles

Peabody Developmental Motor Scales Activity Cards

Gross Motor
- Jumping forward
- Jumping down
- Walking balance beam
- Walking backward
- Standing on one foot

Portage Guide to Early Education Activity Cards

Motor
- Jumps forward
- Jumps over
- Jumps up
- Jumps in place
- Jumps from height
- Jumps backward
- Walks balance beam
- Stands on one foot

GOAL 2.0 Runs avoiding obstacles

Objective 2.1 Runs

GM B

CONCURRENT GOALS

Cog A   Participation (all goals)
Cog B:4.0   Demonstrates understanding of 10 different qualitative concepts
Cog B:6.0   Demonstrates understanding of 12 different spatial relations concepts
Cog D:1.0   Follows directions of three or more related steps that are not routinely given
Cog G   Play (all goals)
SC B:1.0   Uses verbs
SC B:5.0   Uses descriptive words

DAILY ROUTINES

Routine events that provide opportunities for children to run include indoor (if appropriate) and outdoor play times. Close supervision of running activities is important to assist children in developing an awareness of their bodies in space and to promote mastery of the gross motor skill.

Example   The doctor informed Timmy's mother that it is important for Timmy to gradually increase his endurance for physical activity. During outdoor play time in their fenced backyard, his mother chooses the game Hide-and-Seek. She runs a few steps in front of him and hides behind the tree, saying, "Run, Timmy. Come and find me!" *(GM B2.1)*

ENVIRONMENTAL ARRANGEMENTS

■ Arrange the classroom into activity areas, including a gross motor area. Include an open space (with mats or carpets to protect children if they fall) and an outdoor space (grassy areas are nice) where children have room to run. Sometimes long hallways free of obstacles provide space to run.

■ Create safe running opportunities for children as part of a daily routine by arranging an environment with appropriate running surface and evaluating the space for obstacles or other safety hazards. Children begin running with a hurried walk. Not until 2 to 3 years of age do children truly run with a period of nonsupport (at some point in the running cycle neither leg is on the surface). Running becomes more refined and efficient, with evidence of increased speed, by age 5.

■ "Running" is in the eyes of the beholder. Children may run on two feet, with a walker, in a wheelchair, or in a wagon pulled by another person. Consult a qualified motor specialist to determine if running is an attainable gross motor goal for a particular child and to discuss adaptations to activities and equipment.

PLANNED ACTIVITIES

Two examples of how to embed this goal and the associated objective within activities are presented here. For a complete set of activities that address goals and objectives across domains, see Section V.

Duck, Duck, Goose

This is a favorite among children. Children sit in a circle, and one child is chosen to be "it." The child who is "it" walks around the outside of the circle, tapping each child's head gently and calling the child either a duck or a goose. Whoever the child chooses as "goose" stands up and chases and tries to tag the first child before he or she sits down at his or her place in the circle. The goose then becomes "it."

Example   Children playing Duck, Duck, Goose in the classroom with Alice begin the game sitting in chairs facing out of the circle. The group chooses a special style of running (running sideways or backward) before the game begins. If Alice is the "goose," she runs in her wheelchair. When Alice is "it," the "goose" has a chance to practice an alternative method of running that will also improve coordination and speed and give Alice an opportunity to avoid being tagged by the "goose." *(GM B:2.1, with adaptation)*

Chick, Chick, Chickens

Children pretend to be baby chicks following after the mother chicken. The mother "chicken" leads the chicks in such activities as walking, running, or jumping. Cones or chairs can be set up to weave in and out of when a "fox" appears. This provides opportunities for the children to run avoiding obstacles.

Example   The interventionist pairs the children with a buddy, including Eric, who has a visual impairment. The activity is conducted in the large grassy field free of obstacles, and Eric can run confidently. *(GM B:2.1)*

PRESCHOOL CURRICULA WITH SIMILAR GOALS

The following preschool curricula provide information on this goal or similar goals. Interventionists whose programs have access to one or more of these curricula may refer to the referenced sections for additional programming strategies.

The Carolina Curriculum for Preschoolers with Special Needs
Locomotion
■ Running

The Creative Curriculum
Outdoors

High Scope—Young Children in ACTION
Active Learning
■ Using the large muscles

Peabody Developmental Motor Scales Activity Cards
Gross Motor
■ Running

Portage Guide to Early Education Activity Cards

Motor

- Picks up object from ground while running
- Runs changing direction
- Runs short distance

GOAL 3.0   Bounces, catches, kicks, and throws ball

Objective 3.1   Bounces ball

Objective 3.2   Catches ball

Objective 3.3   Kicks ball

Objective 3.4   Throws ball

CONCURRENT GOALS

Cog A	Participation (all goals)
Cog B:4.0	Demonstrates understanding of 10 different qualitative concepts
Cog B:6.0	Demonstrates understanding of 12 different spatial relations concepts
Cog D:1.0	Follows directions of three or more related steps that are not routinely given
Cog G	Play (all goals)
Cog H:2.0	Counts 10 objects
SC B:1.0	Uses verbs
SC B:5.0	Uses descriptive words
Soc A:2.0	Initiates cooperative activity

DAILY ROUTINES

Routine events that provide opportunities for children to practice gross motor skills with balls include indoor and outdoor play times. Close supervision ensures safety during gross motor activities.

Example   During recess, the interventionist selects several different-size balls for the play area. She places a lighter, medium-size ball in front of her and demonstrates kicking by modeling the action of moving her leg through the ball. Timmy watches and smiles. The interventionist brings a ball over, places it in front of Timmy, and says, "Kick it, Tim." *(GM B:3.3)*

ENVIRONMENTAL ARRANGEMENTS

- Provide balloons, beanbags, beach balls, Nerf balls, and other balls of different sizes and weights to create opportunities for practice and to promote mastery in bouncing, catching, kicking, and throwing a ball during indoor and outdoor play periods. Trash cans, boxes, or hoops may become a target for the game.

■ The ideal environmental arrangement for ball activities includes not only the close supervision of adults for safety but active participation of family members and classroom personnel to assist in developing the children's awareness of body position in space (body image).

■ An understanding of the developmental sequence of bouncing, catching, kicking, and throwing balls promotes environmental arrangements that allow children to successfully practice ball activities at their present skill level while offering opportunities to achieve a higher level of mastery. The sequence of kicking a ball initially involves simply pushing against the ball. Later the child will stand still and kick at the ball with the leg straight. Finally, as the child learns to kick through the ball, the lower leg will bend, swinging backward and forward with the arms to provide balance. The maturational sequence of throwing a ball begins with only an arm movement and eventually includes rotation of the body and stepping forward with the leg on the same side as the throwing arm. Children learning to catch a ball will initially use both body and hands before learning to catch with only hands. For successful catching activities, initially use larger balls before advancing to smaller balls. After a period of simply chasing balls, a child's attempt to catch a ball with the arms will appear delayed. Modeling and verbal cues are required for a child to learn how to position the arms for catching. For a 3- to 4-year-old, fear of a thrown ball (turning the head away) is a normal response.

PLANNED ACTIVITIES

Two examples of how to embed this goal and the associated objectives within activities are presented here. For a complete set of activities that address goals and objectives across domains, see Section V.

Basketball

Children can play basketball with a child-size hoop (e.g., a trash can, laundry basket) and child-size basketballs (e.g., red rubber balls, plastic beach balls). This activity provides opportunities for the children to practice bouncing, catching, and throwing balls. Rules are modified depending on the skill level of the children participating; other modifications include changes in the game rules, special equipment needs of the children to ensure participation, and the optimal combination of physical assistance and verbal cues. It is important to emphasize developmentally appropriate motor skill acquisition, rather than winning, when children participate in sports activities.

Example The interventionist and Alice have designed a breakaway play. When Alice's team has the ball, she propels her wheelchair as fast as she can to the basket. Her teammates practice bouncing, throwing, and catching the ball down the court. When Alice is in position, her friends pass her the ball and Alice shoots. *(GM B:3.2, 3.4, with adaptation)*

One Fly Up

This game is played with small groups of children in a field or in a gym. One child becomes the "thrower." The other children are assisted in finding their own special spot away from each other and a few feet from the thrower. The interventionist selects a ball of appropriate size and weight for the gross motor skill level of the group. The "thrower" throws the ball. The "catchers" cannot move their feet, and whoever catches the ball gets to be the "thrower." The interventionist should make sure the children are facing the "thrower" and have their hands ready to catch the ball. Children will require different combinations of physical assistance and verbal cues to locate a position in space and to catch and throw the ball.

Example   The interventionist selects a ball of medium size and weight that makes a sound when it moves. She reminds the "thrower" to signal the "catcher" by saying, "Ready, Eric, hold your arms out to catch" before throwing the ball. The sound of the ball approaching and the verbal cues give everyone, including Eric, who has a visual impairment, a greater chance to successfully catch the ball and become the "thrower." *(GM B:3.2)*

PRESCHOOL CURRICULA WITH SIMILAR GOALS

The following preschool curricula provide information on this goal or similar goals. Interventionists whose programs have access to one or more of these curricula may refer to the referenced sections for additional programming strategies.

The Carolina Curriculum for Preschoolers with Special Needs
Balls
- Catching balls
- Throwing balls

Balance
- Dynamic balance

The Creative Curriculum
Outdoors

High Scope—Young Children in ACTION
Active Learning
- Using the large muscles

Peabody Developmental Motor Scales Activity Cards
Gross Motor
- Bouncing ball
- Catching ball
- Kicking ball
- Throwing ball

Portage Guide to Early Education Activity Cards
Motor
- Bounces and catches large ball
- Catches ball
- Kicks ball
- Throws ball

GOAL 4.0 Skips

Objective 4.1 Hops

CONCURRENT GOALS

Cog A   Participation (all goals)
Cog B:3.0   Demonstrates understanding of six different size concepts
Cog B:4.0   Demonstrates understanding of 10 different qualitative concepts
Cog B:6.0   Demonstrates understanding of 12 different spatial relations concepts
Cog D:1.0   Follows directions of three or more related steps that are not routinely given
Cog G   Play (all goals)
SC B:1.0   Uses verbs
SC B:5.0   Uses descriptive words
Soc A:2.0   Initiates cooperative activity

DAILY ROUTINES

Daily routines that provide opportunities for children to practice hopping and skipping include the following:

Indoor and outdoor play times
Transitions (moving from one activity or place to another)

Close supervision ensures safety during gross motor activities.

Example   Manuel and his family have been playing tag in the park. The game has been modified to allow Manuel and his brothers and sisters to practice jumping, hopping, galloping, and skipping. The person who is "it" calls the gross motor skill. When Manuel's father is "it," he points to a child in the park skipping and says, "Look at that boy skipping, Manuel. Do you want to try?" Manuel's father allows time out from the tag game for the whole family to practice skipping. After observing Manuel and his brothers and sisters skipping, Manuel's father continues the tag game with skipping as the targeted gross motor skill. *(GM B:4.0)*

ENVIRONMENTAL ARRANGEMENTS

■ Arrange the classroom into activity areas, including a gross motor area. Include an open space (mats or carpets make it less painful to fall!) where children have the space to hop and skip and an outdoor play area (grassy areas are nice). Sometimes long hallways free of obstacles provide the space to practice hopping and skipping.

Example   During recess, the interventionist introduces skipping to a group of interested children. Standing in front of the group and facing away from the children, the interventionist models the action of skipping and calls out, "Step hop, step hop," to assist the children in development of the appropriate timing and movement

sequence for skipping. Children practice skipping by following the leader (the interventionist). After a rest, children take turns leading the skipping activity. *(GM B:4.0)*
- Environmental arrangements should allow children to successfully participate in
  hopping and skipping activities at their present skill level while promoting higher
  levels of mastery and independence in games involving hopping and skipping. Safety
  considerations associated with environmental arrangements should include a large
  space and organized pattern of movement to allow a group of young children to successfully explore movement in space.

PLANNED ACTIVITIES

Two examples of how to embed this goal and the associated objective within activities
are presented here. For a complete set of activities that address goals and objectives
across domains, see Section V.

Simon Says

The interventionist (or a child) is "Simon" and leads the children in movement activities. Simon directs and models a specific gross motor skill and direction of movement,
such as "Simon says hop forward." Children imitate the leader's movement and follow
the designated direction. The interventionist might take one or more turns being
Simon to offer the children an equal opportunity to participate in a variety of movement experiences.

Skip, Skip, Skip, to My Lou

Children skip or dance during group circle time while singing the song "Skip, Skip,
Skip, to My Lou."

> Skip, skip, skip, to my Lou,
> Skip, skip, skip, to my Lou,
> Skip, skip, skip, to my Lou,
> Skip to my Lou, my darlin'.

PRESCHOOL CURRICULA WITH SIMILAR GOALS

The following preschool curricula provide information on this goal or similar goals.
Interventionists whose programs have access to one or more of these curricula may
refer to the referenced sections for additional programming strategies.

The Carolina Curriculum for Preschoolers with Special Needs
Locomotion
- Galloping/skipping
- Hopping

The Creative Curriculum
Outdoors

High Scope—Young Children in ACTION
Active Learning
- Using large muscles

GM B

Peabody Developmental Motor Scales Activity Cards

Gross Motor
- Skipping
- Hopping

Portage Guide to Early Education Activity Cards

Motor
- Skips
- Hops

GOAL 5.0   Rides and steers two-wheel bicycle

Objective 5.1   Pedals and steers two-wheel bicycle with training wheels

---

CONCURRENT GOALS

Cog A	Participation (all goals)
Cog D:1.0	Follows directions of three or more related steps that are not routinely given
SC B:1.0	Uses verbs
SC B:5.0	Uses descriptive words
Soc A:2.0	Initiates cooperative activity

DAILY ROUTINES

Routine activities that provide opportunities for children to practice riding and steering a two-wheel bicycle include outdoor play times. Close adult supervision and use of a child's bicycle helmet ensure a fun and safe biking experience.

Example   Latifa's mother and Joey's mother bring their children's bikes to the park so the children can practice riding their two-wheel bicycles with training wheels. *(GM B:5.1)*

ENVIRONMENTAL ARRANGEMENTS

- Include a range of bicycle-riding equipment to create opportunities for children to practice at their existing level of bicycle-riding ability. Provide small and large tricycles for children learning bike skills, and introduce obstacles (e.g., cones, chairs, blocks) as children become adept at peddling and steering. Two-wheel bikes with and without training wheels will challenge children with more advanced skills. Arrange play areas to include a large open space with a hard surface where children can be adequately supervised.
- A qualified motor specialist can assist in recommendations for tricycle and bicycle adaptations. Tricycles and bicycles may be modified with a safety belt, an addition to

the back of the seat, or both to provide increased support of a child's trunk; adaptations to the pedals offer assistance with foot position while pedaling. Modifications to the pedaling system create an opportunity for children to use a variety of arm and leg patterns to pedal, steer, and turn.

PLANNED ACTIVITIES

Two examples of how to embed this goal and the associated objective within activities are presented here. For a complete set of activities that address goals and objectives across domains, see Section V.

Trains

Children line up with different vehicles (e.g., bikes, tricycles, wagons) and form a "train." Children take turns wearing a hat and pretending to be the train engineer. The engineer leads the group and blows the horn.

Police Officers

Children ride around on their bicycles pretending to be police officers. This can be planned as an outdoor dramatic play activity, using an outdoor climbing structure or a large cardboard box as a police station. Children can use blue shirts for uniforms, make "tickets" and "badges" from paper, and label different outdoor bikes and tricycles with the words "police car." Opportunities to ride bicycles occur as children ride around handing out "tickets" or helping adults or peers in trouble.

Example   The interventionist selects Latifa, Joey, and Maria to be the police officers. Joey's police car is a two-wheel bicycle with training wheels. Latifa feels safer patrolling the streets on a tricycle, although she has practiced on a two-wheel bike. Maria's adapted tricycle has a seat belt and an additional back support to assist her with sitting balance while she concentrates on pedaling and steering with her arms. Eric travels downtown in his wagon, and Manuel offers to pull the wagon. Latifa notices them traveling too quickly and gives them a ticket for speeding. Eric receives a warning for not wearing a seat belt in the wagon. *(GM B:5.0, 5.1, with adapted materials)*

PRESCHOOL CURRICULA WITH SIMILAR GOALS

The following preschool curricula provide information on this goal or similar goals. Interventionists whose programs have access to one or more of these curricula may refer to the referenced sections for additional programming strategies.

The Carolina Curriculum for Preschoolers with Special Needs
Outdoor Equipment

High Scope—Young Children in ACTION
Active Learning
- Using the large muscles

Portage Guide to Early Education Activity Cards
Motor
- Rides bicycle
- Pedals tricycle

ADAPTIVE DOMAIN

Newborns are almost totally dependent on their caregivers to provide them with necessary nutrition, warmth, safety, and emotional support. For several months following birth, infants are dependent on caregivers to be fed, clothed, and kept clean. Gradually, as infants mature and develop motor skills, they begin to exercise partial control over these activities. Preschoolers are typically able to conduct many daily living activities independently. The Adaptive Domain is focused on selected daily living skills, including eating/dining, personal hygiene, and dressing and undressing. The ability to independently meet personal needs contributes to children's positive self-image and fosters autonomy.

Considerable time is spent initially by caregivers in feeding, changing, and protecting their infants from harm. Although babies are dependent on adults, they are competent in a number of ways that help ensure their survival. At birth, babies are able to eat, eliminate body waste, and regulate their body temperature, which is subject to frequent variation. Newborn infants exhibit reflexive behaviors when they orient to a food source, close their lips around a nipple, suck, and swallow. Some of these early reflexes remain, but others disappear as higher brain functioning and learning provide the 3- to 4-month-old baby with new responses needed for interaction with the environment.

Through the continuing interaction between infants and environments, along with neurological maturation, fine and gross motor skills develop. As infants become familiar with caregiving routines, they begin to cooperate, to anticipate, and to perform actions independently. For example, a child may pull an arm out of a sleeve during undressing or open his or her mouth on seeing a spoon full of food. The caregiver should maintain a balance between encouraging the development of new skills and still providing assistance as necessary. With each developing skill, caregivers should reduce the amount of assistance yet still provide enough support for children to successfully complete tasks. Children should always be encouraged to move toward independent performance of an activity, even when it initially takes the child longer to complete the activity without assistance.

During the preschool years, eating/dining, personal hygiene, and dressing skills are refined as children's motor, cognitive, and social skills develop. Many preschool children are able to meet most of their personal needs but may need practice with more intricate aspects of a task (e.g., buttoning buttons). Children learn to eat and drink a variety of foods, handle utensils, prepare simple foods, and use social dining skills such as wiping hands with a napkin or remaining seated during mealtimes. Most children learn to use the toilet during the preschool years.

In the area of dressing, children initially learn to pull off clothing, particularly shoes, socks, and hats. This requires less refinement of motor skills than putting on the same items. Next children learn to pull off and wiggle out of jackets, sweaters, shirts, and pants. Caregivers often find that toddlers resist putting on clothes but are gleeful in removing them from their bodies. As preschoolers gain independence, most develop an intense desire to dress themselves, which may be frustrating for them and their caregivers. With practice, most preschoolers are able to dress and undress independently.

Children's ability to perform adaptive skills is dependent on other areas of their development. Adaptive skills generally have motor, social, and cognitive components. A goal that requires a child to select appropriate clothing and dress independently at designated times requires the gross and fine motor skills necessary to have access to the clothing and manipulate fasteners. In addition, this goal requires the cognitive and social skills necessary to discriminate which clothing will meet the child's physical needs in a socially appropriate way (e.g., choosing a sweater to wear when it is cold outside). The goals in the Adaptive Domain require children to coordinate a variety of skills and information. Consequently, these goals address multiple targets, are functional, and can usually be addressed in routine activities throughout the day.

The Adaptive Domain is composed of three strands. Strand A (Dining) focuses on the child's ability to eat and drink a variety of foods using utensils, prepare and serve food, and demonstrate social dining skills. Strand B (Personal Hygiene) focuses on the child's ability to conduct toileting functions and to wash and groom him- or herself. Strand C (Dressing and Undressing) examines the child's ability to fasten and unfasten fasteners on garments, as well as the ability to select appropriate clothing and dress independently. Earlier eating, toileting, and dressing skills are targeted in the *AEPS Curriculum for Birth to Three Years*.

The Adaptive Domain curriculum is divided into four sections: 1) Intervention Considerations, 2) Suggested Activities, 3) Using Activity-Based Intervention, and 4) Domain Goals. Intervention Considerations addresses important factors an interventionist may wish to consider prior to and when working with children at risk for or who have disabilities. Suggested Activities provides a selected list of activities that may be particularly helpful when working on adaptive skills. This section also provides suggestions for additional materials that increase the opportunities for children to practice targeted adaptive skills. The third section provides an illustration of how to target IEP/IFSP goals in the Adaptive Domain using an activity-based intervention approach. The final section, Domain Goals, discusses suggestions for concurrent goals, daily routines, environmental arrangements, and planned activities in the home and classroom for each goal identified in the Adaptive Domain of the AEPS Test for Three to Six Years. This section also lists other commercially available curricula that provide intervention activities for each goal.

INTERVENTION CONSIDERATIONS

General considerations when working on adaptive goals are discussed below.

- Adaptive skills should be practiced throughout children's daily routines in a variety of settings, with a variety of people. Routines such as dressing and undressing, mealtimes, and children's unstructured play times are natural contexts for children to learn adaptive skills.
- An occupational therapist, physical therapist, or both can help assess children to determine if an adaptive goal is functional or realistically attainable for children with

motor impairments. Children with motor impairments may demonstrate a variety of feeding difficulties that require intervention from a qualified specialist. Children may need additional support to improve their oral-motor control (facilitating chewing and swallowing) and their self-feeding skills. In addition to providing information concerning the modification of activities and utilization of adaptive equipment, a therapist may recommend some type of preparation, such as therapy to help normalize a child's muscle tone to assist the child to participate in adaptive activities.

■ Children will benefit from planned activities that provide practice on adaptive goals. Children with motor skill impairments may require compensatory strategies such as modification to the environment or adaptive equipment to increase their independence. Adaptive equipment such as hand splints, nonslip surfaces, shortened or built-up utensils, Velcro fasteners, and handrails for toilets and sinks can provide the support necessary for children to participate in a variety of activities. Consult a qualified specialist to obtain information concerning special equipment and adaptations to the environment, activities, or materials.

■ Be aware of how adaptive devices may prevent children from interacting with their peers. Positioning is an important consideration for children with motor impairments. To participate in activities such as mealtimes, the child needs to be upright and well supported. However, adaptive equipment such as a wheelchair often places the child higher than other children, and lap trays create a physical barrier between a child and peers. Whenever possible, particularly during activities that are social events such as mealtimes, children should be seated in regular chairs or adapted chairs (if extra support is required).

■ Plan enough time for children to complete tasks. During busy schedules at home and school, adults often find themselves rushing children through feeding, clothing, and toileting routines to keep on schedule. When possible, allot adequate time for children to complete tasks independently, or with as little assistance as necessary. Creating sufficient opportunities to practice is necessary if a child is to achieve independence in personal care.

■ Children with visual impairments may benefit from adaptations to materials during activities. The use of brightly colored, high-contrasting materials may assist a child with limited vision. In addition, keeping materials (e.g., clothing, washcloths, soap, cups, plates, utensils, food items) in predictable locations and using modified materials (e.g., bowls and plates with a lip) help the child acquire independence in adaptive skills more rapidly.

SUGGESTED ACTIVITIES

Art activities provide opportunities for adaptive skills such as dressing and undressing, washing, and grooming when children put on and take off smocks and wash up after the activity. The following list of activities and materials may be particularly helpful for eliciting skills within the Adaptive Domain. For a complete list of activities, see Section V.

Dramatic Play Activities

Children can practice dining, personal hygiene, and dressing and undressing skills as they act out dramatic play scenarios. The following activity is particularly helpful for embedding adaptive goals: House Play.

Other Activities

- Painting
- Teddy Bear Picnic
- Washing Babies
- Restaurant
- Shoe Store
- Cooking
- Exploratory activities
- Messy art activities

USING ACTIVITY-BASED INTERVENTION

An illustration of how an interventionist can incorporate activity-based strategies to enhance the development of a child's adaptive skills is provided below. The child's targeted IEP/IFSP objective is to use any functional means to fasten buttons, snaps, and Velcro fasteners when dressing.

- The interventionist observes Maria playing in the dramatic play center. She *follows the child's lead* by joining Maria in her play and encourages peers to join. The interventionist *expands on the child's initiation* by opening up the chest with dress-up clothing such as aprons with snaps, brightly colored shirts with oversize buttons, and shoes and slippers with Velcro fasteners.
- The interventionist *models* how to fasten buttons by putting on a shirt, using *self-talk* to comment on her own actions (e.g., "I'm going to put on this pretty shirt. First I'll line up the buttons and holes...").
- The interventionist draws Maria's attention to peers who are displaying more advanced skills (e.g., "Look at Latifa! She's putting on an apron and snapping the snaps"). The classroom consists of a *heterogeneous* (at varied skill levels) group of children, providing opportunities for Maria to learn new skills by observing peer models or to enhance skills by assisting children with different strengths.
- The interventionist uses additional strategies to encourage *multiple opportunities* for Maria to practice targeted goals. She comments, "Don't forget to wear an apron," when Maria is playing at the stove, providing an opportunity for her to practice fastening the snaps on the apron.
- The interventionist provides the *least amount of assistance* necessary for Maria to fasten fasteners while playing in the dramatic play center.

DOMAIN GOALS

This section provides suggestions for concurrent goals, daily routines, environmental arrangements, and planned activities for all the adaptive goals listed in the AEPS Test for Three to Six Years. If an objective has been targeted, the interventionist can turn to the corresponding goal and determine which suggestions are relevant to facilitate that objective. A standard format is used for each goal: 1) Strand, 2) Goal, 3) Objective(s), 4) Concurrent Goals, 5) Daily Routines, 6) Environmental Arrangements, 7) Planned Activities, and 8) Preschool Curricula with Similar Goals. Concurrent Goals list the AEPS goals that can often be worked on at the same time the child works on the target goal or associated objectives. Daily Routines present a list of routine activities that provide opportunities to practice targeted skills. Environmental Arrangements should be considered when designing children's programs around child-initiated, routine, and planned activities. The Planned Activities offer examples of how to embed targeted goals within the context of planned activities.

Finally, Preschool Curricula with Similar Goals lists other curricula that can be used to supplement the AEPS Curriculum for Three to Six Years. If a given program has one or more of these preschool curricula, the interventionist can refer to the referenced sections to find additional programming strategies for the targeted goal or objective. Additional information on daily routines, environmental arrangements, planned activities, and themes is provided in Section III.

Strand A   Dining

      G1.0   Eats and drinks a variety of foods using appropriate utensils with little or no spilling
          1.1   Eats a variety of food textures
          1.2   Selects and eats a variety of food types
          1.3   Eats with fork and spoon
      G2.0   Prepares and serves food
          2.1   Prepares food for eating
          2.2   Uses knife to spread food
          2.3   Pours liquid into a variety of containers
          2.4   Serves food with utensil
      G3.0   Displays social dining skills
          3.1   Puts proper amount of food in mouth, chews with mouth closed, swallows before taking another bite
          3.2   Takes in proper amount of liquid and returns cup to surface
          3.3   Remains seated during meal or until excused
          3.4   Uses napkin to clean face and hands
          3.5   Assists in clearing table

Strand B   Personal Hygiene

      G1.0   Carries out all toileting functions
          1.1   Uses toilet paper, flushes toilet, washes hands after using toilet
          1.2   Uses toilet
          1.3   Indicates need to use toilet
      G2.0   Washes and grooms self
          2.1   Uses tissue to clean nose
          2.2   Brushes teeth
          2.3   Bathes and dries self
          2.4   Brushes or combs hair
          2.5   Washes and dries face

Strand C   Dressing and Undressing

      G1.0   Unfastens fasteners on garments
          1.1   Unfastens buttons/snaps/Velcro fasteners on garments
          1.2   Unties string-type fastener
          1.3   Unzips zipper
      G2.0   Selects appropriate clothing and dresses self at designated times
          2.1   Puts on long pants
          2.2   Puts on front-opening garment
          2.3   Puts on pullover garment
          2.4   Puts on shoes
          2.5   Puts on underpants, shorts, or skirt

Adap

G3.0   Fastens fasteners on garments
    3.1   Ties string-type fastener
    3.2   Fastens buttons, snaps, and Velcro fasteners
    3.3   Threads and zips zipper

Adap

Strand A   Dining

GOAL 1.0   Eats and drinks a variety of foods using appropriate utensils with little or no spilling

Objective 1.1   Eats a variety of food textures
Objective 1.2   Selects and eats a variety of food types
Objective 1.3   Eats with fork and spoon

CONCURRENT GOALS

FM A:1.0	Manipulates two small objects at same time
Cog A	Participation (all goals)
Cog B	Demonstrates Understanding of Concepts (all goals)
Cog C:1.0	Groups objects, people, or events on the basis of specified criteria
SC A	Social-Communicative Interactions (all goals)
SC B	Production of Words, Phrases, and Sentences (all goals)
Soc B	Interaction with Environment (all goals)
Soc C:1.0	Communicates personal likes and dislikes

DAILY ROUTINES

Routine events that provide opportunities for children to eat and drink a variety of foods using appropriate utensils include the following:

Mealtime
Snack time
Unstructured play times

Example   During mealtime and snack time, a variety of foods with different textures is provided. The interventionist encourages children to try new foods and to eat using the appropriate utensils. *(Adap A:1.1, 1.2, 1.3)*

ENVIRONMENTAL ARRANGEMENTS

- Arrange the classroom into activity areas including a dramatic play center. Although a dramatic play center usually uses pretend foods, as a special treat the interventionist may want to provide real foods for the children to serve and eat. Include forks, spoons, cups, and bowls to provide opportunities for children to practice handling utensils, with or without real food.

■ Provide foods from the different food groups (e.g., dairy, meat, fruit, vegetables, breads) as well as foods with different textures. A range of foods helps children learn to use a variety of utensils. Choose foods such as the following:

  – Semisolid foods (e.g., applesauce, yogurt)
  – Chewy foods (e.g., meat, dried fruits)
  – Hard foods (e.g., apples, raw vegetables, pretzels)
  – Soft foods (e.g., bananas, cooked vegetables, macaroni)
  – Liquids (e.g., milk, water, juice)

■ To encourage children to practice eating with a fork and spoon, offer foods during mealtime and snack time that can be scooped (e.g., applesauce, yogurt, pudding, ice cream) or speared (e.g., meat, vegetables, chunks of fruit). Provide utensils that can be easily managed by children.
■ Positioning is an important consideration for children with motor impairments. Make sure the child is upright and well supported during mealtimes.
■ Adaptations to utensils may be necessary for children with special needs to perform this skill independently. For example, children with motor impairments may benefit from using utensils with built-up or shortened grips. Adapted utensils are available commercially or can be fabricated. Contact a qualified specialist for adaptation needs of children with sensory and/or motor impairments.

  Example   During snack time, Maria uses an adapted spoon and places the elbow and forearm of her free hand on the table to provide balance and support to her upper body. Her interventionist sits close by and uses verbal cues and the least level of assistance necessary for Maria to successfully eat her pudding. Maria grasps her spoon, scoops pudding, brings it to her mouth, removes the food from the spoon, and returns the spoon to the bowl. The interventionist fades assistance as soon as possible. *(Adap A:1.3)*

PLANNED ACTIVITIES

Two examples of how to embed this goal and the associated objectives within activities are presented here. For a complete set of activities that address goals and objectives across domains, see Section V.

Super Soup

A nutritious soup can be made for lunch or snack. Children can actively participate by washing and cutting (with adult assistance) the vegetables and then combining the vegetables, broth, and spices. The five senses are explored throughout the process by looking, touching, smelling, listening (e.g., to the snap of celery being broken), and tasting the ingredients. Opportunities can be provided for children to sample foods of different textures (e.g., meat, raw and cooked vegetables, raw and cooked macaroni, vegetable broth). The soup can be served with dairy products and fruits to encourage children to select and eat foods from different food groups. The interventionist should observe children's ability to use utensils when eating soup or when scooping or spearing other food items.

Fruit Salad

Children will enjoy preparing fruit salad for snack. The interventionist can provide fruits with different textures (e.g., bananas, pineapple, raisins, oranges, apples) and let the children take an active part in preparing the food by washing, peeling, slicing, and scooping foods into bowls. Vanilla yogurt, granola, almonds, or wheat germ can be added to the salad if desired. The interventionist should encourage children to sample foods of different textures while preparing the snack, and offer foods from the different food groups during snack. Children use utensils while preparing foods (e.g., spoons to scoop yogurt, forks to spear fruits) and while eating their snack.

Example The interventionist allows Eric, who has a visual impairment, time to explore through touch his food and utensils. The interventionist provides a deep bowl with a lip that Eric and the other children can use to practice scooping. When it is time to eat the fruit salad, the interventionist provides brightly colored utensils that contrast with the placemat, helping Eric to locate his spoon. The interventionist also provides verbal feedback as to where utensils and food are located and places them in predictable locations (e.g., the spoon on the right-hand side of his plate). *(Adap A:1.3)*

PRESCHOOL CURRICULA WITH SIMILAR GOALS

The following preschool curricula provide information on this goal or similar goals. Interventionists whose programs have access to one or more of these curricula may refer to the referenced sections for additional programming strategies.

The Carolina Curriculum for Preschoolers with Special Needs
Self-Help Skills
- Eating

High Scope—Young Children in ACTION
Active Learning
- Taking care of one's own needs

Portage Guide to Early Education Activity Cards
Self Help
- Uses correct utensils for food
- Feeds self meal
- Uses fork
- Uses spoon
- Drinks from cup

Adap A

GOAL 2.0   Prepares and serves food

Objective 2.1	Prepares food for eating
Objective 2.2	Uses knife to spread food
Objective 2.3	Pours liquid into a variety of containers
Objective 2.4	Serves food with utensil

CONCURRENT GOALS

FM A:1.0   Manipulates two small objects at same time
SC A   Social-Communicative Interactions (all goals)
SC B   Production of Words, Phrases, and Sentences (all goals)
Soc A:2.0   Initiates cooperative activity
Soc B   Interaction with Environment (all goals)
Soc C:1.0   Communicates personal likes and dislikes

DAILY ROUTINES

Routine events that provide opportunities for children to prepare and serve food include the following:

Mealtime
Snack time
Unstructured play time

   Example   During snack, Latifa peels a banana, spreads peanut butter on bread, and pours juice from a small pitcher into her cup. Latifa's mother sits by her, providing verbal cues and the least level of physical assistance necessary for Latifa to prepare her snack. *(Adap A:2.0)*

ENVIRONMENTAL ARRANGEMENTS

■ Arrange the classroom into activity areas that include a dramatic play center. Although a dramatic play center usually uses pretend foods, as a special treat the interventionist might provide real foods for the children to serve and eat. Include forks, spoons, knives, pitchers, and cups for children to practice preparing and serving food, with or without real food.
■ Present materials during snack or mealtimes that provide opportunities for children to practice the following:

 – Preparing food (e.g., wrapped crackers, foods in containers, bananas with skin, hardboiled eggs with shell, cheese with plastic wrappers)
 – Using a knife to spread (e.g., dull knives to spread peanut butter on bread, cream cheese on crackers, jam on toast)

- Pouring liquid into containers (e.g., juice from a child-size pitcher into a cup, milk from a small bottle into a cup)
- Serving food with a utensil (e.g., scooping applesauce or yogurt into a bowl, spearing melon with a fork and transferring to a bowl or plate)

  Example Alice uses a knife to practice spreading cream cheese on a cracker. The interventionist uses verbal cues and the least level of physical assistance to prompt Alice to stabilize the cracker with her left hand while she spreads the cheese with her right. *(Adap A:2.2)*

■ Positioning is an important consideration for children with motor impairments. Make sure the child is upright and well supported during mealtimes.

■ Adaptations to materials may be necessary for children with special needs. Contact a qualified specialist for adaptation needs of children with sensory and/or motor impairments. Children with motor impairments may benefit from the use of nonslip surfaces to stabilize materials (e.g., bowls, plates) or by using utensils with built-up or shortened grips.

PLANNED ACTIVITIES

Two examples of how to embed this goal and the associated objectives within activities are presented here. For a complete set of activities that address goals and objectives across domains, see Section V.

Animal Cookies

Children make cookies with a favorite sugar cookie dough and animal cookie cutters. They can actively participate in making the cookies by opening containers, transferring ingredients from containers to the bowl, pouring liquids into the bowl, and stirring ingredients together. When the cookies have been baked, children can use dull knives to spread frosting or jam on them. Close supervision during cooking activities will ensure safety.

Fruit Animals

Children practice food preparation and serving skills while making animals from fruit. The interventionist can provide canned fruit such as pineapple slices, maraschino cherries, and pear halves, as well as sliced bananas, oranges, raisins, grapes, and apricot halves. Children create animals on paper plates using the pineapple rings or pear halves as faces, cherries or raisins for eyes, wedges of oranges or apricot halves for ears, and bananas for mouths. Children practice food preparation skills as they peel bananas, remove raisins from boxes, and spoon or spear fruit while transferring it from bowls to paper plates. Children eat their creations during snack time.

PRESCHOOL CURRICULA WITH SIMILAR GOALS

The following preschool curricula provide information on this goal or similar goals. Interventionists whose programs have access to one or more of these curricula may refer to the referenced sections for additional programming strategies.

The Carolina Curriculum for Preschoolers with Special Needs
Self-Help Skills
■ Eating

High Scope—Young Children in ACTION
Active Learning
■ Taking care of one's own needs

Portage Guide to Early Education Activity Cards
Self-Help
■ Prepares own sandwich
■ Uses knife
■ Pours from pitcher
■ Serves self at table

Adap A

GOAL 3.0   Displays social dining skills

Objective 3.1	Puts proper amount of food in mouth, chews with mouth closed, swallows before taking another bite
Objective 3.2	Takes in proper amount of liquid and returns cup to surface
Objective 3.3	Remains seated during meal or until excused
Objective 3.4	Uses napkin to clean face and hands
Objective 3.5	Assists in clearing table

CONCURRENT GOALS

FM A:1.0	Manipulates two small objects at same time
Cog C:1.0	Groups objects, people, or events on the basis of specified criteria
Cog D:1.0	Follows directions of three or more related steps that are not routinely given
SC A	Social-Communicative Interactions (all goals)
SC B	Production of Words, Phrases, and Sentences (all goals)
Soc A:2.0	Initiates cooperative activity
Soc B	Interaction with Environment (all goals)
Soc C:1.0	Communicates personal likes and dislikes

DAILY ROUTINES

Routine events that provide opportunities for children to practice social dining skills include the following:

Mealtime
Snack time
Unstructured play time
Visit to restaurant

Example   After snack time, Latifa starts to leave the table and the interventionist reminds her, "If you are finished with snack, throw away your napkin and put your cup in the tub. Then you can go outside to play." Latifa puts her napkin in the trash and places her cup in the plastic tub by the table. *(Adap A:3.5)*

ENVIRONMENTAL ARRANGEMENTS

Arrange the classroom into activity areas that include a dramatic play center (see Environmental Arrangements in Section III and Dramatic Play Activities in Section V). To encourage children to engage in mealtime activities, provide materials such as a child-size table with chairs; a tablecloth; cups; plates; bowls; utensils, napkins; serving bowls; and a pretend kitchen with a stove, sink, and sponges.

- Whenever possible, mealtimes and snack times should occur at a consistent time and location with consistent expectations for children. Provide child-size tables and chairs, cups and napkins, food that is in small pieces or easily cut up by a child, and a location for children to throw away garbage and put away dirty dishes.

  Example   During dinner, Timmy takes a piece of bread and wanders away from the table. His mother reminds him, "We eat at the table," and brings him back to the table. She gives Timmy attention while he is at the table, talking to him and occasionally rubbing his back. While Timmy is learning how to stay at the table for meals, his mother does not let him eat dinner in other locations. *(Adap A:3.3)*

- Positioning is an important consideration for children with motor impairments. Make sure the child is upright and well supported during mealtimes.

- Adaptations to materials may be necessary for children with special needs. Contact a qualified specialist for adaptation needs of children with sensory and/or motor impairments. Children with motor impairments may benefit from the use of nonslip surfaces to stabilize materials (e.g., bowls, plates) or from the use of utensils with built-up or shortened grips.

PLANNED ACTIVITIES

Two examples of how to embed this goal and the associated objectives within activities are presented here. For a complete set of activities that address goals and objectives across domains, see Section V.

Tasting Party

This activity is particularly interesting when a classroom is composed of children from different cultural backgrounds. Children can indicate different foods that they enjoy and caregivers can be asked what foods they eat in their households. Some examples include salsas, curries, sweet rice, and spring rolls. The interventionist should help the children prepare their favorite foods for snack. Children can practice their social dining skills when sitting down to taste the different foods and when helping to clean up.

Adap A

Restaurant Field Trip

A field trip can be arranged to eat at a restaurant with foods from a different country. Before the trip, the interventionist facilitates a discussion about eating out at restaurants, reviewing dining skills such as staying at the table and using napkins. During the meal, the interventionist encourages the children to use appropriate social dining skills.

PRESCHOOL CURRICULA WITH SIMILAR GOALS

The following preschool curricula provide information on this goal or similar goals. Interventionists whose programs have access to one or more of these curricula may refer to the referenced sections for additional programming strategies.

The Carolina Curriculum for Preschoolers with Special Needs
Self-Help Skills
- Eating

High Scope—Young Children in ACTION
Active Learning
- Taking care of one's own needs

Portage Guide to Early Education Activity Cards
Self-Help
- Uses napkin
- Clears place

Adap A

Strand B   Personal Hygiene

GOAL 1.0   Carries out all toileting functions

Objective 1.1	Uses toilet paper, flushes toilet, washes hands after using toilet
Objective 1.2	Uses toilet
Objective 1.3	Indicates need to use toilet

CONCURRENT GOALS

FM A:1.0	Manipulates two small objects at same time
Adap A:1.0	Eats and drinks a variety of foods using appropriate utensils with little or no spilling
Adap C:3.0	Fastens fasteners on garments
SC A	Social-Communicative Interactions (all goals)
SC B	Production of Words, Phrases, and Sentences (all goals)
Soc B	Interaction with Environment (all goals)

DAILY ROUTINES

When children are first learning to use the toilet, it may be useful to incorporate consistent and frequent visits to the bathroom into their daily routine. It is important not to pressure children about toilet training and to avoid punishing them for noncompliance. Caregivers and interventionists should realize that toilet training is a gradual process, so even if a child is toilet trained, accidents may occur if a child is tired or upset. In some conditions, such as spina bifida, toilet training may not be an appropriate goal because of the lack of bowel and bladder sensation and control. A developmental psychologist may provide useful suggestions to promote the emotional and psychological well-being of older children working on toileting goals.

ENVIRONMENTAL ARRANGEMENTS

- Children require access to a toilet, toilet paper, a sink, hand soap, paper towels, and a garbage can to independently carry out toileting functions.
- Clothing that is easily removed by the child (e.g., skirts, dresses, pants that have a stretch waist, fasteners that are easily engaged) may facilitate a child's independently carrying out toileting functions. As the child increases independence in toileting, this activity can provide opportunities to embed goals addressing manipulation of more complex fasteners.

- Children who use augmentative communication systems should be provided with a means to communicate their need to use the toilet (e.g., a sign for toilet, a picture of a toilet on the communication board).
- Some children require adaptations to successfully reach this goal. The following considerations may influence the child's ability to independently carry out toileting functions: the size/model of the toilet (child-size toilets, toilets that flush by hand or foot levers, potty chairs), handrails on the side of the toilet, the location/type of toilet paper roll dispenser, the size/model of the sink (a step stool, handrails, or both may be necessary for the child to have access to the sink), and the type of dispensers provided for soap and paper towels. Children with visual impairments will benefit from consistent and predictable location of all necessary materials. Consult qualified specialists for programming suggestions.

PLANNED ACTIVITIES

Although planned activities are not appropriate for this goal, subskills such as washing hands or dressing can be targeted within activities (e.g., washing hands before cooking or after messy play, changing clothes during pretend play). For a complete set of activities that address goals and objectives across domains, see Section V.

PRESCHOOL CURRICULA WITH SIMILAR GOALS

The following preschool curricula provide information on this goal or similar goals. Interventionists whose programs have access to one or more of these curricula may refer to the referenced sections for additional programming strategies.

The Carolina Curriculum for Preschoolers with Special Needs
Self-Help Skills
- Toileting

High Scope—Young Children in ACTION
Active Learning
- Taking care of one's own needs

Portage Guide to Early Education Activity Cards
Self-Help
- Toileting
- Finds correct bathroom in public places
- Independent toileting
- Dry at night/nap
- Recognizes need to use toilet

GOAL 2.0 Washes and grooms self

Objective 2.1	Uses tissue to clean nose
Objective 2.2	Brushes teeth
Objective 2.3	Bathes and dries self
Objective 2.4	Brushes or combs hair
Objective 2.5	Washes and dries face

CONCURRENT GOALS

FM A:1.0	Manipulates two small objects at same time
FM A:3.0	Ties string-type fastener
SC A	Social-Communicative Interactions (all goals)
SC B	Production of Words, Phrases, and Sentences (all goals)
Soc B:1.0	Meets physical needs in socially appropriate ways
Soc C:1.0	Communicates personal likes and dislikes

DAILY ROUTINES

Routine events that provide opportunities for children to wash and groom themselves include the following:

Dressing
Mealtime
Snack time
Unstructured play times
Transition times
Bathtime
Bedtime

Example   Eric, who has a visual impairment, has a goal to bathe and dry himself. Eric's mother keeps towels, soap, and shampoo in consistent locations in the bathroom. She guides Eric's hand and talks to him, familiarizing him with the hot and cold faucets and how to test the water before getting into the tub. *(Adap B:2.3)*

Example   Children practice brushing their teeth after snack at school. *(Adap B:2.2)*

ENVIRONMENTAL ARRANGEMENTS

■ Present materials in the home and classroom environments that provide opportunities for children to independently wash and groom themselves. For example, provide a child-size sink (or a step stool) in the bathroom and a mirror at child height. Children should have access to their own toothbrushes, brushes or combs, washcloths or paper towels, and tissues. To prevent the spread of infection, children should not share any items they use while washing and grooming themselves. Consult qualified specialists for adaptations to materials for children with disabilities.

PLANNED ACTIVITIES

Two examples of how to embed this goal and the associated objectives within activities are presented here. For a complete set of activities that address goals and objectives across domains, see Section V.

Trip to the Police Station

Children may enjoy going on a trip to the local police station. Reading a story or discussing police officers prior to the trip will help prepare children for the visit. Children can practice grooming skills by getting ready for the trip, washing their faces, and brushing their hair (mirrors should be provided). Before leaving, let children eat a small snack so they do not get hungry on the trip. Children may brush their teeth afterward. The interventionist should carry tissues and provide the least amount of assistance necessary for children to thoroughly clean their noses if necessary.

The Fire Station

The children will enjoy setting up a fire station in the dramatic play center. The station can reflect the daily life of firefighters and where they sleep, eat, and work. The interventionist may want to facilitate a discussion on how community helpers are careful about their grooming and try to stay neat and clean when not fighting fires. Provide a mirror in the dress-up area, clean uniforms (e.g., white shirts, firehats, yellow raincoats, boots), individual children's brushes or combs, tissues, and dining materials (e.g., utensils, cups, pitchers, napkins, pretend food, small table and chairs).

PRESCHOOL CURRICULA WITH SIMILAR GOALS

The following preschool curricula provide information on this goal or similar goals. Interventionists whose programs have access to one or more of these curricula may refer to the referenced sections for additional programming strategies.

The Carolina Curriculum for Preschoolers with Special Needs
Self-Help Skills
- Grooming

High Scope—Young Children in ACTION
Active Learning
- Taking care of one's own needs

Portage Guide to Early Education Activity Cards
Self-Help
- Wipes and blows nose
- Brushes teeth
- Bathes self
- Combs/brushes hair
- Washes hands/face

Adap B

Strand C   Dressing and Undressing

GOAL 1.0   Unfastens fasteners on garments

Objective 1.1	Unfastens buttons/snaps/Velcro fasteners on garments
Objective 1.2	Unties string-type fastener
Objective 1.3	Unzips zipper

CONCURRENT GOALS

FM A:1.0   Manipulates two small objects at same time
FM A:3.0   Ties string-type fastener
Adap C:3.0   Fastens fasteners on garments
Cog G:1.0   Engages in imaginary play
Soc B:1.0   Meets physical needs in socially appropriate ways

DAILY ROUTINES

Routine events that provide opportunities for children to manipulate different types of fasteners include the following:

Dressing/undressing
Arrival/departure
Unstructured play times
Bathtime
Bedtime

Example   Timmy arrives at school and walks over to the children playing with Play-Doh. His interventionist leads him back to his cubby and says (signing), "TAKE OFF YOUR COAT, TIM. THEN YOU CAN GO PLAY WITH THE PLAY-DOH." When Timmy does not respond, the interventionist points to the zipper and says, "First you need to unzip your coat." Timmy unzips his coat, and the interventionist provides verbal cues and the least amount of physical assistance for Timmy to detach the zipper. *(Adap C:1.3)*

ENVIRONMENTAL ARRANGEMENTS

■ Present a large selection of materials that provide opportunities for the children to manipulate different types of fasteners (e.g., dolls with doll clothes that have different types of fasteners such as snaps, laces, zippers, buttons, or Velcro fasteners; dress-up clothes with different types of fasteners). Arrange the classroom into activity areas that include a dramatic play center, and store materials so children have easy access. Dress-up clothes should include clothing with buttons, snaps, Velcro fasteners, string-type fasteners, and zippers. (See Environmental Arrangements in Section III and Dramatic Play Activities in Section V.)

■ Consultation with a qualified motor specialist may assist the interventionist in designing activities to include children with sensory and/or motor impairments. Adaptations for manipulating fasteners to maximize a child's potential for functional independence should include a discussion of position (standing or sitting), sequence of activity, type of fastener or modification of clothes, assistive devices for the arm or hand, and the optimal combination of modeling, physical assistance, and verbal cues.

■ Children who have limitations in fine motor control may require the assistance of peers, family members, or classroom personnel. Typically children with motor impairments require significantly greater amounts of time to complete dressing activities. The interventionist should schedule adequate time to manipulate fasteners during dressing and play activities rather than simply offering assistance to save time.

PLANNED ACTIVITIES

Two examples of how to embed this goal and the associated objectives within activities are presented here. For a complete set of activities that address goals and objectives across domains, see Section V.

Doctor's Office

Children will enjoy setting up a doctor's office in the dramatic play center of the classroom. The interventionist can provide props such as bandages, pretend stethoscopes, a cot for the patients, a wagon for an ambulance, and uniforms. Opportunities can be provided for children to unfasten fasteners on garments as they engage in this dramatic play. Patients can untie their shoes or unzip their coats before lying on the cot, and doctors and nurses can take off their uniforms, unfastening buttons/snaps or Velcro fasteners after "surgery" (smocks make excellent "scrubs").

Body Tracing

Children paint an outline of their body. This activity can begin by having children put on smocks with fasteners. The outline is created by having a child lie down on a piece of butcher paper while either the interventionist or another child outlines the child's body with a marker. The outline is taped to the wall, and the children are allowed to paint in their facial features, clothing, and background decorations. The interventionist should prepare the paint before the activity, making sure it is quite thick to keep it from dripping. Children practice unfastening fasteners when they complete the activity and take off their smocks.

PRESCHOOL CURRICULA WITH SIMILAR GOALS

The following preschool curricula provide information on this goal or similar goals. Interventionists whose programs have access to one or more of these curricula may refer to the referenced sections for additional programming strategies.

Adap C

The Carolina Curriculum for Preschoolers with Special Needs
Self-Help Skills
■ Dressing

High Scope—Young Children in ACTION
Active Learning
■ Taking care of one's own needs

Portage Guide to Early Education Activity Cards
Self-Help
■ Unbuttons own clothing
■ Unfastens snaps

GOAL 2.0 Selects appropriate clothing and dresses self at
designated times

Objective 2.1   Puts on long pants

Objective 2.2   Puts on front-opening garment

Objective 2.3   Puts on pullover garment

Objective 2.4   Puts on shoes

Objective 2.5   Puts on underpants, shorts, or skirt

Adap C

CONCURRENT GOALS

FM A:1.0	Manipulates two small objects at same time
FM A:3.0	Ties string-type fastener
Adap C:1.0	Unfastens fasteners on garments
Adap C:3.0	Fastens fasteners on garments
Cog B:1.0	Demonstrates understanding of eight different colors
Cog B:3.0	Demonstrates understanding of six different size concepts
Cog B:6.0	Demonstrates understanding of 12 different spatial relations concepts
Cog D:1.0	Follows directions of three or more related steps that are not routinely given
Soc B:1.0	Meets physical needs in socially appropriate ways
Soc C:1.0	Communicates personal likes and dislikes

DAILY ROUTINES

Routine events that provide opportunities for children to practice selecting appropriate clothing and dressing themselves at designated times include the following:

Dressing
Departure
Unstructured play time
Bedtime

Example   Timmy can put on his shoes without assistance but sometimes puts his shoes on the wrong feet. Timmy's interventionist puts a small red sticker on the inside edge of each sneaker, near the toes. Timmy puts on his shoes before going outside to play, and if necessary the interventionist reminds Timmy to make the two stickers touch. She also draws Timmy's attention to the way the shoes curve at the toes, and as soon as possible fades the use of the stickers. *(Adap C:2.4)*

ENVIRONMENTAL ARRANGEMENTS

- Children should be able to independently retrieve clothing in the home and school environment. Cubbies or lockers provide a location for personal belongings at school, and child-size dressers or low shelves provide opportunities for children to select clothing and dress themselves at home.
- Offer clothing that is simple to put on when children are first learning to dress (e.g., pants with an elastic waist, oversize tops). As children become more confident in dressing, other types of clothing can be introduced.
- Include a dramatic play center in the classroom and provide interesting clothing or uniforms that allow opportunities for children to practice skills (e.g., sweatshirts, post office shirt and pants, blouses, fancy shoes). (See Environmental Arrangements in Section III and Dramatic Play Activities in Section V.)

  Example   Joey sits in a chair, and his interventionist hands him (in the correct position) a pair of "police" pants. She draws his attention to the label in the back of the pants. Joey sits in the chair until the pants are at his knees and then stands to pull them up all the way. The interventionist helps him fasten the button. *(Adap C:2.1)*
- Consultation with a qualified motor specialist may assist the interventionist in designing activities to include children with sensory and/or motor impairments. Adaptations for selecting clothing and dressing self to maximize a child's potential for functional independence should include a discussion of position (standing or sitting); sequence of activity; type of fastener or modification of clothes; assistive devices for the arm or hand; and the optimal combination of modeling, physical assistance, and verbal or visual cues. Some children may need additional adaptations to the environment to make clothing accessible (e.g., lowering a coat hook for a child who uses a wheelchair, returning clothing to predictable locations for a child with a visual impairment).
- Children who have limitations in fine motor control may require the assistance of peers, family members, or classroom personnel. Typically children with motor impairments require significantly greater amounts of time to complete dressing activities. The interventionist should schedule adequate time during dressing and play activities rather than simply offering assistance to save time.

Adap C

PLANNED ACTIVITIES

Two examples of how to embed this goal and the associated objectives within activities are presented here. For a complete set of activities that address goals and objectives across domains, see Section V.

Forest Ranger

The interventionist reads a book to children or facilitates a discussion on what forest rangers do at work (e.g., teach people about the environment, maintain campgrounds, watch for forest fires). A campground is set up in the dramatic play center with props such as a tent (tarps or sheets draped over chairs make nice tents), a campfire (stones that form a ring with sticks for wood), cooking pots and utensils, backpacks, water bottles and canteens, old blankets or bed rolls, and pictures of the forest and animals. Materials should be included that allow the children to select clothing and dress themselves, such as flannel shirts, raincoats, pants, rain or snow boots, and a forest ranger's uniform (e.g., green dress shirt, green pants, ranger hat, belt, boots).

Let's Go Fishing!

Children go fishing and bring the fish to the "market" to sell. Fishing poles can be created by attaching one end of a string to the end of a dowel and attaching a magnet to the other end of the string for the "hook." The children make fish from construction paper, with a paper clip attached to each fish so that it will be attracted to the magnet. Children practice selecting clothing (e.g., overalls, boots, raincoats, sweaters, coats, socks, clerk smocks, shirts, skirts) and dressing themselves while they pretend to be fisherpeople, market workers, or shoppers. Set up a marketplace with small tables, cash registers, pretend money, and grocery sacks.

PRESCHOOL CURRICULA WITH SIMILAR GOALS

The following preschool curricula provide information on this goal or similar goals. Interventionists whose programs have access to one or more of these curricula may refer to the referenced sections for additional programming strategies.

The Carolina Curriculum for Preschoolers with Special Needs
Self-Help Skills
- Dressing

High Scope—Young Children in ACTION
Active Learning
- Taking care of one's own needs

Portage Guide to Early Education Activity Cards
Self-Help
- Chooses appropriate clothing
- Dresses self completely
- Dresses self with some assistance
- Puts on shoes

Adap C

GOAL 3.0   Fastens fasteners on garments

Objective 3.1   Ties string-type fasteners
Objective 3.2   Fastens buttons, snaps, and Velcro fasteners
Objective 3.3   Threads and zips zipper

CONCURRENT GOALS

FM A:1.0   Manipulates two small objects at same time
FM A:3.0   Ties string-type fastener
Adap C:1.0   Unfastens fasteners on garments
Soc B:1.0   Meets physical needs in socially appropriate ways

DAILY ROUTINES

Routine events that provide opportunities for children to practice fastening fasteners on garments include the following:

Dressing
Departure
Unstructured play time
Bedtime

Example   Eric, who has a visual impairment, gets dressed in the morning before breakfast. Eric chooses his clothes, which are kept in consistent locations, but needs assistance buttoning the buttons on his shirt. His mother first guides Eric's hands to feel all the buttons and holes, starting at the top and moving to the bottom. She then provides verbal cues and the least level of physical assistance for Eric to button his shirt. *(Adap C:3.0, 3.2)*

ENVIRONMENTAL ARRANGEMENTS

■ Present a large selection of materials that provide opportunities for the child to manipulate different types of fasteners (e.g., dolls with doll clothes that have different types of fasteners such as snaps, laces, zippers, buttons, or Velcro fasteners; dress-up clothes with different types of fasteners). Arrange the classroom into activity areas with easy access that include a dramatic play center and store materials. Dress-up clothes should include clothing with buttons, snaps, Velcro fasteners, string-type fasteners, and zippers. (See Environmental Arrangements in Section III and Dramatic Play Activities in Section V.)
■ Consultation with a qualified motor specialist may help the interventionist design activities to include children with sensory and/or motor impairments. Possible adap-

tations for manipulating fasteners to maximize a child's potential for functional independence should include a discussion of position (standing or sitting); sequence of
activity; type of fastener or modification of clothes; assistive devices for the arm or
hand; and the optimal combination of modeling, physical assistance, and verbal cues.

■ Children who have limitations in fine motor control may require the assistance of
  peers, family members, or classroom personnel. Typically children with motor
  impairments require significantly more time to complete dressing activities. The
  interventionist should schedule adequate time to manipulate fasteners during dressing and play activities rather than simply offering assistance to save time.

PLANNED ACTIVITIES

Two examples of how to embed this goal and the associated objectives within activities
are presented here. For a complete set of activities that address goals and objectives
across domains, see Section V.

Going on a Picnic

Children prepare food and invite family members to a picnic. It may be helpful to hold
this event after school or on a weekend so that working family members can participate. Before inviting family members to a picnic, the children can practice holding pic-
nics during school hours by eating snack outside once or twice a week. Children
practice fastening fasteners as they get ready for the picnic, either dressing up in special
clothing or putting on coats in cool weather. If the weather is warm, children may
enjoy taking off their shoes in a grassy area and can practice tying a string-type fastener
when they put the shoes back on.

Washing Babies

Children wash their "babies" (washable baby dolls) in tubs of water. The interventionist
should provide shampoo, soap, soft brushes, washcloths, towels, and baby clothing that
has different types of fasteners (e.g., snaps, buttons, Velcro fasteners, zippers). Children
practice their fastening skills as they get ready (e.g., putting on smocks with fasteners)
and participate in (e.g., dressing their baby dolls after their bath, tying the doll's shoes)
this activity.

PRESCHOOL CURRICULA WITH SIMILAR GOALS

The following preschool curricula provide information on this goal or similar goals.
Interventionists whose programs have access to one or more of these curricula may
refer to the referenced sections for additional programming strategies.

The Carolina Curriculum for Preschoolers with Special Needs
Self-Help Skills
■ Dressing

High Scope—Young Children in ACTION
Active Learning
■ Taking care of one's own needs

Adap C

Portage Guide to Early Education Activity Cards

Self-Help
- Ties strings
- Ties shoes
- Buttons clothing
- Snaps or hooks clothing

COGNITIVE DOMAIN

Cognition refers to thinking and learning processes used by humans to obtain desired goals, solve problems, and adapt to environmental demands. The development of cognitive abilities in children appears to result from the interaction between their genetic and physiological characteristics and their environmental training and experiences. Clearly the development of cognitive abilities is fundamentally important to the well-being of children and their success in becoming independent and functional individuals.

The Cognitive Domain of this curriculum is designed to enhance and expand the reciprocal interactions between children and their social and physical environment. The activities and strategies are designed to encourage children to actively engage their environment and to capitalize on children's inherent motivation to explore and expand their repertoires. Piaget's (1970) constructivist theory of cognitive development provides the general framework to organize the series of goals and intervention activities in this domain. A brief review of early cognitive development is offered before the introduction to these goals and activities.

During the early stages of the *sensorimotor period* of cognitive development described by Piaget, an infant's interactions with the environment are governed by sensory and primitive motor behaviors such as sight, sound, and touch. The infant learns by reaching, grasping, mouthing, and acting on objects and then processing the feedback received from these actions. During the entire sensorimotor period, which lasts from birth to approximately 2 years, children gradually acquire the ability to use symbols to represent objects, events, and social agents and to manipulate these symbols mentally. For example, the development of the *object permanence concept* during the second year is dependent on the child's ability to form and maintain mental representations or images of objects not present in the visual field. Children who master mental manipulation of symbols move into a period of cognitive development not tied to concrete and immediate experiences. Children learn to perform actions "in their head" and to anticipate outcomes before they occur.

The transition from the sensorimotor to the *preoperational period,* which occurs between 24 and 36 months, finds children learning to mentally represent objects and events and learning to "think" about past, current, and future activities. They learn to use symbols, beginning with those that are concrete and moving to those that are increasingly abstract. For example, a child may first learn that a toy cat represents an actual cat and then that a black and white sketch represents a cat.

Three- to 5-year-old children who are in the preoperational period come to understand that the world operates in a predictable fashion. Children recognize invariants of objects even though the conditions of size, shape, placement, and other dimensions may change. They also recognize invariants of functions (e.g., there are several ways to retrieve an object out of reach). Language is used to exchange information, and children in the preoperational period can learn from the communication of others. Extensive dialogues are managed on topics not immediately present or that happened earlier. Grammar expands and becomes more refined. Children are able to seek feedback by using questions or restatements and are able to follow complex instructions.

Associated with the development of symbolic thinking is children's growing ability to imitate responses observed earlier and to engage in pretend play. For example, children can pretend to be someone or something else observed previously, can use objects to substitute for other objects (e.g., a block becomes a train), and can conduct pretend activities (e.g., give a doll a drink from an imaginary cup). During this period, concepts are developed and understood, indicating that children are learning to organize information so that it is applicable not only to a specific entity but also to similar constellations of objects, people, and events. Children learn to appreciate the differences and similarities between entities, which permits them to classify and arrange items along a number of dimensions (e.g., size, color, use). In addition, children begin to learn number, time, and spatial relations concepts.

The growth in cognitive abilities of the young child during the sensorimotor and preoperational periods is remarkable. Appreciation of and knowledge about the substantial qualitative changes in the cognitive skills of young children are both necessary if interventionists and caregivers are to develop and deliver effective intervention services to children whose cognitive development is delayed or atypical. Those who would benefit from additional information on cognitive growth and development in young children are referred to Flavell (1977) and McCormick (1990).

It is important for three reasons for interventionists to observe children across a range of settings and activities before drawing firm conclusions about their cognitive abilities. First, children with disabilities often have uneven repertoires, so that they may perform differently as conditions vary. For example, a child may show more advanced problem-solving skills when engaged in familiar activities than when engaging in unfamiliar activities. Second, cognitive skills do not develop in isolation. Rather, early cognitive, communication, motor, and social processes appear to develop interdependently in young children, and the lack of development in one area can adversely affect development in another area. For example, acquisition of means ends, and causality concepts might be significantly delayed in children with severe motor impairments because of their reduced opportunity to physically act on their environment, not because of inherent cognitive limitations. Third, many activities and tasks require children to draw on skills from more than one behavioral domain. For example, a child's ability to follow a three-step direction (e.g., clean up your toys, put on your coat, and line up at the door) requires gross and fine motor skills (e.g., walking and zipping), adaptive skills (e.g., putting on the coat), language skills (e.g., understanding the words), and cognitive skills (e.g., attention and memory). The child may have adequate attention and memory skills but be unable to follow the directions because of deficient language skills.

Children with disabilities often require adaptation of activities if meaningful participation is to occur. The challenge is to design activities that maximize children's independent participation but still provide ample opportunity for children to practice targeted goals and objectives. Providing alternative methods of responding, working in conjunction with specialists, and being sensitive to children's subtle cues can lead to the successful adaptation of activities so that participation and benefits are maximal for children with disabilities.

Cog

The Cognitive Domain is composed of nine strands. Strand A (Participation) focuses on the child's ability to initiate and maintain participation in age-appropriate activities, including participation in small and large groups. Strand B (Demonstrates Understanding of Concepts) involves the child's ability to follow directions, answer questions, or identify objects according to color, shape, size, qualitative, quantitative, spatial, or temporal dimensions. Strand C (Categorizing) involves the child's ability to group objects, people, or events on the basis of category, function, or physical attributes. Strand D (Sequencing) involves the child's ability to follow directions, place objects in a series according to length or size, and retell events in sequence. Strand E (Recalling Events) involves the child's ability to recall events with or without contextual cues, as well as the ability to recall verbal information about him- or herself. Strand F (Problem Solving) examines the child's ability to evaluate solutions to problems as well as reasoning skills. Strand G (Play) involves the child's ability to engage in imaginary play and games with rules. Strand H (Premath) involves the child's ability to recite numbers, count objects, identify printed numerals, and match printed numerals to sets of 1–10 objects. Strand I (Prereading) examines the child's prereading and auditory skills as well as the ability to sound out words and read words by sight.

The Cognitive Domain curriculum is divided into four sections: 1) Intervention Considerations, 2) Suggested Activities, 3) Using Activity-Based Intervention, and 4) Domain Goals. Intervention Considerations addresses important factors an interventionist may wish to consider prior to and when working with children at risk for or who have disabilities. Suggested Activities provides a selected list of activities that may be particularly helpful when working on cognitive skills. This section also provides suggestions for additional materials that will increase opportunities for children to practice targeted cognitive skills. The third section provides an illustration of how to target IEP/IFSP goals in the Cognitive Domain using an activity-based intervention approach. The final section, Domain Goals, discusses suggestions for concurrent goals, daily routines, environmental arrangements, and planned activities in the home and classroom for each goal listed in the Cognitive Domain of the AEPS Test for Three to Six Years. This section also lists other commercially available curricula that provide intervention activities or suggestions for each goal.

INTERVENTION CONSIDERATIONS

General considerations when working on cognitive goals are discussed below.

- Some preschool special education programs emphasize school skills (e.g., numbers, letters, colors, writing skills) in an attempt to have children seem as "normal" as possible and to give them an academic head start on their peers. If the child does not understand the concepts that underlie academic skills, however, working on these skills can be very frustrating for both the child and the interventionist. Other nonacademic skills such as effective communication, social skills, following directions, attending for short periods of time without supervision, and the ability to move easily from one activity to the next are as important for success in public school environments as academic skills.

- When choosing goals and objectives for a child, consider the functionality of the goals for the child's immediate needs. How many times a day will the child actually use the targeted goal? Will it give him or her more independence? Because children with cognitive impairments may take longer to learn new skills, it is particularly

Cog

important to target goals that will be functional and generalizable in their immediate and future environments.

- Observe children carefully and work with familiar adults to determine each child's methods of communication, and provide nonverbal children with alternative forms of communication when assessing cognitive skills (see Social-Communication Domain).

- Observe children carefully across a range of settings and activities as well as across developmental domains before drawing firm conclusions about their cognitive abilities. Children may show more advanced problem-solving skills when engaged in familiar activities, or in the presence of familiar adults, peers, and settings.

- Children with disabilities may require additional considerations to facilitate generalization of responses. Observe children's learning styles carefully to determine where their strengths are (e.g., visual, auditory, kinesthetic, a combination of styles). Many examples of objects, people, and events across different activities and settings may need to be explored by children to understand different concepts (e.g., these are all balls, but they have features that are different).

- Spatial concepts are particularly difficult for children with visual impairments and should be emphasized. When applicable, it is helpful to go from three-dimensional objects (e.g., a sphere) to two-dimensional objects (e.g., a picture with raised print).

- The inability of a child to move freely in the environment can inhibit cognitive development. The interventionist should work closely with specialists to determine adaptations to the environment, activities, and materials that allow the child to actively explore and manipulate objects, participate in activities, and interact with peers.

- Be aware of the amount of noise and distraction in the environment. Some children may have difficulty attending to the appropriate stimuli (e.g., a direction, a book being read) with other distractions occurring (e.g., peers talking, loud noises).

SUGGESTED ACTIVITIES

The following list of activities and materials may be particularly helpful for eliciting skills within the Cognitive Domain. For a complete list of activities, see Section V.

Dramatic Play Activities

Dramatic play scenarios are excellent contexts for children to practice cognitive skills. When selecting props, include materials that will provide opportunities for children to practice targeted goals. For example, if a child has a goal to sort objects on the basis of physical attribute, include materials such as socks, utensils, and coins that can be sorted by color, shape, or size. The following themes are particularly helpful when embedding cognitive goals: House Play, Shoe Store, and Airplane.

Other Activities

- Marble Painting
- Collages
- Planting a Garden
- Board Games
- Ramps
- Expressive Arts
- What's Missing?

- Teddy Bear Counting Game
- Art Activities
- Books/Book Making
- Water/Sand Play
- Play-Doh
- Construction/Manipulation Activities
- Cooking

USING ACTIVITY-BASED INTERVENTION

An illustration of how an interventionist can incorporate strategies to enhance the development of a child's cognitive skills is provided below. The child's targeted IEP/IFSP objectives are to 1) indicate solutions to problems (adult can provide general cues) and 2) correctly count five objects.

- The interventionist observes Alice choosing to play with Play-Doh. She *follows the child's lead* by joining Alice in her play and encourages peers to join. The classroom consists of a *heterogeneous* (at varied skill levels) group of children, providing opportunities for Alice to learn new skills by observing peer models or to enhance skills by assisting children who are less able.
- The interventionist *"forgets"* to put rolling pins with the Play-Doh, providing an opportunity for Alice to recognize the missing materials and indicate a solution to the problem.
- During the activity, Alice says, "Me making hotdogs." The interventionist *expands on the child's initiation,* providing an opportunity for Alice to practice counting by commenting, "Hmm—I wonder how many hotdogs you have?"
- If necessary, the interventionist *models* counting for Alice (e.g., "I'm going to count my hotdogs...1, 2, 3, 4, 5") or encourages a child with more advanced skills to model by asking, "How many hotdogs do you have, Maria?"
- The interventionist encourages *multiple opportunities* for Alice to practice counting different materials such as rolling pins, cookie cutters, colors of Play-Doh, or the number of people participating in the activity.
- The interventionist *"violates the child's expectations"* of the activity by using a cookie cutter incorrectly (upside down) and commenting, "Hmm—This isn't working!" Alice may be able to recognize the problem and offer a solution or may learn by observing a peer's solution to the problem.
- Throughout the activity, the interventionist uses the *least amount of assistance* necessary for Alice to successfully practice counting or solving problems.

DOMAIN GOALS

This section provides suggestions for concurrent goals, daily routines, environmental arrangements, and planned activities for the cognitive goals listed in the AEPS Test for Three to Six Years. If an objective has been targeted, the interventionist can turn to the corresponding goal and determine which suggestions are relevant to facilitate that objective. A standard format is used for each goal: 1) Strand, 2) Goal, 3) Objective(s), 4) Concurrent Goals, 5) Daily Routines, 6) Environmental Arrangements, 7) Planned Activities, and 8) Preschool Curricula with Similar Goals. Concurrent Goals list the AEPS goals that can often be addressed at the same time the child works on the target goal or associated objectives. Daily Routines present a list of routine activities that may provide opportunities to practice targeted skills. The Environmental Arrangements should be considered when designing children's programs around child-initiated, routine, and planned activities. The Planned Activities offer examples of how to embed targeted goals within the context of planned activities. Finally, Preschool Curricula with Similar Goals list other curricula that can be used to supplement the AEPS Curriculum for Three to Six Years. If a given program has one or more of these preschool curricula, the interventionist can refer to the referenced sections to find additional programming strategies for the targeted goal or objective. Additional information on daily routines, environmental arrangements, planned activities, and themes is provided in Section III.

Strand A   Participation

G1.0   Initiates and completes age-appropriate activities

1.1   Responds to request to finish activity

1.2   Responds to request to begin activity

G2.0   Watches, listens, and participates during small group activities

2.1   Interacts appropriately with materials during small group activities

2.2   Responds appropriately to directions during small group activities

2.3   Looks at appropriate object, person, or event during small group activities

2.4   Remains with group during small group activities

G3.0   Watches, listens, and participates during large group activities

3.1   Interacts appropriately with materials during large group activities

3.2   Responds appropriately to directions during large group activities

3.3   Looks at appropriate object, person, or event during large group activities

3.4   Remains with group during large group activities

Strand B   Demonstrates Understanding of Concepts

G1.0   Demonstrates understanding of eight different colors

1.1   Demonstrates understanding of six different colors

1.2   Demonstrates understanding of three different colors

G2.0   Demonstrates understanding of five different shapes

2.1   Demonstrates understanding of three different shapes

2.2   Demonstrates understanding of one shape

G3.0   Demonstrates understanding of six different size concepts

3.1   Demonstrates understanding of four different size concepts

3.2   Demonstrates understanding of two different size concepts

G4.0   Demonstrates understanding of 10 different qualitative concepts

4.1   Demonstrates understanding of six different qualitative concepts

4.2   Demonstrates understanding of four different qualitative concepts

4.3   Demonstrates understanding of two different qualitative concepts

G5.0   Demonstrates understanding of eight different quantitative concepts

5.1   Demonstrates understanding of five different quantitative concepts

5.2   Demonstrates understanding of two different quantitative concepts

G6.0   Demonstrates understanding of 12 different spatial relations concepts

      6.1   Demonstrates understanding of nine different spatial relations concepts

      6.2   Demonstrates understanding of six different spatial relations concepts

      6.3   Demonstrates understanding of three different spatial relations concepts

G7.0   Demonstrates understanding of seven different temporal relations concepts

      7.1   Demonstrates understanding of five different temporal relations concepts

      7.2   Demonstrates understanding of three different temporal relations concepts

Strand C   Categorizing

G1.0   Groups objects, people, or events on the basis of specified criteria

      1.1   Groups objects, people, or events on the basis of category

      1.2   Groups objects on the basis of function

      1.3   Groups objects on the basis of physical attribute

Strand D   Sequencing

G1.0   Follows directions of three or more related steps that are not routinely given

      1.1   Follows directions of three or more related steps that are routinely given

G2.0   Places objects in series according to length or size

      2.1   Fits one ordered set of objects to another

G3.0   Retells event in sequence

      3.1   Completes sequence of familiar story or event

Strand E   Recalling Events

G1.0   Recalls events that occurred on same day, without contextual cues

      1.1   Recalls events that occurred on same day, with contextual cues

      1.2   Recalls events immediately after they occur

G2.0   Recalls verbal sequences

      2.1   Recalls verbal information about self

Strand F   Problem Solving

G1.0   Evaluates solutions to problems

      1.1   Suggests acceptable solutions to problems

      1.2   Identifies means to goal

G2.0   Makes statements and appropriately answers questions that require reasoning about objects, situations, or people

      2.1   Gives reason for inference

      2.2   Makes prediction about future or hypothetical events

      2.3   Gives possible cause for some event

Strand G   Play

G1.0   Engages in imaginary play

      1.1   Enacts roles or identities

      1.2   Plans and acts out recognizable event, theme, or story line

Cog

        1.3   Uses imaginary props
G2.0   Engages in games with rules
        2.1   Maintains participation
        2.2   Conforms to game rules

Strand H   Premath

G1.0   Recites numbers from 1 to 20
        1.1   Recites numbers from 1 to 10
        1.2   Recites numbers from 1 to 5
        1.3   Recites numbers from 1 to 3
G2.0   Counts 10 objects
        2.1   Counts five objects
        2.2   Counts two objects
        2.3   Demonstrates understanding of one-to-one correspondence
G3.0   Identifies printed numerals 1–10
        3.1   Identifies printed numerals 1–8
        3.2   Identifies printed numerals 1–5
        3.3   Identifies printed numerals 1–3
G4.0   Matches printed numerals to sets of 1–10 object(s)
        4.1   Matches printed numerals to sets of 1–8 object(s)
        4.2   Matches printed numerals to sets of 1–5 object(s)
        4.3   Matches printed numerals to sets of 1–3 object(s)

Strand I   Prereading

G1.0   Demonstrates prereading skills
        1.1   Demonstrates functional use of books
        1.2   Tells about pictures in book
        1.3   Participates actively in storytelling
G2.0   Demonstrates prereading auditory skills
        2.1   Blends sounds
        2.2   Rhymes words
G3.0   Sounds out words
        3.1   Produces phonetic sounds for letters
G4.0   Reads words by sight
        4.1   Identifies letters

Strand A Participation

GOAL 1.0 Initiates and completes age-appropriate activities

Objective 1.1 Responds to request to finish activity
Objective 1.2 Responds to request to begin activity

CONCURRENT GOALS

Adap A:1.0 Eats and drinks a variety of foods using appropriate utensils with little or no spilling
Adap B Personal Hygiene (all goals)
SC A Social-Communicative Interactions (all goals)
Soc A:1.0 Has play partners
Soc A:2.0 Initiates cooperative activity
Soc B:2.0 Follows context-specific rules outside home and classroom

DAILY ROUTINES

Routine events that provide opportunities for children to participate in activities include unstructured play times.

Example During play time at home, Latifa's mother says, "I need to start dinner. Please go get your Legos or coloring books to play with." Latifa gets the Legos from her room and plays with them on the kitchen table. (*Cog A:1.2*)

ENVIRONMENTAL ARRANGEMENTS

■ Provide materials that are age appropriate and appealing and arrange the classroom into activity centers (see Environmental Arrangements in Section III).

Example During free play, Joey chooses to work at the water table. After 10 minutes, the interventionist tells him that in 5 minutes it will be time to clean up and go outside. After 5 minutes, the interventionist says, "It's time to clean up." Joey finishes pouring water through the water wheel, puts away the water toys in a bucket, and lines up to go outside. (*Cog A:1.1*)

■ Create a daily routine that includes unstructured play times. Provide the children with opportunities to make choices about activities and materials as often as possible during free play and planned activities.

■ It may be necessary to adapt materials and/or the environment to make activities accessible to children with special needs. Contact qualified specialists for programming suggestions. Some children may require additional support and guidance from an adult to initially participate in meaningful activities.

Cog A

PLANNED ACTIVITIES

Two examples of how to embed this goal and the associated objectives within activities are presented here. For a complete set of activities that address goals and objectives across domains, see Section V.

Leaf Collage

During the fall season, the interventionist and the children take a walk and gather leaves. On returning to school, the children make collages with leaves they have gathered, gluing their favorites to construction paper.

Fall Colors

Children paint with fall colors such as red, orange, and yellow on any type of paper. They cut out leaf shapes to paint or to use as stencils. The interventionist cuts out a large tree trunk to put on the wall of the classroom, and the children hang their leaves on the class tree.

PRESCHOOL CURRICULA WITH SIMILAR GOALS

The following preschool curricula provide information on this goal or similar goals. Interventionists whose programs have access to one or more of these curricula may refer to the referenced sections for additional programming strategies.

The Carolina Curriculum for Preschoolers with Special Needs
Assuming Responsibility
Interpersonal Skills
Self-Concept

The Creative Curriculum
Blocks
House Corner
Table Toys
Art
Sand and Water
Library
Outdoors

High Scope—Young Children in ACTION
Active learning
■ Choosing materials, activities, purposes

Portage Guide to Early Education Activity Cards
Social
■ Plays near and talks with other children when working on own project
■ Works alone at chore
■ Cooperates with adult requests

Cog A

GOAL 2.0 Watches, listens, and participates during small group activities

---

Objective 2.1   Interacts appropriately with materials during small group activities

Objective 2.2   Responds appropriately to directions during small group activities

Objective 2.3   Looks at appropriate object, person, or event during small group activities

Objective 2.4   Remains with group during small group activities

---

CONCURRENT GOALS

GM B   Play Skills (all goals)
Adap A:3.0   Displays social dining skills
Cog D:1.0   Follows directions of three or more related steps that are not routinely given
Cog G   Play (all goals)
SC A   Social-Communicative Interactions (all goals)
Soc A   Interaction with Others (all goals)
Soc B   Interaction with Environment (all goals)
Soc C:1.0   Communicates personal likes and dislikes

DAILY ROUTINES

Routine events that provide opportunities for children to participate during small group activities include the following:

Circle time
Snack time

Example   During circle time, the interventionist asks children to get a carpet square and come sit in the circle. Timmy watches and imitates the other children as they follow the direction. (*Cog A:2.2*)

ENVIRONMENTAL ARRANGEMENTS

■ Provide materials that are age appropriate and interesting and arrange the classroom into activity centers (see Environmental Arrangements in Section III).

Example   During a Play-Doh activity, the interventionist models rolling out Play-Doh for Eric, who has a visual impairment, by having him feel the Play-Doh; then she hand-over-hand prompts Eric to roll out the Play-Doh. (*Cog A:2.1*)

Cog A

- Small chairs or carpet squares for children to sit on during circle time help children define their space and stay with the group. Putting away their chairs or carpet squares signals the end of the activity.
- During circle time, the use of props such as puppets, pictures, or tactile items maintains interest and increases understanding of children in the group (e.g., real flowers to look at and touch when discussing spring, samples of foods to taste and smell when discussing nutrition). Children with visual, communicative, or other impairments should be given special attention, providing opportunities for their participation during circle time. Consult qualified specialists for individual programming suggestions.

    Example   While discussing where animals live, the interventionist holds up a picture of a fish and a horse and asks a child who communicates with eye gazes to look at the animal that lives in the water. The child gazes at the fish. (*Cog A:2.2*)

PLANNED ACTIVITIES

Two examples of how to embed this goal and the associated objectives within activities are presented here. For a complete set of activities that address goals and objectives across domains, see Section V.

Snow Painting

Children make "snow" with two cups of soap flakes and one cup of water. Children take turns whipping up the mixture with an egg beater or an electric mixer in a large bowl. Then they use paint brushes to create snow pictures (dark construction paper makes a good background), let them dry overnight, and hang them in the classroom or at home.

   Example   Latifa is interested in using the electric mixer but is starting to wander away from the table. The interventionist notices Latifa getting restless and reminds the children, "The children who are at the table will get a chance to whip up the snow!" Latifa rejoins the group and gets the next turn to use the mixer. (*Cog A:2.4*)

Snow Flakes

Children move to music while twirling white scarves or white paper streamers, pretending to be snowflakes. When the music is loud, the "snowflakes" twirl fast; as the music softens, the "snowflakes" slow down; and when the music stops, the "snowflakes" fall to the ground. Children take turns suggesting other things (e.g., birds, leaves) they will pretend to be.

PRESCHOOL CURRICULA WITH SIMILAR GOALS

The following preschool curricula provide information on this goal or similar goals. Interventionists whose programs have access to one or more of these curricula may refer to the referenced sections for additional programming strategies.

The Carolina Curriculum for Preschoolers with Special Needs

Assuming Responsibility
Self-Concept
Interpersonal Skills

The Creative Curriculum

Blocks
House Corner
Table Toys
Art
Sand and Water
Library
Outdoors

High Scope—Young Children in ACTION

Active Learning
■ Choosing materials, activities, purposes
Language
■ Talking with other children and adults about personally meaningful experiences
■ Having fun with language

Portage Guide to Early Education Activity Cards

Social
■ Plays with four to five children in cooperative activity without constant supervision
■ Plays with two to three children in cooperative activity
■ Cooperates with adult requests
■ Explains rules of game or activity to others
■ Explains rules in group games led by an older child
■ Follows rules in group games led by adult

GOAL 3.0 Watches, listens, and participates during large group activities

---

Objective 3.1	Interacts appropriately with materials during large group activities
Objective 3.2	Responds appropriately to directions during large group activities
Objective 3.3	Looks at appropriate object, person, or event during large group activities
Objective 3.4	Remains with group during large group activities

Cog A

CONCURRENT GOALS

GM B	Play Skills (all goals)
Adap A:3.0	Displays social dining skills
Cog G	Play (all goals)
SC A	Social-Communicative Interactions (all goals)

Soc A:1.0   Has play partners
Soc A:2.0   Initiates cooperative activity
Soc C:1.0   Communicates personal likes and dislikes

DAILY ROUTINES

Routine events that provide opportunities for children to participate in large group activities include the following:

Circle time
Snack time
Cleanup time

   Example   During cleanup, the interventionist gives directions. "When you hear music playing, it's time to clean up; but when the music stops, freeze!" Manuel follows the directions, participating in this game during cleanup time. (*Cog A:3.2*)

ENVIRONMENTAL ARRANGEMENTS

- Plan activities that are age appropriate and appealing to children during group times (see Section V).
- Structure the daily routine to include large group activities. Circle time and snack time provide opportunities for large groups of children to participate in activities. Whenever possible, provide children with opportunities to make choices about activities, direct the way activities are carried out, and actively participate throughout activities.
   Example   During snack time, children pour juice, request preferred food items, and prepare their food (e.g., peel bananas, spread peanut butter on crackers). When Joey gets fidgety and starts to leave the group, the interventionist asks him, "Are you finished Joey, or do you want some more?" (*Cog A:3.4*)
- Small chairs or carpet squares for children to sit on during circle time help children define space and stay with the group. Putting away their chairs or carpet squares signals the end of the activity.
   Example   Every few minutes Timmy's interventionist reinforces him for sitting in the circle. She rubs Timmy's back, asks him a question, gives him something to hold, or praises him for sitting in the circle. Timmy sits on a carpet square, and, if he gets up, the interventionist reminds him, "Stay on your square until we are all finished." (*Cog A:3.4*)
- During circle time, the use of props such as puppets, pictures, or tactile items maintains interest and increases understanding of children in the group (e.g., real flowers to look at and touch when discussing spring, samples of foods to taste and smell when discussing nutrition). Children with visual, communicative, or other impairments should be given special attention, providing methods for their active participation during circle time. Consult qualified specialists for individual programming suggestions.

PLANNED ACTIVITIES

Two examples of how to embed this goal and the associated objectives within activities are presented here. For a complete set of activities that address goals and objectives across domains, see Section V.

Musical Parade

Children play musical instruments and march in a "parade." They take turns being the leader and lead the other children inside or outside.

Example   Timmy chooses a drum to play during the parade. At first he shakes it up and down to make a noise, so the interventionist models how to hit the drum. Timmy joins the parade, hitting the drum to make noise. (*Cog A:3.1*)

Circus Acrobats

Children gather around a tumbling mat and pretend to be circus acrobats. They go one at a time to the mat and perform a somersault, log roll, or any movement they can do. Children who are watching clap for each performer.

Example   Manuel watches Maria roll on the mat, claps when Maria finishes, and waits for his turn to be called. (*Cog A:3.3*)

PRESCHOOL CURRICULA WITH SIMILAR GOALS

The following preschool curricula provide information on this goal or similar goals. Interventionists whose programs have access to one or more of these curricula may refer to the referenced sections for additional programming strategies.

The Carolina Curriculum for Preschoolers with Special Needs

Assuming Responsibility
Self-Concept
Interpersonal Skills

The Creative Curriculum

Blocks
House Corner
Table Toys
Art
Sand and Water
Library
Outdoors

High Scope—Young Children in ACTION

Active Learning
■ Choosing materials, activities, purposes
Language
■ Talking with other children and adults about personally meaningful experiences
■ Having fun with language

Portage Guide to Early Education Activity Cards

Social
■ Will take turns with eight or nine other children
■ Cooperates with adult requests

Cog A

Strand B   Demonstrates Understanding of Concepts

GOAL 1.0   Demonstrates understanding of eight different colors

Objective 1.1   Demonstrates understanding of six different colors

Objective 1.2   Demonstrates understanding of three different colors

CONCURRENT GOALS

FM A:2.0	Cuts out shapes with curved lines
Adap C:2.0	Selects appropriate clothing and dresses self at designated times
Cog C	Categorizing (all goals)
SC A:1.0	Uses words, phrases, or sentences to inform, direct, ask questions, and express anticipation, imagination, affect, and emotions
SC B:5.0	Uses descriptive words
Soc C:1.0	Communicates personal likes and dislikes

DAILY ROUTINES

Routine events that provide opportunities for children to demonstrate understanding of color concepts include the following:

Dressing	Snack time
Mealtime	Unstructured play time
Travel time	Transition time
Arrival and departure	Bathtime
Circle time at school	Bedtime

Example   While caregivers help children get dressed, they reinforce color concepts by commenting about, describing, and requesting by color. (*Cog B:1.0*)

ENVIRONMENTAL ARRANGEMENTS

■ Arrange the classroom into activity areas that include an art center and provide age-appropriate and appealing materials of different colors:

– Art materials with different colors, such as markers, crayons, paints, construction paper, and tissue paper
– Materials of different colors, such as Play-Doh, Lego toys and Tinkertoys, counting bears, small colored blocks, clothing in the dress-up area

Cog B

– Games with color themes, such as Candyland or Color Bingo
– Materials of different colors used in daily routines (e.g., cups and bowls, food items, chairs and carpet squares)

■ Include books in the library and story audiotapes in the music area that are about colors.
■ Paint the classroom or home environment in bright, appealing colors. Hang pictures or include decorations in the environment that provide examples of different colors.
■ Include special color days or weeks in the classroom plan. For example, Monday is blue day, and the color blue is highlighted throughout the day with special activities such as painting with different shades of blue, eating blueberries for snack, and having a scavenger hunt to find blue things.

PLANNED ACTIVITIES

Two examples of how to embed this goal and the associated objectives within activities are presented here. For a complete set of activities that address goals and objectives across domains, see Section V.

Tie-Dyed Flowers

Children make tie-dyed flowers with colored water and coffee filters. They fill baby food jars half full with water and add a few drops of food coloring to make different colors. Children fold the filters, drop colored water on them with an eye dropper, unfold the filters, and hang them up with clothespins on a line to dry. Children can demonstrate understanding of different colors as they get ready for the activity (e.g., "Can I make the red water?"), follow directions (e.g., "Pass the green water"), and participate in the activity. The interventionist reinforces the concept by labeling, commenting on, and describing materials by their color.

Example   The interventionist comments on Joey's flower while pointing to the colors, "You used green, blue, and..." Joey says, "Red." (*Cog B:1.0*)

Butterfly Blots

Children use construction paper and paint in squeeze bottles (e.g., plastic ketchup or mustard bottles) to make "butterflies." They 1) choose colored paper, 2) fold the paper in half lengthwise, 3) open the paper, 4) choose paint colors, 5) squirt small blobs of paint on *one half* of the paper, 6) fold the paper in half, 7) press and smooth out, and 8) open up the butterfly and let it dry.

PRESCHOOL CURRICULA WITH SIMILAR GOALS

The following preschool curricula provide information on this goal or similar goals. Interventionists whose programs have access to one or more of these curricula may refer to the referenced sections for additional programming strategies.

The Carolina Curriculum for Preschoolers with Special Needs
Concepts
■ Labels all primary colors
■ Identifies red, blue, and yellow
■ Sorts objects by color, form, or name

Cog B

The Creative Curriculum
Blocks
House Corner
Table Toys
Art
Library

High Scope—Young Children in ACTION
Classification
■ Investigating and describing the attributes of things
■ Noticing and describing how things are the same and how they are different; sorting and matching
■ Talking about the characteristics something does not possess or the class it does not belong to

Portage Guide to Early Education Activity Cards
Cognitive
■ Names colors

GOAL 2.0   Demonstrates understanding of five different shapes

---

Objective 2.1   Demonstrates understanding of three different shapes

Objective 2.2   Demonstrates understanding of one shape

CONCURRENT GOALS

FM A:2.0	Cuts out shapes with curved lines
FM B	Prewriting (all goals)
Cog C	Categorizing
SC A:1.0	Uses words, phrases, or sentences to inform, direct, ask questions, and express anticipation, imagination, affect, and emotions
SC B:5.0	Uses descriptive words

DAILY ROUTINES

Routine events that provide opportunities for children to demonstrate understanding of shape concepts include the following:

Dressing	Snack time
Mealtime	Unstructured play time
Travel time	Transition time
Arrival and departure	Bathtime
Circle time at school	Bedtime

Cog B

Example   Manuel's father often describes shapes they see while driving in the car. One day Manuel points to a traffic sign and says, "Look, a triangle." (*Cog B:2.0*)

ENVIRONMENTAL ARRANGEMENTS

■ Include materials of different shapes during unstructured play times and routine events that provide opportunities for the child to learn shape concepts:

- Art materials such as shape stencils, construction paper, and sponges cut into different shapes to use as paint stamps
- Games with shape themes, such as Shape Bingo
- Food items such as crackers of different shapes, cheese cut into shapes
- Materials of different shapes, such as parquetry blocks, shape sorters, puzzles, Play-Doh rolled and cut with cookie cutters

■ Display pictures or decorations in the environment that provide examples of different shapes. Include books about shapes in the library area. Labeling tables/chairs/activity areas with shapes may make transitions more smooth and reinforce children's shape concepts (e.g., "When you get inside, go to the star table for the painting activity").

PLANNED ACTIVITIES

Two examples of how to embed this goal and the associated objectives within activities are presented here. For a complete set of activities that address goals and objectives across domains, see Section V.

Shape Search

Children search the classroom for examples of different shapes. Depending on the skill level of the child, the interventionist can 1) tell the child what to look for (e.g., "Find something shaped like a circle"); 2) show the child a model of a circle and then have the child look for one; or 3) have the child hold the model while looking for another object shaped like a circle.

Example   The interventionist provides a tactile model of a circle for Eric, who has a visual impairment. Eric "feels" the circle and finds a puzzle that has a circle piece to match. (*Cog B:2.0*)

Tasting Party

Children smell, touch, and taste different foods. The interventionist presents small amounts of unfamiliar food to the children that are of a wide variety of different tastes (e.g., sweet, sour, salty). The foods might be presented in different shapes (e.g., pineapple and kiwi sliced into circles; cheese cut in rectangles, squares, hearts, or stars). Children demonstrate understanding of shapes as they get ready for the activity (e.g., "Go to the star table"), follow directions (e.g., "Can you find one that looks like a circle?"), and participate in the activity. The interventionist reinforces shape concepts by labeling, commenting on, and describing the different foods by their shapes.

Cog B

PRESCHOOL CURRICULA WITH SIMILAR GOALS

The following preschool curricula provide information on this goal or similar goals. Interventionists whose programs have access to one or more of these curricula may refer to the referenced sections for additional programming strategies.

The Carolina Curriculum for Preschoolers with Special Needs

Concepts
- Labels square, triangle, and circle
- Identifies square and round
- Sorts objects by color, form, or name

The Creative Curriculum

Blocks
House Corner
Table Toys
Art
Library

High Scope—Young Children in ACTION

Spatial Relations
- Distinguishing and describing shapes
Classification
- Investigating and describing the attributes of things
- Noticing and describing how things are the same and how they are different; sorting and matching
- Talking about the characteristics something does not possess or the class it does not belong to

Portage Guide to Early Education Activity Cards

Cognitive
- Names three shapes—square, triangle, and circle
- Matches geometric form with picture of shape

GOAL 3.0   Demonstrates understanding of six different size concepts

---

Objective 3.1   Demonstrates understanding of four different size concepts

Objective 3.2   Demonstrates understanding of two different size concepts

---

CONCURRENT GOALS

FM B   Prewriting (all goals)
Cog B:4.0   Demonstrates understanding of 10 different qualitative concepts

Cog C	Categorizing (all goals)
Cog D:2.0	Places objects in series according to length or size
SC A:1.0	Uses words, phrases, or sentences to inform, direct, ask questions, and express anticipation, imagination, affect, and emotions
SC B:5.0	Uses descriptive words
Soc C:1.0	Communicates personal likes and dislikes
Soc C:2.0	Relates identifying information about self and others

DAILY ROUTINES

Routine events that provide opportunities for children to demonstrate understanding of size concepts include the following:

Dressing	Snack time
Mealtime	Unstructured play time
Travel time	Transition time
Arrival and departure	Bathtime
Circle time at school	Bedtime

Example   During cleanup time, the interventionist asks Joey to pick up all the long blocks and Latifa to pick up all the short blocks. (*Cog B:3.0*)

ENVIRONMENTAL ARRANGEMENTS

■ Have materials with two or more sizes available during unstructured play times and routine events:

– Art materials such as thin and fat markers, crayons, or paintbrushes; big and little scissors; and various sizes of construction paper
– Collage materials such as beans, macaroni, yarn, and buttons
– Materials with several sizes such as blocks, Lincoln Logs, stacking/nesting cups, Tinkertoys, Lego toys, plastic people/animals, cars and trucks, dress-up clothes (e.g., big and small hats), books, balls, bikes, and wagons; water table materials of various sizes such as cups, funnels, pitchers, and big and little tables and chairs
– Snack items of various sizes, such as tiny crackers and big cookies and fruit, as well as cups, plates, utensils, and pitchers of different sizes.

■ Incorporate books and story audiotapes in the library and music centers that include information about sizes (e.g., "Goldilocks and the Three Bears").
■ Present pictures and decorations in the environment that provide examples of objects and people of different sizes.

PLANNED ACTIVITIES

Two examples of how to embed this goal and the associated objectives within activities are presented here. For a complete set of activities that address goals and objectives across domains, see Section V.

Water Music

Children experiment with tones by tapping jars filled with water. Glass jars provide the clearest tones, but safety should be considered when choosing containers. The interventionist should provide several sizes of water containers and items to tap with (e.g., spoons, chopsticks, wooden sticks). Children can vary the amount of water in each jar and tap the jar to produce different sounds. The interventionist should model how to "tap" softly. Children demonstrate understanding of size concepts as they get ready for the activity (e.g., "Use the big bucket to get some water"), follow directions (e.g., "Hand me the long chopstick"), and participate in the activity. The interventionist reinforces concepts by labeling, commenting, and describing materials by size. This activity is best done at the water table and needs to be supervised closely.

Make it Move

Children experiment with using ramps to make objects move. The interventionist provides children with big and little cars and trucks, short and long boards or planks, and different sizes of blocks or other supports on which to lean the planks. The interventionist asks, "How can we use this ramp to make the cars go without pushing them?" (The interventionist may need to model how to set up the ramps.) Children experiment with making a ramp higher or lower and changing the length of a ramp to see how these variables affect the speed and distance the cars and trucks move.

PRESCHOOL CURRICULA WITH SIMILAR GOALS

The following preschool curricula provide information on this goal or similar goals. Interventionists whose programs have access to one or more of these curricula may refer to the referenced sections for additional programming strategies.

The Carolina Curriculum for Preschoolers with Special Needs
Concepts
- Compares sizes of familiar objects not in view
- Understands fat, skinny, thick, and thin

The Creative Curriculum
Blocks
House Corner
Table Toys
Art
Sand and Water
Library

High Scope—Young Children in ACTION
Seriation
- Making comparisons
- Arranging several things in order and describing their relations

Classification
- Investigating and describing the attributes of things
- Noticing and describing how things are the same and how they are different; sorting and matching
- Talking about the characteristics something does not possess or the class it does not belong to

Portage Guide to Early Education Activity Cards

Cognitive
- Arranges objects in sequence of width and length
- Names long and short
- Points to long and short objects
- Names big and little objects
- Points to big and little objects upon request

GOAL 4.0   Demonstrates understanding of 10 different qualitative concepts

---

Objective 4.1	Demonstrates understanding of six different qualitative concepts
Objective 4.2	Demonstrates understanding of four different qualitative concepts
Objective 4.3	Demonstrates understanding of two different qualitative concepts

---

CONCURRENT GOALS

Adap A:1.0	Eats and drinks a variety of foods using appropriate utensils with little or no spilling
Cog C	Categorizing (all goals)
SC A:1.0	Uses words, phrases, or sentences to inform, direct, ask questions, and express anticipation, imagination, affect, and emotions
SC B:5.0	Uses descriptive words
Soc C:1.0	Communicates personal likes and dislikes
Soc C:3.0	Accurately identifies affect/emotions in others and self consistent with demonstrated behaviors

DAILY ROUTINES

Routine events that provide opportunities for children to demonstrate understanding of qualitative concepts include the following:

Dressing	Snack time
Mealtime	Unstructured play time
Travel time	Transition time
Arrival and departure	Bathtime
Circle time at school	Bedtime

Example   During dinner, Joey takes a bite of his food and says, "Ow!" His mother prompts him by asking, "Is it hot, Joey?" and Joey responds, "Yeah, hot." (*Cog B:4.0*)

Cog B

ENVIRONMENTAL ARRANGEMENTS

■ Arrange the classroom into activity areas that include a science and nature center where children can explore objects with different qualitative attributes. Children add to the table by bringing natural objects they find outside, such as pinecones, rocks, shells, and feathers. Provide materials with different qualitative features:

 – Art materials such as cotton balls, fabrics such as velvet and denim, paper products such as sandpaper and tissue paper, paint that has been given a rough texture by adding sand
 – Food and snack items with contrasting qualitative features, such as sweet and sour tastes, hot and cold temperatures, smooth and rough surfaces (e.g., apple and pineapple), wet and dry qualities
 – Materials such as blocks (heavy/light), musical instruments (loud/soft), clay and Play-Doh (hard/soft), sand or water table filled with different materials (e.g., sand, cornmeal, flour, warm or cold water)

■ Provide a weather chart with pictures depicting sunny, rainy, cloudy, or snowy days. Discuss the weather during group time. Pictures help children visualize concepts such as wet/dry, light/dark, and hot/cold. Whenever possible, go outside or look out a window to see the clouds, feel the warm sun, and touch the wet rain or cold snow.

PLANNED ACTIVITIES

Two examples of how to embed this goal and the associated objectives within activities are presented here. For a complete set of activities that address goals and objectives across domains, see Section V.

Nature Collage

Children go outside on a scavenger hunt and later make collages with items they find. The interventionist specifies the characteristics of items (e.g., hard/soft, prickly/smooth, light/heavy), and children go in teams to hunt for items with those characteristics. Children should be encouraged to gather only items that have fallen to the ground, so that plants can continue to grow! Children demonstrate understanding of qualitative concepts as they get ready for the activity (e.g., "What's the weather like outside? Yes, it's cold, so we need to wear our coats"), follow directions (e.g., "Find something smooth"), and participate in the activity. The interventionist reinforces the concepts by labeling, commenting on, and describing objects, people, or events according to qualitative concepts. After finding several items, the children can glue items onto a heavy piece of cardboard.

Example   After Jose completes his project, his interventionist encourages him to talk about his collage, prompting him to use qualitative terms. "How does the moss feel? Is the pebble rough or smooth?" (*Cog B:4.0*)

Feely Bag

Children gather small objects from a nature walk (e.g., leaves, flowers, pebbles, pinecones, seeds) and put them in one bag. Each child puts a hand in the bag, feels one object, describes the object he or she is touching, and guesses what the object is without looking at it.

PRESCHOOL CURRICULA WITH SIMILAR GOALS

The following preschool curricula provide information on this goal or similar goals. Interventionists whose programs have access to one or more of these curricula may refer to the referenced sections for additional programming strategies.

The Carolina Curriculum for Preschoolers with Special Needs
Concepts
- Understands rough and smooth
- Understands heavy and light
- Understands fast and slow
- Understands soft and hard

The Creative Curriculum
Blocks
House Corner
Table Toys
Art
Sand and Water
Library

High Scope—Young Children in ACTION
Seriation
- Making comparisons

Classification
- Investigating and describing the attributes of things
- Noticing and describing how things are the same and how they are different; sorting and matching
- Talking about the characteristics something does not possess or the class it does not belong to

Portage Guide to Early Education Activity Cards
Cognitive
- Names objects as same or different
- Tells if object is heavy or light
- Matches textures

Cog B

> ## GOAL 5.0 Demonstrates understanding of eight different quantitative concepts

---

Objective 5.1 Demonstrates understanding of five different quantitative concepts

Objective 5.2 Demonstrates understanding of two different quantitative concepts

---

CONCURRENT GOALS

Adap A:2.0 Prepares and serves food
Adap A:3.0 Displays social dining skills
Adap C:2.0 Selects appropriate clothing and dresses self at designated times
Cog C   Categorizing (all goals)
Cog H   Premath (all goals)
SC A:1.0   Uses words, phrases, or sentences to inform, direct, ask questions, and express anticipation, imagination, affect, and emotions
SC B:5.0   Uses descriptive words

DAILY ROUTINES

Routine events that provide opportunities for children to demonstrate understanding of quantitative concepts include the following:

Dressing   Snack time
Mealtime   Unstructured play time
Travel time   Transition time
Arrival and departure   Bathtime
Circle time at school   Bedtime

Example Joey plays with plastic cups during bathtime. His father plays too, filling a cup and saying, "My cup is full" and emptying the cup with, "Oops, now it's empty." Joey says, "Mine full!" (*Cog B:5.0*)

Example During circle time, the interventionist asks, "Has anyone ever been to the zoo?" Maria responds, "I've been there three times!" (*Cog B:5.0*)

ENVIRONMENTAL ARRANGEMENTS

Provide materials during free play and routine events that have many parts to count, as well as materials that can be poured and measured according to volume:

– Art supplies with many pieces, such as collage materials (e.g., beans, buttons, scraps of paper, pieces of yarn), crayons, pencils, and markers

- Food and snack items in many pieces (e.g., mini crackers, raisins) as well as liquid or semiliquid items (e.g., juice, applesauce) that can be poured or scooped into cups or bowls
- Materials with many pieces, such as blocks, Tinkertoys, Lego toys, plastic animals and people, cars; sorting materials, such as counting bears, nuts and bolts
- Sand or water table filled with different materials, such as sand, cornmeal, birdseed, and water, as well as cups, pitchers, and funnels to explore the materials

These types of materials will provide opportunities for children to make comparisons according to number and volume, and demonstrate use of quantitative concepts.

■ Arrange the classroom into activity areas that include art, manipulative, and dramatic play areas.

    Example   Latifa and Manuel are pretending to have dinner in the play house. Manuel holds up a bowl of pretend food and asks Latifa, "You want some?" (*Cog B:5.0*)

■ Include pictures, books, and tapes that give children opportunities to learn about or demonstrate understanding of quantitative concepts. For example, a picture of a family eating dinner provides opportunities to compare food quantity using concepts such as more, empty, full, or lots.

PLANNED ACTIVITIES

Two examples of how to embed this goal and the associated objectives within activities are presented here. For a complete set of activities that address goals and objectives across domains, see Section V.

Bubbles

This activity is fun to do outside. The recipe for bubbles is ¼ cup glycerine (available in drug stores), ¾ cup dishwashing liquid (Dawn or Joy works best), and 8 cups water. Children pour about ¼ cup of this mixture into a cup and use straws to blow bubbles. Children should practice blowing through straws because some children suck through the straw by mistake. Children practice using quantitative concepts as they get ready for the activity (e.g., "Pour the soap in the big cup"), follow directions (e.g., "Let Joey have some"), and participate in the activity (e.g., "I have lots! I made more bubbles than you"). The interventionist reinforces the quantitative concepts by using such terms to describe objects, people, or events.

Wading Pool

This activity is fun to do outside when it is very hot. Children bring swimsuits and towels from home. Introduce the activity by asking if any of the children have a wading pool at home or if they go swimming in the summer. Provide buckets, cups, and pitchers of different sizes and let the children help fill up the wading pool with a hose or buckets of water.

    Example   Eric and a friend work together to fill a bucket of water and pour it into the pool. The interventionist describes their actions by saying, "Your bucket is *empty*. Better get some *more* water." The next time Eric empties his bucket, the interventionist says, "Uh oh, your bucket is ...," and pauses to give Eric an opportunity to say, "Empty." (*Cog B:5.0*)

Cog B

PRESCHOOL CURRICULA WITH SIMILAR GOALS

The following preschool curricula provide information on this goal or similar goals. Interventionists whose programs have access to one or more of these curricula may refer to the referenced sections for additional programming strategies.

The Carolina Curriculum for Preschoolers with Special Needs

Concepts
■ Size and number

The Creative Curriculum

Blocks
House Corner
Table Toys
Art
Sand and Water
Library

High Scope—Young Children in ACTION

Numbers
■ Comparing amounts

Classification
■ Distinguishing between "some" and "all"

Portage Guide to Early Education Activity Cards

Language
■ Can point to most, least, few
■ Can point to some, many, several

GOAL 6.0	**Demonstrates understanding of 12 different spatial relations concepts**

Objective 6.1	Demonstrates understanding of nine different spatial relations concepts
Objective 6.2	Demonstrates understanding of six different spatial relations concepts
Objective 6.3	Demonstrates understanding of three different spatial relations concepts

---

CONCURRENT GOALS

GM B   Play Skills (all goals)
Adap C   Dressing and Undressing (all goals)

Cog B

SC A:1.0   Uses words, phrases, or sentences to inform, direct, ask questions, and
              express anticipation, imagination, affect, and emotions
SC B:5.0   Uses descriptive words

DAILY ROUTINES

Routine events that provide opportunities for children to demonstrate understanding
of spatial relations concepts include the following:

Dressing	Snack time
Mealtime	Unstructured play time
Travel time	Transition time
Arrival and departure	Bathtime
Circle time at school	Bedtime

Example   Getting in the car, Manuel's father asks him, "Do you want to sit in front
or back?" Manuel replies, "Front" and goes to open the front door of the car. (*Cog B:6.0*)

ENVIRONMENTAL ARRANGEMENTS

■ Present materials during free play and routine events that provide opportunities for
the child to demonstrate an understanding of different spatial relations concepts:

  – Blocks, cars, and trucks with little people or animals to move in relation to each
    other
  – Sand/water table with cups, scoops, funnels, pitchers, and water wheels
  – Dolls, playhouse with people, barn with animals
  – Bikes, wagons, and other vehicles
  – Slides, tunnels, and climbing structures

    Example   While playing with the barn and animals, Alice puts all the cows in
    the barn. The interventionist says, "I wonder where the cows are?" and Alice points
    and says, "In barn." (*Cog B:6.0*)
■ Provide children with choices about where they want to sit or stand during activities
  such as circle time, snack time, and transition times. Comment on the relative position of the children (e.g., "Eric's sitting next to Maria").
■ Spatial concepts are particularly difficult for children with visual impairments and
  should be emphasized. When applicable, it is helpful to go from three-dimensional
  objects (e.g., a sphere) to two-dimensional objects (e.g., a picture with raised print).
■ Present pictures, posters, books, and magazines that give children opportunities to
  think about and demonstrate understanding of spatial relations.
    Example   Looking at a picture in a book, Latifa says, "She on horse!" (*Cog B:6.0*)

PLANNED ACTIVITIES

Two examples of how to embed this goal and the associated objectives within activities
are presented here. For a complete set of activities that address goals and objectives
across domains, see Section V.

Cog B

My Town

Children make a town on a tabletop by creating houses of milk cartons and boxes, tunnels of paper tubes or boxes with ends cut off, ponds or rivers with blue paper, and roads with masking tape. The children decorate their houses with markers, crayons, and construction paper and choose a spot on the table to tape their house. Children decide together where the roads, tunnels, and ponds should be located. After the "town" is created, small cars, animals, and people are added to the activity. Children demonstrate knowledge of spatial relations as they get ready for the activity (e.g., "I want to sit next to Eric"), follow directions (e.g., "Put the rest of the paper under the table"), and participate in the activity (e.g., "My dog's in the pond"). The interventionist reinforces spatial concepts by commenting about and describing objects, people, or events using spatial relations concepts.

Example   Alice's interventionist says, "Look Alice. The boy is standing in front of his house, but where is his dog?" Alice responds, "In back," while pointing to the back of the house. (*Cog B:6.0*)

My Home

Children draw pictures of their houses, including their family, pets, cars, and trees. Children should be as detailed as possible (some may want to paste precut shapes such as trees or people). As the children tell about their pictures, opportunities arise to use spatial relations.

Example   Latifa's interventionist says, "Tell me about your picture." Latifa responds, "Here is my house. This is my sister." "What's that on the bottom?" the interventionist asks (without pointing). Latifa responds, "My dog." (*Cog B:6.0*)

PRESCHOOL CURRICULA WITH SIMILAR GOALS

The following preschool curricula provide information on this goal or similar goals. Interventionists whose programs have access to one or more of these curricula may refer to the referenced sections for additional programming strategies.

The Carolina Curriculum for Preschoolers with Special Needs

Concepts
- Understands around, in front of, in back of, between, high, and low
- Understands under, over, next to, and beside
- Follows directions including in, out, and on

The Creative Curriculum

Blocks
House Corner
Table Toys
Art
Sand and Water
Library

High Scope—Young Children in ACTION

Spatial Relations
- Experiencing and describing the relative positions, directions, and distances of things
- Observing and describing things from different spatial viewpoints

- Interpreting representations of spatial relations in drawings, pictures, and photographs

Language

- Describing objects, events, and relations

Portage Guide to Early Education Activity Cards

Cognitive

- Names first, middle, and last position
- Places objects behind, beside, next to
- Places objects in, on, and under upon request

GOAL 7.0 Demonstrates understanding of seven different temporal relations concepts

---

Objective 7.1 Demonstrates understanding of five different temporal relations concepts

Objective 7.2 Demonstrates understanding of three different temporal relations concepts

---

CONCURRENT GOALS

Cog D:3.0	Retells event in sequence
Cog E	Recalling Events (all goals)
SC A:1.0	Uses words, phrases, or sentences to inform, direct, ask questions, and express anticipation, imagination, affect, and emotions
SC A:2.0	Uses conversational rules
SC B:5.0	Uses descriptive words
Soc A:2.0	Initiates cooperative activity

DAILY ROUTINES

Routine events that provide opportunities for children to demonstrate understanding of temporal relations concepts include the following:

Dressing	Snack time
Mealtime	Unstructured play time
Travel time	Transition time
Arrival and departure	Bathtime
Circle time at school	Bedtime

Example Maria's mother asks her, "What would you like to do after dinner?" and waits for Maria to respond with her communication board. Maria points to the picture of books. (*Cog B:7.0*)

Cog B

ENVIRONMENTAL ARRANGEMENTS

■ Present materials during free play and routine events that provide opportunities for the child to demonstrate an understanding of different temporal relations:

- Sequenced story cards
- Sand/water tables, block play, and other exploratory activities that provide opportunities for children to anticipate or recall events
- Art, construction, and cooking activities that require several steps to accomplish
- Pets and other animals, particularly interesting animals to observe such as those that metamorphose (e.g., polliwog into a frog, caterpillar into a butterfly)

■ Arrange the classroom into activity areas that include a science area with experiments (e.g., growing seeds) that allow children to track progress day to day.

■ Establish a predictable routine to the classroom day that includes an opening and closing circle time. During opening circle, the daily schedule and special events (e.g., birthdays, holidays, field trips, unusual activities) are discussed. A calender is a visual means to discuss events of yesterday, today, and tomorrow. Closing circle gives children an opportunity to discuss the day's events.

■ Include pictures, posters, books, and magazines in the library area that give children opportunities to recall events on the basis of temporal relations.

PLANNED ACTIVITIES

Two examples of how to embed this goal and the associated objectives within activities are presented here. For a complete set of activities that address goals and objectives across domains, see Section V.

Making Applesauce

The interventionist and children take a trip to a farm to pick or buy apples if possible. Peel, core, and slice four apples and place in a saucepan (children may cut apples with plastic knives). Add ½ cup water and simmer until the apples are soft. Stir in ¼ cup brown sugar or honey and a sprinkle of cinnamon. Children demonstrate understanding of temporal relations concepts as they get ready for the activity (e.g., "We're going to go to the farm today!"), follow directions (e.g., "First you need to wash your hands"), and participate in the activity ("Can I put in my apples after him?"). The interventionist reinforces the concepts by commenting and describing events using spatial relations concepts. Close supervision will ensure safety during cooking activities.

Example   While waiting for the apples to cook, Eric's interventionist asks him, "Tell me how we made this applesauce." Eric does not respond, and the interventionist prompts, "Yesterday we went to the farm and got the apples, then..." Eric says, "Today we cut them up and cooked them." (*Cog B:7.0*)

Leaf Rubbings

The children take a walk and gather leaves in small bags. They make rubbings by placing a leaf under a piece of lightweight paper and rubbing with the side of a crayon or pencil over the paper. The imprint of the leaf will appear. Children describe how and when they made their leaf rubbings during closing circle or to a parent.

PRESCHOOL CURRICULA WITH SIMILAR GOALS

The following preschool curricula provide information on this goal or similar goals. Interventionists whose programs have access to one or more of these curricula may refer to the referenced sections for additional programming strategies.

The Creative Curriculum

Blocks
House Corner
Table Toys
Art
Sand and Water
Library

High Scope—Young Children in ACTION

Time
- Anticipating future events
- Describing and representing past events
- Using conventional time units when talking about past and future events
- Noticing, describing, and representing the order of events

Portage Guide to Early Education Activity Cards

Language
- Uses yesterday and tomorrow meaningfully

Strand C   Categorizing

GOAL 1.0   Groups objects, people, or events on the basis of specified criteria

Objective 1.1   Groups objects, people, or events on the basis of category

Objective 1.2   Groups objects on the basis of function

Objective 1.3   Groups objects on the basis of physical attribute

CONCURRENT GOALS

Adap A:1.0   Eats and drinks a variety of foods using appropriate utensils with little or no spilling

Cog B   Demonstrates Understanding of Concepts (all goals)

SC A:1.0   Uses words, phrases, or sentences to inform, direct, ask questions, and express anticipation, imagination, affect, and emotions

SC B:5.0   Uses descriptive words

Soc C:1.0   Communicates personal likes and dislikes

DAILY ROUTINES

Routine events that provide opportunities for children to group objects, people, or events on the basis of devised criteria include the following:

Mealtime
Snack time
Unstructured play time
Transition time
Cleanup time (e.g., sorting laundry, dishes, toys)

Example   During cleanup time, the interventionist asks Joey to put all the toy animals in one basket and Latifa to put all the toy people in another. (*Cog C:1.1*)

ENVIRONMENTAL ARRANGEMENTS

■ Present materials during free play and routine events that are interesting and appealing to the children and provide opportunities to group objects, people, or events on the basis of devised criteria. For example, present toys and materials that can be sorted according to the following:

- Different functions (e.g., art materials, tools, toys that go in the water, things to eat, things to wear)
- Different categories (e.g., food from different food groups)
- Physical attributes (e.g., blocks of different sizes, foods with different textures such as crunchy or chewy, crayons of different colors, puzzle pieces of different shapes)

Example While playing in the house play area, Manuel cleans house, putting away the food in the refrigerator and clothing in the dresser. (*Cog C:1.2*)

■ Include pictures, posters, books, and magazines in the environment that give children opportunities to group objects, people, or events on the basis of certain criteria. For example, a poster of children playing could be categorized on the basis of sex, age, hair color, eye color, or any other criterion selected by the children or interventionist.

PLANNED ACTIVITIES

Two examples of how to embed this goal and the associated objectives within activities are presented here. For a complete set of activities that address goals and objectives across domains, see Section V.

What Am I Thinking Of?

One child thinks of an object, and other children try to guess what it is. The interventionist provides miniature objects that represent different categories (e.g., animals that fly, animals that live in water, animals of different colors, farm or zoo animals). Other children each ask a question to narrow down the possibilities. A child might ask, "Does it live in the water?" and, if the answer is yes, all animals that do not live in water are removed. If each child has made a guess about the animal and no one has guessed correctly, the first child gives another clue. The interventionist should provide the least level of assistance necessary for children to think up questions and subsequently categorize the objects.

Animal Books *(see Books/Book Making in Section V)*

Children cut pictures of animals from magazines and paste them in their books (use big paper for the books). Encourage children to glue on the same page animals that can be categorized together. Some children may come up with their own categories, whereas others need more assistance (e.g., "See if you can find pictures of animals with feathers for this page").

Example Eric's interventionist provides him with pictures of animals with tactile surfaces glued on (e.g., birds with feathers, mammals with furry material, fish with smooth surfaces). Eric glues animals that go together on different pieces of paper in his book. (*Cog C:1.3*)

PRESCHOOL CURRICULA WITH SIMILAR GOALS

The following preschool curricula provide information on this goal or similar goals. Interventionists whose programs have access to one or more of these curricula may refer to the referenced sections for additional programming strategies

Cog C

The Carolina Curriculum for Preschoolers with Special Needs

Concepts
- Sorts by categories
- Sorts objects by color, form, or name

The Creative Curriculum

Blocks
House Corner
Table Toys
Art

High Scope—Young Children in ACTION

Classification
- Investigating and describing the attributes of things
- Noticing and describing how things are the same and how they are different; sorting and matching
- Using and describing objects in different ways
- Talking about the characteristics something does not possess or the class it does not belong to
- Holding more than one attribute in mind at a time

Portage Guide to Early Education Activity Cards

Cognitive
- Arranges objects into categories

Strand D   Sequencing

GOAL 1.0   Follows directions of three or more related steps that are not routinely given

Objective 1.1   Follows directions of three or more related steps that are routinely given

CONCURRENT GOALS

GM B   Play Skills (all goals)
Cog A   Participation (all goals)
Soc B:2.0   Follows context-specific rules outside home and classroom

DAILY ROUTINES

Routine events that provide opportunities for children to follow directions include the following:

Dressing	Unstructured play time
Mealtime	Transition time
Travel time	Cleanup time
Arrival and departure	Bathtime
Circle time at school	Bedtime
Snack time	

Example   Latifa's mother tells her, "It's time for bed, Latifa. Turn off the television, brush your teeth, and get in bed. Then I'll come read you a story." (*Cog D:1.1*)

ENVIRONMENTAL ARRANGEMENTS

■ Provide children with independent access to materials they used during free play and routine activities. Place coat hooks at the child's height, a child-size sink (or step stool) and soap and towels within reach, and free choice materials at the child's level. The caregiver or interventionist also provides opportunities for children to follow directions.

Example   During free play, Joey asks the interventionist if he can paint. The interventionist says, "Sure you can. First get a smock. Then get a piece of paper and bring it to the easel." (*Cog D:1.0*)

PLANNED ACTIVITIES

Two examples of how to embed this goal and the associated objective within activities are presented here. For a complete set of activities that address goals and objectives across domains, see Section V.

Simon Says

The interventionist is "Simon" and gives three-step directions to the children. Children enjoy doing silly things, so be creative!

Example   Simon says, "Put your hands on your head, make a funny face, and say 'hamburger.'" (*Cog D:1.0*)

My Body

Children lie down on large pieces of paper, and another person traces their bodies. Children color in their skin color, features, and clothing with markers, crayons, or paint. Children follow directions getting ready for the activity, participating in the activity, and cleaning up.

Example   Timmy's interventionist signs him a three-step direction, "Get a piece of paper, get a crayon, and put them on the floor." (*Cog D:1.0, with adaptation*)

PRESCHOOL CURRICULA WITH SIMILAR GOALS

The following preschool curricula provide information on this goal or similar goals. Interventionists whose programs have access to one or more of these curricula may refer to the referenced sections for additional programming strategies.

The Carolina Curriculum for Preschoolers with Special Needs

Receptive Skills
- Follows one-step commands related to two objects or an object and a place
- Follows two-step commands involving sequence

The Creative Curriculum

Blocks
House Corner
Table Toys
Art
Library
Outdoors

Portage Guide to Early Education Activity Cards

Language
- Carries out a series of three directions

GOAL 2.0 Places objects in series according to length or size

Objective 2.1 Fits one ordered set of objects to another

CONCURRENT GOALS

Adap A:2.0   Prepares and serves food
Cog B:3.0   Demonstrates understanding of six different size concepts
Cog C:1.0   Groups objects, people, or events on the basis of specified criteria
SC A   Social-Communicative Interactions (all goals)
SC B:5.0   Uses descriptive words

DAILY ROUTINES

Routine events that provide opportunities for children to place objects in series according to length or size include the following:

Mealtime
Snack time
Cleanup time
Unstructured play time
Transition time

    Example   While getting ready to go outside, children line up from shortest to tallest (and from tallest to shortest to come inside) (*Cog D:2.0*)

ENVIRONMENTAL ARRANGEMENTS

- Present materials in the environment of varying length and sizes that provide opportunities for children to make comparisons (e.g., blocks, Lego toys, cups, pitchers, paint brushes, crayons, books, balls). In addition, provide objects of different sizes that have two or more parts children can fit together (e.g., bowls with lids, nuts and bolts, dolls with doll clothes, cars and "garages").
- Arrange the classroom into activity areas and encourage children to return materials in an orderly way to designed locations. Children place objects in a series according to length or size while cleaning up.

PLANNED ACTIVITIES

Two examples of how to embed this goal and the associated objective within activities are presented here. For a complete set of activities that address goals and objectives across domains, see Section V.

Cog D

Goldilocks and the Three Bears

Children work together to make a flannel board set of Goldilocks and the Three Bears. The interventionist provides stencils or outlines for three bowls, chairs, beds, and bears (small, medium, and large) and, of course, Goldilocks. Children help cut out the figures, decorate them, or make a stage for the play. The "stage" can be a flannel board made of sturdy cardboard covered with flannel. The interventionist models the story of Goldilocks and the Three Bears and provides opportunities for children to sequence the props while they retell the story.

Driving Cars

Have available a set of cars of varying sizes (i.e., small, medium, and large). Also have a set of garages (cardboard boxes of varying sizes). Children work together to drive their cars into the "right" garage.

PRESCHOOL CURRICULA WITH SIMILAR GOALS

The following preschool curricula provide information on this goal or similar goals. Interventionists whose programs have access to one or more of these curricula may refer to the referenced sections for additional programming strategies.

The Creative Curriculum
Blocks
House Corner
Table Toys
Art

High Scope—Young Children in ACTION
Seriation
■ Arranging things in order
■ Fitting one ordered set of objects to another through trial and error

Portage Guide to Early Education Activity Cards
Cognitive
■ Arranges objects in sequence of width and length
■ Matches one to one (three or more objects)
■ Puts together four-part nesting toy

GOAL 3.0   Retells event in sequence

Objective 3.1   Completes sequence of familiar story or event

CONCURRENT GOALS

Cog B:7.0	Demonstrates understanding of seven different temporal relations concepts
Cog D:1.0	Follows directions of three or more related steps that are not routinely given
Cog E	Recalling Events (all goals)
SC A	Social-Communicative Interactions (all goals)
SC B	Production of Words, Phrases, and Sentences (all goals)

DAILY ROUTINES

Routine events that provide opportunities for children to retell events in sequence include the following:

Dressing	Snack time
Mealtime	Unstructured play time
Travel time	Transition time
Arrival and Departure	Bathtime
Circle time at school	Bedtime

Example   Manuel helps his mother make cookies. During dinner she asks him, "Manuel, can you tell your father how you made cookies?" and Manuel responds, "I put flour and eggs in a bowl, stirred it up, put it on the tray, and set it in the oven to bake." (*Cog D:3.0*)

ENVIRONMENTAL ARRANGEMENTS

■ Provide opportunities to retell events or complete a familiar story in sequence, and present activities and materials in the environment that are interesting and appealing to children:

- Sequenced story cards
- Books, flannel board materials, and story audiotapes
- Pictorial descriptions of activities (e.g., a painting activity uses pictures of a child putting on a smock, getting a piece of paper, painting a picture on the easel, and hanging the picture up on the wall)
- Art, construction, or cooking activities that require several steps to accomplish

■ Arrange the classroom into activity areas that include a science center and dramatic play center. Experiments such as growing seeds can be ongoing in the science area, allowing children to track progress from day to day and retell events in sequence.

Cog D

Dramatic play centers provide opportunities for children to role play familiar situations or stories.

■ Establish a predictable routine to the classroom day, including an opening and closing circle time. During opening circle, the daily schedule and special events (e.g., birthdays, holidays, field trips, unusual activities) are discussed. Establishing a predictable daily routine will help the children respond appropriately to questions about the sequence of events in the classroom (e.g., "What do we do next?"). Closing circle provides opportunities for children to discuss the day's events in the sequence in which they occurred.

PLANNED ACTIVITIES

Two examples of how to embed this goal and the associated objective within activities are presented here. For a complete set of activities that address goals and objectives across domains, see Section V.

Planting a Garden

Planting a garden is an exciting and rewarding project for children. This activity involves several steps (e.g., hoeing the ground, planting the seeds, watering the ground, weeding) and provides opportunities for the child to retell events in sequence. Reading a story about growing things (e.g., *The Carrot Seed*), discussing the sequence of steps ahead of time, or making sequenced cards of the event may help children answer questions about the sequence of the event or retell the event in correct sequence.

Making Popcorn

The interventionist makes popcorn using a heavy pan with a lid or an electric popper, ⅓ cup popcorn, 2 tablespoons oil, salt, and a large bowl. The children can examine the corn kernels before popping them. Oil and popcorn are added to the saucepan or electric popper (if a pan is used, the lid is closed and the pan shaken over medium heat). The popcorn can be served once it cools, and children can retell the event.

Note   Popcorn must be chewed thoroughly while the children are sitting down. This activity is not recommended for children who have difficulties chewing or swallowing or for very young children.

PRESCHOOL CURRICULA WITH SIMILAR GOALS

The following preschool curricula provide information on this goal or similar goals. Interventionists whose programs have access to one or more of these curricula may refer to the referenced sections for additional programming strategies.

The Carolina Curriculum for Preschoolers with Special Needs
Attention and Memory
■ Recalls most essential elements in a story
■ Recalls three to four elements from a story without prompts

The Creative Curriculum
Blocks
House Corner

Table Toys
Art
Sand and Water
Library Corner
Outdoors

High Scope—Young Children in ACTION

Time
- Noticing, describing, and representing the order of events
- Using conventional time units when talking about past and future events

Portage Guide to Early Education Activity Cards

Cognitive
- Retells five main facts from story heard three times
- Repeats familiar rhymes
- Repeats finger plays with words and actions
- Describe two events or characters from familiar story or television program

Language
- Puts together and tells 3- to 5-part sequence story
- Tells two events in order of occurrence

Strand E   Recalling Events

GOAL 1.0   Recalls events that occurred on same day, without contextual cues

Objective 1.1   Recalls events that occurred on same day, with contextual cues
Objective 1.2   Recalls events immediately after they occur

CONCURRENT GOALS

Cog B:7.0	Demonstrates understanding of seven different temporal relations concepts
Cog D	Sequencing (all goals)
SC A	Social-Communicative Interactions (all goals)
SC B	Production of Words, Phrases, and Sentences (all goals)

DAILY ROUTINES

Routine events that provide opportunities for children to recall events include the following:

Dressing	Snack time
Mealtime	Unstructured play time
Travel time	Bathtime
Arrival and departure	Bedtime
Circle time at school	

Example   On the drive home from school, Timmy's mother asks, "What did you do at school today?" Timmy takes a picture from his bag and signs, PAINT. (*Cog E.1.0*)

ENVIRONMENTAL ARRANGEMENTS

■ Provide materials and activities in the environment that are age appropriate and appealing to children (see Section V). Field trips to community sites such as the post office, fire station, zoo, or museum provide exciting topics for later discussions.
■ Include in the daily routine group times when children come together to share special events in their home lives and discuss classroom events.
  Example   Eric arrives at group time after the other children. They say, "We missed you, Eric. Where have you been?" Eric replies, "In the bathroom." (*Cog E:1.2*)
■ Keep a notebook for each child and send it from school to home with the child. The child's caregivers describe special events that occurred at home, and the school staff

describe the activities at school. This information is then used to prompt the child to recall events.

PLANNED ACTIVITIES

Two examples of how to embed this goal and the associated objectives within activities are presented here. For a complete set of activities that address goals and objectives across domains, see Section V.

Sharing Time

Children take turns telling about something they did or something special that occurred during the day at school. Whereas some children will be able to recall events without contextual cues, the interventionist may need to provide cues (e.g., examples of artwork, materials that the child played with) to prompt others. Limiting the number of children who share each day to two or three keeps the other children from becoming restless.

Hand Prints

Children make "hand prints" by pressing a hand in a tray with paint (Styrofoam trays work well) or by having a friend paint the palm of one hand; then they press the painted hand on paper. Some children will enjoy making careful prints, whereas others enjoy smearing the paint. The interventionist provides opportunities to recall events by asking the children what activity they just came from (e.g., "Hi Joey. What were you just doing?") or by asking questions during the activity about events that occurred earlier in the day (e.g., "What did you have for snack?"). At the end of the day, during group time, the interventionist asks children what they did in art and provides pictures of the painting for a contextual cue if necessary.

PRESCHOOL CURRICULA WITH SIMILAR GOALS

The following preschool curricula provide information on this goal or similar goals. Interventionists whose programs have access to one or more of these curricula may refer to the referenced sections for additional programming strategies.

The Carolina Curriculum for Preschoolers with Special Needs

Attention and Memory
- Describes events that happened in the past
- Recalls one or two elements from a story just read
- Remembers incidental information

The Creative Curriculum

Blocks
House Corner
Table Toys
Art
Sand and Water
Library Corner
Outdoors

High Scope—Young Children in ACTION

Time

■ Using conventional time units when talking about past and future events
■ Describing and representing past events
■ Noticing, describing, and representing the order of events

Portage Guide to Early Education Activity Cards

Language

■ Tells daily experiences
■ Tells about immediate experiences

GOAL 2.0   Recalls verbal sequences

Objective 2.1   Recalls verbal information about self

CONCURRENT GOALS

Cog D	Sequencing (all goals)
Cog H	Premath (all goals)
Cog I	Prereading (all goals)
SC A	Social-Communicative Interactions (all goals)
SC B	Production of Words, Phrases, and Sentences (all goals)
Soc C:2.0	Relates identifying information about self and others

DAILY ROUTINES

Routine events that provide opportunities for children to recall verbal sequences include the following:

Dressing	Snack time
Mealtime	Unstructured play time
Travel time	Bathtime
Circle time at school	Bedtime

Example   During dinner, Latifa says, "I'm going to be four!" Her uncle asks her, "When is your birthday?" Latifa replies, "April 24th." (*Cog E:2.1*)

Example   While playing Hide-and-Seek, Manuel counts to 20 and yells, "Ready or not, here I come!" (*Cog E:2.0*)

ENVIRONMENTAL ARRANGEMENTS

■ During opening circle, use a calendar with removable numbers and symbols to denote special days (e.g., a heart for Valentine's Day, cake for a child's birthday). The class recites the days of the week, counts the days of the month on the calendar to the present date, and highlights birthdays and special events in the month.

■ Place examples of children's names around the classroom. Label the children's cubbies, personal belongings, and artwork. Display "birthday balloons" that label children's names and birthdates. Provide posters or examples of the alphabet and numbers on the walls. As the interventionist or caregiver comments on these decorations, children hear appropriate models of the different verbal sequences (e.g., "Here's your cubby, Joey. It says J-o-e-y. Joey.")

■ Arrange the classroom into activity centers that include a listening center and a dramatic play center. In the listening center, provide music tapes about the alphabet, numbers, and days of the week. Using props such as telephones, calendars, and clocks in the dramatic play center and themes such as post office or police station provides children with opportunities to recall verbal sequences.

   Example   After a discussion facilitated by the interventionist on what to do if you are lost, the class sets up a police station in the dramatic play center. Manuel goes up to a "police officer" and says, "I'm lost." The "officer" asks, "What's your name? How do you spell it?" (*Cog E:2.1*)

PLANNED ACTIVITIES

Two examples of how to embed this goal and the associated objective within activities are presented here. For a complete set of activities that address goals and objectives across domains, see Section V.

Let's Write a Letter

Children write letters (or draw pictures) to a family member or a friend. The interventionist provides pens, pencils, crayons, markers, stamps, paper, and envelopes for children to use. The interventionist prompts children to talk about their families and name their siblings and parents. Children are encouraged to "write" about themselves, telling their birthdays and how old they are. When finished with their letters, children can write their names, spell their names for the interventionist to write, or recite their names.

Pretend Birthday

Children have a pretend birthday party at school. They decorate a "cake" (shaving cream and whipped cream are fun), make birthday cards or gifts, sing happy birthday, and wear party hats. When children finish writing their cards, the interventionist reminds them to write their names or spell their names aloud, and encourages them to include their telephone numbers so their friends can call. The interventionist provides opportunities to recall verbal information by asking children who they would like to invite to their birthday party and by encouraging them to tell their full names, birthdays, and ages when it is their turn to be the "birthday child." Children count to 20 while waiting for the cake to be brought out.

PRESCHOOL CURRICULA WITH SIMILAR GOALS

The following preschool curricula provide information on this goal or similar goals. Interventionists whose programs have access to one or more of these curricula may refer to the referenced sections for additional programming strategies.

Cog E

The Carolina Curriculum for Preschoolers with Special Needs

Concepts
- Counts correctly to 20
- Tells current age

High Scope—Young Children in ACTION

Time
- Noticing, describing, and representing the order of events

Portage Guide to Early Education Activity Cards

Cognitive
- Counts by rote 1 to 100
- Names days of week in order
- Prints own first name
- Says letters of alphabet in order
- Counts up to 20 items and tells how many
- Tells month and day of birthday

Language
- Tells telephone number
- Tells address
- Tells full name when requested

Strand F   Problem Solving

GOAL 1.0   Evaluates solutions to problems

Objective 1.1   Suggests acceptable solutions to problems

Objective 1.2   Identifies means to goal

CONCURRENT GOALS

Cog F:2.0   Makes statements and appropriately answers questions that require reasoning about objects, situations, or people

SC A   Social-Communicative Interactions (all goals)

SC B   Production of Words, Phrases, and Sentences (all goals)

Soc A:3.0   Resolves conflicts by selecting effective strategy

DAILY ROUTINES

Routine events that provide opportunities for children to evaluate solutions to problems include the following:

Dressing	Snack time
Mealtime	Unstructured play time
Travel time	Transition time
Arrival and departure	Bathtime
Circle time at school	Bedtime

As children follow directions and get ready for and participate in activities, caregivers or
interventionists reinforce the ability to solve problems by discussing reasons why and
how routine activities are conducted, answering why or how questions children ask
about routine events, and providing reasons for requests made of children. Eventually
caregivers begin to question children, providing opportunities for children to evaluate
their own solutions to problems.

Example   When Latifa's mother helps her get dressed in the morning, she talks
about the weather. If Latifa complains about wearing her sweater, her mother reminds
her that when it is cold, a sweater keeps her warm. The next day Latifa runs to her
mother at the playground and says, "I'm cold—I need a sweater." (*Cog F:1.1*)

ENVIRONMENTAL ARRANGEMENTS

■ Provide materials and activities during routine and planned activities that are interesting and appealing to children (see Section V). Activities should be child directed

and open ended whenever possible, providing opportunities for the child to explore materials and evaluate solutions to problems as they arise during play.

- Arrange the classroom into activity centers and keep materials in predictable locations accessible to children, unless the materials are potentially dangerous.

    Example   Timmy and Joey are going shopping at the "grocery store" in the dramatic play center. The interventionist asks, "What will you carry your groceries in?" Joey runs to get a paper bag from the art center. (*Cog F:1.2*)

- Do something deliberate to interfere with the conduct of an activity (e.g., unplug the record player prior to a group music activity). This strategy should be used sparingly and with caution; however, when employed selectively, it provides opportunities for children to solve problems.

- "Forget" to provide necessary equipment or overlook an important component of a routine or familiar activity. For example, do not have food immediately available for snack time or books for story time.

- Place objects that are desirable or necessary to complete an activity within sight but out of reach of the child.

- Omit or change a familiar step or element in a well-practiced or routine activity. For example, provide children with Popsicle sticks to draw with instead of crayons.

- Provide the least level of assistance necessary when helping a child solve a problem. Encourage children to provide an acceptable solution to the problem (e.g., "What can you try?"). If necessary, go to the next level of assistance. For example, set a cup of water near a child who "can't make the paint work."

PLANNED ACTIVITIES

Two examples of how to embed this goal and the associated objectives within activities are presented here. For a complete set of activities that address goals and objectives across domains, see Section V.

Pinecone Birdfeeders

Children spread peanut butter on large pinecones and then roll the pinecones in birdseed to make birdfeeders. The interventionists can have children direct the activity and use problem-solving skills by asking them questions like, "I wonder what we can use to spread the peanut butter on the pine cones?", "How can we keep the table clean?", "How can we cover the pinecones in birdseed?", and "Where should we put the feeders so the birds can get to them?" When the class goes outside to hang the birdfeeders, have children suggest solutions about how to hang them on high branches (you might have a ladder nearby). Often children will suggest solutions to problems that do not work very well. If possible, their solutions should be tried even if they will not work. This provides children with the necessary information to reevaluate their suggestions and come up with new ideas that do work.

Bug Search

Children look for insects on the playground and collect them to observe briefly. Before searching, children can suggest possible containers to hold the insects and evaluate whether the containers will work. Children look around the classroom for containers, or the interventionist provides containers to choose from (clear plastic containers with lids with holes poked in them make good bug viewers). Once the class is outside, the interventionist can ask children where they can find bugs and how they will collect them. Throughout the activity, opportunities can be provided for children to solve problems (e.g., the problem of how to overturn a heavy rock). After observing collected bugs for a few minutes, children return the bugs to their homes.

Note This activity may not be safe in certain areas of the country where bugs are found that bite or are poisonous. Have children show insects to an adult before touching. Young children should be supervised closely and often need to be reminded to treat living things carefully.

PRESCHOOL CURRICULA WITH SIMILAR GOALS

The following preschool curricula provide information on this goal or similar goals. Interventionists whose programs have access to one or more of these curricula may refer to the referenced sections for additional programming strategies.

The Carolina Curriculum for Preschoolers with Special Needs
Reasoning
- Reasons about future events
- Reasons about experiences and asks and answers questions
- Describes what "will happen next"
- Responds appropriately to "tell me how" or "how do you" questions
- Answers two or more "what do you do when" questions
- Answers at least one "why do" question correctly
- Experiments with cause and effect in play

The Creative Curriculum
Blocks
House Corner
Table Toys
Art
Sand and Water
Library Corner
Outdoors

High Scope—Young Children in ACTION
Active Learning
- Exploring actively with all the senses
Time
- Anticipating future events

Portage Guide to Early Education Activity Cards
Cognitive
- Predicts what happens next
Language
- Answers question "what happens if…?"
- Answers why question with an explanation
- Expresses future occurrences with "going to," "have to," "want to"
- Answers simple "how" questions

GOAL 2.0   Makes statements and appropriately answers questions that require reasoning about objects, situations, or people

---

Objective 2.1   Gives reason for inference

Objective 2.2   Makes prediction about future or hypothetical events

Objective 2.3   Gives possible cause for some event

CONCURRENT GOALS

Adap C:2.0	Selects appropriate clothing and dresses self at designated times
Cog F:1.0	Evaluates solutions to problems
SC A	Social-Communicative Interactions (all goals)
SC B	Production of Words, Phrases, and Sentences (all goals)
Soc A:3.0	Resolves conflicts by selecting effective strategy
Soc B:1.0	Meets physical needs in socially appropriate ways
Soc C:3.0	Accurately identifies affect/emotions in others and self consistent with demonstrated behaviors

DAILY ROUTINES

Routine events that provide opportunities for children to use reasoning skills include the following:

Dressing	Snack time
Mealtime	Unstructured play time
Travel time	Transition time
Arrival and departure	Bathtime
Circle time at school	Bedtime
Story time	

The caregiver or interventionist reinforces this skill by modeling 1) making inferences (e.g., "That must have hurt, you fell down hard"); 2) making predictions (e.g., "If you walk in that puddle, your shoes will get wet"); and 3) giving possible causes for events (e.g., "You hurt your knee. Did you fall off your bike?").

    Example   While giving Manuel a bath, his father asks him, "What do you think would happen if you never took a bath?" Manuel answers, "I'd get real dirty." (*Cog F:2.2*)

Cog F

ENVIRONMENTAL ARRANGEMENTS

■ Provide materials and activities during routine and planned activities that are interesting and appealing to children (see Section V). The activities should be open ended,
allowing children opportunities to experiment and problem-solve to carry them out.
Provide opportunities for children to brainstorm solutions to problems as they arise
(e.g., "What will happen if you let go of the block?"). Take time with children after
activities to evaluate solutions that were chosen, how they worked, and how other
solutions might have worked.

■ Arrange the classroom into activity centers that include a science and nature area
where children can observe plants, animals, objects, or events and use reasoning
skills to explain what they see. Interesting events to observe include watching ice
cubes melt, insects eat a leaf, fish swim in a tank, or seeds grow day by day.

    Example   While watching the school bunny eat a carrot, Timmy signs, HUNGRY.
The interventionist asks, "How do you know the rabbit is hungry?" Timmy signs,
EAT. (*Cog F:2.1*)

■ Have a plentiful selection of new books in the library. While reading books to children, stop during an exciting moment and ask what they think will happen next.
Provide magazines, posters, and pictures of objects (e.g., spaceships), situations (e.g.,
thunderstorm), or people (e.g., smiling child) that are interesting and provide opportunities for children to make statements or answer questions that require reasoning.

■ Deliberately "sabotage" or interfere with the conduct of an activity. For example,
remove a piece of track from a train set or unplug the record player prior to a group
music activity.

■ "Forget" to provide necessary equipment or overlook an important component of a
routine or familiar activity. For example, do not have food immediately available for
snack time, or books for story time, and allow children to solve the problem.

PLANNED ACTIVITIES

Two examples of how to embed this goal and the associated objectives within activities
are presented here. For a complete set of activities that address goals and objectives
across domains, see Section V.

The Fire Truck

Large boxes such as refrigerator boxes can be transformed into wonderful make-
believe structures, in this case a fire truck. Opportunities can be provided for children
to solve problems by asking questions such as, "Can anybody think of how we can
make a fire truck out of this box? What do we need?" To make the truck, an adult cuts
the long side of a box, and the children paint it red. Throughout the activity, opportunities can be provided for children to use reasoning skills by asking questions like,
"What might happen if we don't put smocks on while we paint?" or "How do you
think the fire started?"

Doctor's Office

A doctor's office is set up in the dramatic play center of the classroom. The interventionist reads a story about doctors to provide information to get the children actively
involved. Children direct the activity by providing suggestions for what props are needed (e.g., bandages, a cot, white shirts), how the office should be arranged, and what

roles they can play. Opportunities can be provided for children to use their reasoning skills in different roles (e.g., "Why is she crying, Doctor?", What happened to your leg?", "What can you do to make it better?").

PRESCHOOL CURRICULA WITH SIMILAR GOALS

The following preschool curricula provide information on this goal or similar goals. Interventionists whose programs have access to one or more of these curricula may refer to the referenced sections for additional programming strategies.

The Carolina Curriculum for Preschoolers with Special Needs
Reasoning
- Reasons about future events
- Reasons about experiences and asks and answers questions
- Describes what "will happen next"
- Responds appropriately to "tell me how" or "how do you" questions
- Answers two or more "what do you do when" questions
- Answers at least one "why do" question correctly
- Experiments with cause and effect in play

The Creative Curriculum
Blocks
House Corner
Table Toys
Art
Sand and Water
Library Corner
Outdoors

High Scope—Young Children in ACTION
Active Learning
- Exploring actively with all the senses

Time
- Anticipating future events

Portage Guide to Early Education Activity Cards
Cognitive
- Predicts what happens next

Language
- Answers question "what happens if…?"
- Answers why question with an explanation
- Expresses future occurrences with "going to," "have to," "want to"
- Answers simple "how" questions

Cog F

Strand G   Play

GOAL 1.0   Engages in imaginary play

Objective 1.1	Enacts roles or identities
Objective 1.2	Plans and acts out recognizable event, theme, or story line
Objective 1.3	Uses imaginary props

CONCURRENT GOALS

Adap A:3.0	Displays social dining skills
Cog A	Participation (all goals)
SC A	Social-Communicative Interactions (all goals)
SC B	Production of Words, Phrases, and Sentences (all goals)
Soc A	Interaction with Others (all goals)

DAILY ROUTINES

Routine events that provide opportunities for children to engage in imaginary play include the following:

Mealtime
Bathtime
Bedtime
Unstructured play time

Example   At bedtime, Eric's mother brings his favorite stuffed animal to him and says, "Should we read Mickey a story before bed?" (*Cog G:1.3*)

ENVIRONMENTAL ARRANGEMENTS

■ Arrange the classroom into activity areas that include a dramatic play center (see Environmental Arrangements in Section III and Dramatic Play Activities in Section V). Provide materials during free play and routine events that facilitate the child's engagement in imaginary play:

– Dramatic play props
– Puppets
– Dolls of all shapes, sizes, and ethnic origins; doll clothing, diapers, bottles, cribs, blankets
– Dollhouses with little people and furniture

- Blocks and Lego toys with little people, animals, cars
- Stuffed animals
- Outdoor equipment such as climbing structures, wagons, bikes, tricycles, and big boxes for houses or trains

    Example   In the "post office," Latifa scribbles a note on some paper, stuffs it in an envelope, puts a "stamp" on the envelope, and mails it in the mailbox. (*Cog G:1.2*)

■ Include books, pictures, and posters in the home or classroom environment that depict children engaging in imaginary play.

PLANNED ACTIVITIES

Two examples of how to embed this goal and the associated objectives within activities are presented here. For a complete set of activities that address goals and objectives across domains, see Section V.

All Up, All Down

Children pretend to be different animals. They first lie down quietly on the floor, and the interventionist calls, "All up...ducks." Children get up and pretend to be ducks, quacking and waddling around the room until the interventionist calls, "All down." Children lie down quickly on the floor and then take turns choosing the animal they will be next.

Paper Bag Animals

Children make animal puppets out of small lunch sacks and materials such as colored construction paper, fabric, buttons, and yarn. Children make their puppets "talk" by putting a hand in the sack and moving the "mouth" (the bottom flap) up and down. The interventionist should encourage the children to suggest animals on their own and, if necessary, provide models of different animals. When children are finished making their puppets, the interventionist can encourage them to make their animals talk to each other or have a puppet show.

    Example   Joey makes a puppet with feathers, a big trunk, and big teeth, and he names him Max. When he finishes, the interventionist asks him, "Does Max want a cookie?" and hands a pretend cookie to Max. Joey says, "Yes," and pretends to have Max eat the cookie. (*Cog G:1.3*)

PRESCHOOL CURRICULA WITH SIMILAR GOALS

The following preschool curricula provide information on this goal or similar goals. Interventionists whose programs have access to one or more of these curricula may refer to the referenced sections for additional programming strategies.

The Carolina Curriculum for Preschoolers with Special Needs
Symbolic Play

The Creative Curriculum
Blocks
House Corner
Table Toys

Art
Sand and Water
Library Corner
Outdoors

High Scope—Young Children in ACTION

Active Learning

■ Manipulating, transforming, and combining materials

Experiencing and Representing

Role Playing

Portage Guide to Early Education Activity Cards

Social

■ Acts out parts of story, playing part or using puppets
■ Imitates adult roles
■ Plays dress-up in adult clothes

GOAL 2.0   Engages in games with rules

Objective 2.1   Maintains participation
Objective 2.2   Conforms to game rules

CONCURRENT GOALS

GM B:2.0	Runs avoiding obstacles
GM B:3.0	Bounces, catches, kicks, and throws ball
Cog A:2.0	Watches, listens, and participates during small group activities
Cog A:3.0	Watches, listens, and participates during large group activities
SC A	Social-Communicative Interactions (all goals)
SC B	Production of Words, Phrases, and Sentences (all goals)
Soc A:2.0	Initiates cooperative activity
Soc B:2.0	Follows context-specific rules outside home and classroom

DAILY ROUTINES

Routine events that provide opportunities for children to participate in games with rules include unstructured play time.

   Example   Maria's parents play cards together, and sometimes Maria wants to join them. If Maria asks to play a game of cards, her mother says, "Okay, let's play Go Fish, but you need to stay and play the whole game—okay?" If Maria forgets a part of the game, a parent reminds her of the rules. (*Cog G:2.1*)

Cog G

ENVIRONMENTAL ARRANGEMENTS

- Arrange the classroom into activity centers that include one for children to play games. Have materials available during unstructured play times that provide opportunities for children to participate in games with rules:

  - Board games such as Candyland and Color Bingo
  - Age-appropriate games with rules, such as Blockhead, Please Don't Break the Ice, and card games such as Old Maid
  - Basketballs, kickballs, soccer balls, hoops, and goals

- Arrange for children to participate in small group activities with peers who have slightly advanced ability to engage in games with rules.

  Example   Manuel, Latifa, and Timmy are playing Candyland together. When Timmy moves his marker without picking a card first, Manuel says, "Wait Timmy. You need to pick a card first!" (*Cog G:2.2*)

PLANNED ACTIVITIES

Two examples of how to embed this goal and the associated objectives within activities are presented here. For a complete set of activities that address goals and objectives across domains, see Section V.

Hug Tag

One child is chosen to be "it." That child "freezes" other children by tagging them. The children who are frozen stand absolutely still until another child (one who is not "it" and is not yet frozen) gives them a hug. The children can be allowed to take turns being "it," and they should practice giving gentle hugs. The interventionist should observe the children's ability to follow the rules of the game and provide the least level of assistance if children are forgetting rules.

Note   Some children may not feel comfortable getting hugs from their friends. This opportunity can be used to talk about safe touches and personal body space. If a child is very uncomfortable, the rules can be changed to give hand squeezes instead of hugs.

Doggie, Doggie, Who's Got the Bone?

The children sit together in a group and choose one child to be the "doggie." While the doggie hides his or her eyes, a child who is sitting is chosen to hold the "bone" (the bone can be any small object). All children place their hands behind their backs and chant, "Doggie, doggie, who's got the bone?" The doggie opens his or her eyes and gets three chances to guess which child is hiding the bone.

PRESCHOOL CURRICULA WITH SIMILAR GOALS

The following preschool curricula provide information on this goal or similar goals. Interventionists whose programs have access to one or more of these curricula may refer to the referenced sections for additional programming strategies.

The Carolina Curriculum for Preschoolers with Special Needs

Interpersonal Skills
- Spontaneously takes turn and shares

- Plays simple board or card games with other children with adult supervision
- Plays group games with other children, such as Tag and Hide-and-Seek, without constant adult supervision

The Creative Curriculum

Blocks
House Corner
Table Toys
Art
Sand and Water
Library Corner
Outdoors

Portage Guide to Early Education Activity Cards

Social
- Follows rules of verbal reasoning game
- Explains rules of game or activity to others
- Follows rules in group games led by an older child
- Follows rules in group games led by adult

Strand H   Premath

GOAL 1.0   Recites numbers from 1 to 20

Objective 1.1   Recites numbers from 1 to 10
Objective 1.2   Recites numbers from 1 to 5
Objective 1.3   Recites numbers from 1 to 3

CONCURRENT GOALS

GM A:1.0   Alternates feet walking up and down stairs
Cog E:2.0   Recalls verbal sequences
SC A:1.0   Uses words, phrases, or sentences to inform, direct, ask questions, and express anticipation, imagination, affect, and emotions

DAILY ROUTINES

Routine events that provide opportunities for children to recite numbers include the following:

Dressing   Snack time
Mealtime   Unstructured play time
Travel time   Transition time
Arrival and departure   Bathtime
Circle time at school   Bedtime

Example   While running the water for Alice's bath, her mother says, "Let's count to 20 and turn the water off." (*Cog H:1.0*)

ENVIRONMENTAL ARRANGEMENTS

■ Provide materials during free play and routine events that have many pieces to count:

  – Art supplies such as crayons, pencils, markers, or collage materials (e.g., beans, buttons, scraps of paper, pieces of yarn)
  – Food/snack items in many pieces (e.g., mini crackers, raisins)
  – Blocks, Tinkertoys, Lego toys, plastic animals and people, cars
  – Sorting materials such as counting bears, beans, nuts and bolts

■ Include a calendar as a routine circle activity. A calendar can be made with a large piece of cardboard divided into 31 squares with removable numbers. The children count up to the number of the current day.

■ Include in the environment posters, books, and listening tapes about numbers and counting.

PLANNED ACTIVITIES

Two examples of how to embed this goal and the associated objectives within activities are presented here. For a complete set of activities that address goals and objectives across domains, see Section V.

Making Bread

The interventionist chooses a favorite quick bread recipe such as zucchini bread and gathers all necessary ingredients and utensils. Children measure the ingredients, stir the batter, butter the pan, and help clean up afterward. Opportunities can be provided for children to count as they get ready for the activity (e.g., "Let's count to 10 while we wash our hands to make sure they're really clean") and participate in making the bread (each child can stir for the count of 20).

Stairs

While walking up and down stairs, children can count the number of steps. Counting can also be incorporated by having the children count how many seconds it takes for them to walk up and down the stairs.

PRESCHOOL CURRICULA WITH SIMILAR GOALS

The following preschool curricula provide information on this goal or similar goals. Interventionists whose programs have access to one or more of these curricula may refer to the referenced sections for additional programming strategies.

The Carolina Curriculum for Preschoolers with Special Needs
Concepts
■ Counts correctly to 20

The Creative Curriculum
Blocks
Table Toys

High Scope—Young Children in ACTION
Numbers

Portage Guide to Early Education Activity Cards
Cognitive
■ Counts by rote 1 to 20
■ Counts to three in imitation

Cog H

GOAL 2.0 Counts 10 objects

Objective 2.1 Counts five objects

Objective 2.2 Counts two objects

Objective 2.3 Demonstrates understanding of one-to-one correspondence

---

CONCURRENT GOALS

FM A:2.0   Cuts out shapes with curved lines
Cog B:5.0   Demonstrates understanding of eight different quantitative concepts
SC A:1.0   Uses words, phrases, or sentences to inform, direct, ask questions, and express anticipation, imagination, affect, and emotions

DAILY ROUTINES

Routine events that provide opportunities for children to count objects include the following:

Dressing	Snack time
Mealtime	Unstructured play time
Travel time	Transition time
Arrival and departure	Bathtime
Circle time at school	Bedtime

Example   After buttoning Latifa's shirt, her mother says, "Let's see how many buttons you have: one, two, three, four, five. Now you count!" (*Cog H:2.1*)

Example   During snack time, Timmy's interventionist has him pass out one napkin to each of his friends and count as he does so. (*Cog H:2.3*)

ENVIRONMENTAL ARRANGEMENTS

■ Provide materials during free play and routine events that have many pieces to count:

- Art supplies such as collage materials (beans, buttons, scraps of paper, pieces of yarn), crayons, pencils, markers
- Food/snack items in many pieces (e.g., mini crackers, raisins)
- Blocks, Tinkertoys, Lego toys, plastic animals and people, cars
- Sorting materials such as counting bears, beans, nuts and bolts

■ Include posters and books in the environment that provide opportunities for the children to count.

Cog H

PLANNED ACTIVITIES

Two examples of how to embed this goal and the associated objectives within activities are presented here. For a complete set of activities that address goals and objectives across domains, see Section V.

Valentine Cookies

Children help make heart-shaped cookies with a sugar cookie recipe, cookie cutters, and colored frosting for decoration. The children can participate in all aspects of this process by making the dough, rolling it out, cutting the shapes, and decorating and eating the cookies. The activity provides opportunities for children to count objects (e.g., counting children in the group to determine how many chairs are needed, counting number of cookies on a tray, counting napkins).

Potato Prints

Potato prints are made by cutting a raw potato in half, drawing a design on the flat surface (e.g., a heart), and carving around the design with a knife (so the design is raised on the potato surface). Potatoes should be carved by an adult. Children help with the design, watch the carving, and use the potatoes to print. To print, children press the potato in a thin layer of paint, press the painted potato onto a piece of paper, and lift the potato off to see the print. Counting can be incorporated throughout this activity (e.g., count the number of potatoes before and after cutting, count the paint colors, and count the number of prints made on the paper).

PRESCHOOL CURRICULA WITH SIMILAR GOALS

The following preschool curricula provide information on this goal or similar goals. Interventionists whose programs have access to one or more of these curricula may refer to the referenced sections for additional programming strategies.

The Carolina Curriculum for Preschoolers with Special Needs
Concepts
- Gives the correct number of objects when asked—all numbers from 4 to 10
- Counts 10 objects in a row
- Counts up to six objects in a row
- Gives/selects two and three objects

Attention and Memory
- Answers number questions involving one and two objects

The Creative Curriculum
Blocks
Table Toys

High Scope—Young Children in ACTION
Numbers

Portage Guide to Early Education Activity Cards
Cognitive
- Counts up to 20 items and tells how many
- Counts to 10 objects in imitation

Cog H

GOAL 3.0 Identifies printed numerals 1–10

Objective 3.1 Identifies printed numerals 1–8
Objective 3.2 Identifies printed numerals 1–5
Objective 3.3 Identifies printed numerals 1–3

CONCURRENT GOALS

SC A:1.0   Uses words, phrases, or sentences to inform, direct, ask questions, and express anticipation, imagination, affect, and emotions

DAILY ROUTINES

Routine events that provide opportunities for children to identify printed numerals include the following:

Mealtime	Driving time in the car
Snack time	Unstructured play time
Circle time at school	Transition time
Bathtime	Bedtime

Example   Manuel's father points out signs that have numbers while driving to school. Susie's mother points out numerals on a deck of cards. (*Cog H:3.0*)

ENVIRONMENTAL ARRANGEMENTS

■ Arrange the classroom into activity centers that include house play and dramatic play. Place a number from 1 to 10 at each area. Provide materials during free play and routine events that have printed numerals.

– Placemats with numbers printed on them
– Board games with number cards, decks of playing cards
– Magnetic board and numbers
– Number stencils, stamp pad and numbered stamps, variety of number stickers
– Science-related materials such as timers, scales to weigh items, rulers, and old calculators
– A calendar with detachable numbers
– Dramatic play materials such as telephones, toy clocks, play money, signs denoting cost of items, a microwave or stove with numbered controls, cash registers, stamps, and restaurant menus

■ Include colorful and appealing posters, books, and magazines in the environment that have printed numerals.

PLANNED ACTIVITIES

Two examples of how to embed this goal and the associated objectives within activities are presented here. For a complete set of activities that address goals and objectives across domains, see Section V.

Community Helper Book

Children find pictures of community helpers in magazines, cut them out, glue the pictures on paper, and combine pages to make a "book." The interventionist numbers the pages and refers to the numbers as children "read" their books. The interventionist can also take dictation from the children about their books and encourage them to identify printed numbers.

Making Telephones

Children make pretend telephones by attaching a face (paper plate) to a mouthpiece (cardboard cut to look like a telephone mouthpiece) with a piece of string or yarn. Children glue premade numbers to the face from a model, with help from an interventionist. It is good for children to know how to dial 911, the emergency telephone number, as well as how to dial home telephone numbers.

  Note   For children to make real telephone calls, they must practice dialing a telephone, learning how to use both touchtone and rotary telephones, as well as what to do once they have made a connection. This requires many role-play situations, and rules concerning telephone use must be closely monitored. Practice telephone calls to 911 are not looked on favorably by emergency services, and "accidental" calls to Japan are not looked on favorably by parents!

PRESCHOOL CURRICULA WITH SIMILAR GOALS

The following preschool curricula provide information on this goal or similar goals. Interventionists whose programs have access to one or more of these curricula may refer to the referenced sections for additional programming strategies.

The Creative Curriculum
Blocks
Table Toys

High Scope—Young Children in ACTION
Numbers

Portage Guide to Early Education Activity Cards
Cognitive
- Points to named numerals 1–25
- Names 10 numerals

Cog H

GOAL 4.0   Matches printed numerals to sets of 1–10 object(s)

Objective 4.1   Matches printed numerals to sets of 1–8 object(s)

Objective 4.2   Matches printed numerals to sets of 1–5 object(s)

Objective 4.3   Matches printed numerals to sets of 1–3 object(s)

CONCURRENT GOALS

SC A:1.0   Uses words, phrases, or sentences to inform, direct, ask questions, and express anticipation, imagination, affect, and emotions

DAILY ROUTINES

Finding daily events that provide opportunities to match printed numbers to sets of objects may be difficult; however, the activities listed below provide limited opportunities:

Mealtime
Snack time
Circle time at school
Bathtime
Unstructured play time

Example   Maria has a placemat with numbers from 1 to 10 on it. During snack time, Maria's mother provides small crackers and asks Maria how many she would like. If Maria says four, her mother counts out four crackers and places them in a row, under the number four. (*Cog H:4.0*)

ENVIRONMENTAL ARRANGEMENTS

■ Arrange the classroom into activity centers, including a dramatic play center. Some activity areas may require limited occupancy for children to use them effectively (e.g., quiet area). A card that indicates the maximum number of children can be posted at the entrance of the activity area. It may be necessary to provide a visual cue in addition, such as a picture of three children.
■ Provide materials during free play and routine events that have printed numerals:

  – Placemats with numbers printed on them
  – Board games with number cards, decks of playing cards
  – Magnetic numbers with board, additional magnetic figures (e.g., fruits, shapes)
  – Number stencils; stamp pads and number stamps, as well as small stamps of a variety of interesting objects; number stickers
  – Science-related materials such as timers, scales to weigh items, rulers, and old calculators

Cog H

- Calendar with detachable numbers
- Dramatic play materials such as telephones, toy clocks, play money, signs denoting cost of items, microwave stove with numbered controls, cash registers with coins, stamps, and restaurant menus
- Colorful and appealing posters, books, and magazines with printed numerals

PLANNED ACTIVITIES

Two examples of how to embed this goal and the associated objectives within activities are presented here. For a complete set of activities that address goals and objectives across domains, see Section V.

Grocery Store

The dramatic play center is set up as a grocery store, stocked with empty food containers children bring from home. Push toys can be used as grocery carts, and play money bills with numerals 1–10 are provided. Children assume roles (e.g., store clerk, register attendant, bagger, shopper). Children determine what numeral is on their bill and match that to the appropriate food item.

My Number Book

Children create their own book about numbers. Each page is clearly marked with a number from 1 to 10. Children create the numbers independently or with models (e.g., stencils, number stamp, tracing dots, numbers cut out of a magazine). Children then draw, stamp, or cut out pictures that represent the number on each page (e.g., on page 5, child glues five people, draws five dogs, or stamps five stamps).

PRESCHOOL CURRICULA WITH SIMILAR GOALS

The following preschool curricula provide information on this goal or similar goals. Interventionists whose programs have access to one or more of these curricula may refer to the referenced sections for additional programming strategies.

The Creative Curriculum
Blocks
Table Toys

High Scope—Young Children in ACTION
Numbers

Cog H

Strand I   Prereading

GOAL 1.0   Demonstrates prereading skills

Objective 1.1	Demonstrates functional use of books
Objective 1.2	Tells about pictures in book
Objective 1.3	Participates actively in storytelling

CONCURRENT GOALS

FM B:2.0	Prints first name
Cog A	Participation (all goals)
SC A	Social-Communicative Interactions (all goals)
SC B	Production of Words, Phrases, and Sentences (all goals)
Soc A:2.0	Initiates cooperative activity
Soc C:1.0	Communicates personal likes and dislikes
Soc C:3.0	Accurately identifies affect/emotions in others and self consistent with demonstrated behaviors

DAILY ROUTINES

Routine events that provide opportunities for children to demonstrate prereading skills including the following:

Circle time
Driving time in the car
Bedtime
Unstructured play time
Story time

Example Before bedtime, Timmy chooses two books for his father to read to him. Timmy listens carefully and participates by turning pages (*Cog I:1.3*)

ENVIRONMENTAL ARRANGEMENTS

■ Provide materials in the environment that are interesting and appealing to children that allow opportunities to demonstrate prereading skills:

  – Age-appropriate books, magazines
  – Art materials for children to make their own "books" (see Books/Book Making in Section V)
  – Audiotape recorders with headphones and read-along story tapes

- Arrange the classroom into activity areas that include a library area. Make the library area as cozy and comfortable as possible, with carpet, soft pillows, or a mini couch. Decorate the area with posters or children's pictures of favorite story characters. Locate the library area in a quiet part of the classroom. If possible, replenish the area with new books from a local library every week or two.
- Include a story time in the classroom or home routine. Classrooms often have story time at closing circle to give children an opportunity to wind down after a full day of activities.

   Example   As the interventionist tells the story of Goldilocks and the Three Bears, she says, "Then the mama bear said…" and pauses, providing an opportunity for Eric to say, "Somebody's eaten my porridge." (*Cog I:1.3*)

PLANNED ACTIVITIES

Two examples of how to embed this goal and the associated objectives within activities are presented here. For a complete set of activities that address goals and objectives across domains, see Section V.

Library Field Trip

Many children enjoy taking a trip to the community library. The interventionist can call ahead to ask the librarian to give the class a special tour and help locate books about dinosaurs. If possible, the children can be allowed to pick out special books from the library to take home and share with family members.

   Example   Maria's interventionist writes a note home saying: "On the field trip to the library, Maria chose the book, *Danny and the Dinosaur.* She is bringing the book home to share with you. Could you please read it with her and return it to school by Wednesday? Thank you."

Dinosaur Books

Children make their own books about dinosaurs by cutting out pictures of dinosaurs from magazines, drawing their own dinosaurs, or cutting out outlined dinosaurs and coloring them. Children glue the pictures in books (see Books/Book Making in Section V), and the interventionist writes down their stories. Opportunities can be provided for the children to demonstrate prereading skills by asking them to tell about the pictures in their books while they make them. Later the children can share their books during group time.

PRESCHOOL CURRICULA WITH SIMILAR GOALS

The following preschool curricula provide information on this goal or similar goals. Interventionists whose programs have access to one or more of these curricula may refer to the referenced sections for additional programming strategies.

The Creative Curriculum
Library

High Scope—Young Children in ACTION
Experiencing and Representing
- Observing that spoken words can be written down and read back

Language
- Having fun with language
- Having one's own spoken language written down and read back

Portage Guide to Early Education Activity Cards
Cognitive
- Names action pictures

GOAL 2.0   Demonstrates prereading auditory skills

Objective 2.1	Blends sounds
Objective 2.2	Rhymes words

CONCURRENT GOALS

Cog E:2.0   Recalls verbal sequences
SC A   Social-Communicative Interactions (all goals)
SC B   Production of Words, Phrases, and Sentences (all goals)

DAILY ROUTINES

Routine events that provide opportunities for children to demonstrate prereading auditory skills include the following:

Dressing	Snack time
Mealtime	Unstructured play time
Travel time	Transition time
Arrival and departure	Bathtime
Circle time at school	Bedtime
Story time	

Example   While driving to school, Latifa's mother plays rhyming games. "I see a tree and a bee. Stop pop top mop." She sounds out things she sees. "Look Latifa, it's a d-o-g." (*Cog I:2.1, 2.2*)

ENVIRONMENTAL ARRANGEMENTS

- Arrange the classroom into activity areas that include a listening area with audiotape recorders and audiotapes. Include this area as part of the library center if headphones are available so that other children are not disturbed. Present materials in the environment that are interesting and appealing to children and provide opportunities to demonstrate prereading auditory skills:

  – Books with rhyming words, such as nursery rhymes
  – Audiotapes or records of songs with rhymes or that sound out words

■ Include a story time in the classroom or home routine. Classrooms often have story time at closing circle to give children an opportunity to wind down after a full day of activities.

PLANNED ACTIVITIES

Two examples of how to embed this goal and the associated objectives within activities are presented here. For a complete set of activities that address goals and objectives across domains, see Section V.

Spring Walk

The children go on a walk to look for signs of spring. The interventionist provides opportunities for children to rhyme words by thinking up rhyming words for the different things they find. If children see a bee, the interventionist asks if they can think of words that rhyme with bee, such as *tree, see,* and *me.* The interventionist sounds out a word (e.g., "I see a d-o-g") and asks children to blend the sounds to form the word.

Spring Flowers

Children paint a mural of flowers with bright colors on a huge piece of paper. The interventionist can draw the stems ahead of time if desired. To provide opportunities for children to blend sounds, the interventionist says playfully, "I have something behind my back. I'm going to say the sounds and see if you can guess what it is?" Examples of words to use are *cup, mop, top,* and *pen.* Throughout the activity, the interventionist encourages children to rhyme words.

PRESCHOOL CURRICULA WITH SIMILAR GOALS

The following preschool curricula provide information on this goal or similar goals. Interventionists whose programs have access to one or more of these curricula may refer to the referenced sections for additional programming strategies.

The Carolina Curriculum for Preschoolers with Special Needs

Interest in Sounds and Language Functions
■ Makes rhymes to simple words

The Creative Curriculum

Library

High Scope—Young Children in ACTION

Experiencing and Representing
■ Observing that spoken words can be written down and read back
Language
■ Having fun with language
■ Having one's own spoken language written down and read back

Portage Guide to Early Education Activity Cards

Language
■ Tells whether or not two words rhyme

GOAL 3.0   Sounds out words

Objective 3.1   Produces phonetic sounds for letters

CONCURRENT GOALS

Cog E:2.0   Recalls verbal sequences
SC A   Social-Communicative Interactions (all goals)
SC B   Production of Words, Phrases, and Sentences (all goals)

DAILY ROUTINES

Routine events that provide opportunities for children to sound out words include the following:

Circle time at school
Driving time in the car
Unstructured play time
Transition time

   Example   Manuel walks with his father to the park. On the way, his father points to the "S" on a stop sign and says, "Do you know what this letter sounds like?" (*Cog I:3.1*)

ENVIRONMENTAL ARRANGEMENTS

- Provide materials in the environment that are interesting and appealing to children that provide opportunities to demonstrate prereading skills:

  - Age-appropriate books, magazines
  - Art materials for children to make their own "books" (see Books/Book Making in Section V)
  - Audiotape recorders with headphones and read-along story tapes
  - Magnetic board and letters
  - Dramatic play props such as open/closed signs, street signs, menus, patients' charts, labels on grocery store items

- Arrange the classroom into activity centers that include a library and a dramatic play center. Make the library center as cozy and comfortable as possible, with carpet, soft pillows, or a mini couch. Decorate the area with posters or children's pictures and locate the library center in a quiet part of the classroom. If possible, replenish the area with new books from a local library every week or two.
- Display examples of written language in the classroom wherever appropriate. Cubbies are labeled with children's names, labels for materials are posted on shelves, and

Cog I

a menu is created for snack. Pairing written language and pictures (e.g., a picture of Lego toys with the word Legos) will assist children who are just learning to read.

- Include story time in the classroom or home routine. Classrooms often have story time at closing circle to give children the opportunity to wind down after a full day of activities.

PLANNED ACTIVITIES

Two examples of how to embed this goal and the associated objective within activities are presented here. For a complete set of activities that address goals and objectives across domains, see Section V.

Alphabet Soup

Children make alphabet soup from any favorite soup recipe, substituting alphabet noodles for the carbohydrate. Children are given many opportunities to sound out words or produce the phonetic sounds for letters while they make the soup and eat the finished product. The interventionist puts together words consisting of three phonetic units and prompts children to sound out the words, especially encouraging them to sound out words and letters that surface in their soup.

Oatmeal Cookies

Children make oatmeal cookies from a favorite recipe. The interventionist writes out the recipe in simple, easy-to-read words and prompts children to sound out words throughout the activity. Words consisting of three phonetic units that can be included in the recipe are *mix, cup,* and *top.*

   Example   Manuel's interventionist starts to read, "Sprinkle sugar on..." and pauses, pointing to the word "top" to encourage Manuel to sound it out. (*Cog I:3.0*)

PRESCHOOL CURRICULA WITH SIMILAR GOALS

The following preschool curricula provide information on this goal or similar goals. Interventionists whose programs have access to one or more of these curricula may refer to the referenced sections for additional programming strategies.

The Creative Curriculum
Library

High Scope—Young Children in ACTION
Experiencing and Representing
- Observing that spoken words can be written down and read back
Language
- Having fun with language
- Having one's own spoken language written down and read back

GOAL 4.0   Reads words by sight

Objective 4.1   Identifies letters

CONCURRENT GOALS

Cog E:2.0   Recalls verbal sequences
SC A   Social-Communicative Interactions (all goals)
SC B   Production of Words, Phrases, and Sentences (all goals)
Soc C:2.0   Relates identifying information about self and others

DAILY ROUTINES

Routine events that provide opportunities for children to read words by sight include the following:

Circle time at school
Driving time in the car
Unstructured play time
Transition time
Story time

Example   When reading Joey a book at bedtime, his mother sometimes names different letters and asks Joey to identify them in the text. (*Cog I:4.1*)

ENVIRONMENTAL ARRANGEMENTS

■ Present interesting and appealing materials in the environment that provide opportunities for children to identify letters or read words:

- Age-appropriate books, magazines
- Alphabet blocks
- Art materials for children to make their own "books" (see Books/Book Making in Section V)
- Audiotape recorders with headphones and read-along story tapes
- Magnetic board and letters
- Dramatic play props such as open/closed signs, street signs, menus, patients' charts, labels on grocery store items

■ Arrange the classroom into activity areas that include a library and a dramatic play center. Make the library area as cozy and comfortable as possible, with carpet, soft pillows, or a mini couch. Decorate the area with posters or children's pictures of favorite story characters, and locate the library area in a quiet part of the classroom. If possible, replenish the area with new books from a local library every week or two.

■ Display examples of written language wherever appropriate in the classroom environment. Cubbies are labeled with children's names, names of materials are posted on shelves, and a menu is created for snack. Pairing written language with pictures (e.g., a picture of Lego toys with the word Legos) will assist children who are just learning to read.

■ Include a story time in the classroom or home routine. Classrooms often have story time at closing circle to give children an opportunity to wind down after a full day of activities.

PLANNED ACTIVITIES

Two examples of how to embed this goal and the associated objective within activities are presented here. For a complete set of activities that address goals and objectives across domains, see Section V.

Name Cards

Children make name cards on a piece of cardboard and decorate them with crayons, markers, stickers, glitter, and so forth. The interventionist provides the least level of assistance necessary for each child to have a legible model of his or her name. Opportunities can be provided for children to identify letters in their names and other children's names. The cards can be used at different times of the day to provide opportunities for children to recognize their names. During circle time, the interventionist might show name cards as a way to take attendance ("Is this person here today?") or as a way to dismiss children ("When you see your name you can go to the next activity").

Note   Children may seem to be reading their name cards but are actually attending to other stimuli (e.g., the length of their name, a decoration on their cards). To determine if the child is actually recognizing his or her name, the interventionist can have the child identify each letter in his or her name.

Letter Search

Children look through magazines, catalogs, and newspapers for letters. They cut out and identify letters and glue them onto a piece of paper. The interventionist can encourage children to find and identify letters that are in their names and should always have children write their names on art projects.

PRESCHOOL CURRICULA WITH SIMILAR GOALS

The following preschool curricula provide information on this goal or similar goals. Interventionists whose programs have access to one or more of these curricula may refer to the referenced sections for additional programming strategies.

The Creative Curriculum
Library

High Scope—Young Children in ACTION
Experiencing and Representing
■ Observing that spoken words can be written down and read back
Language
■ Having fun with language
■ Having one's own spoken language written down and read back

Portage Guide to Early Education Activity Cards

Cognitive

■ Sight reads 10 printed words

REFERENCES

Flavell, J. (1977). *Cognitive development.* Englewood Cliffs, NJ: Prentice-Hall.

Hoff, S. (1985). *Danny and the dinosaur.* New York: HarperCollins Children's Books.

Kraus, R. (1989). *The carrot seed.* Scranton, PA: HarperCollins.

McCormick, L. (1990). Bases for language and communication development. In L. McCormick & R. Schiefelbusch (Eds.), *Early language intervention* (pp. 37–70). Columbus, OH: Charles E. Merrill.

Piaget, J. (1970). Piaget's theory. In P. Mussen (Ed.), *Carmichael's manual of child psychology* (Vol. 1, pp. 703–732). New York: John Wiley & Sons.

Cog I

SOCIAL-COMMUNICATION DOMAIN

The ability to communicate effectively is fundamental to satisfying relationships and independent functioning throughout life. Communication refers to the exchange of symbolic or nonsymbolic messages or information between speaker and listener. Symbolic communication is generally referred to as language and requires the exchange of words, pictures, tokens, or signs that stand for or represent the actual thing, action, setting, concept, or person. Language is a conventional system that employs a code that represents ideas about the world for the purpose of communication (Bloom & Lahey, 1978). Nonsymbolic communication also conveys messages and information from speaker to listener through gestures, facial expressions, and other actions; however, this form of communication is generally not a conventional system that uses a code to represent ideas about the world.

Infants enter the world as communicators. Their initial communicative efforts are nonsymbolic and indicate to caregivers their pleasure, displeasure, interest, or physiological state. Over time most children learn to understand and use the symbolic communication or the language code of their environment. Acquisition of both nonsymbolic and symbolic communication permits children to become increasingly independent and effective problem solvers. Children who lack effective communication skills are dependent on caregivers to satisfy their needs and solve their problems.

The Social-Communication Domain of the AEPS Curriculum was designed to systematically build and enhance children's symbolic and nonsymbolic communication skills as they use them in daily communicative transactions. This domain provides strategies that will move children from simple early symbolic and nonsymbolic skills to understanding and using increasingly complex language and socially appropriate communication. The preferred approach is to embed training into the activities and routines that occur throughout the child's day.

The Social-Communication Domain is composed of two strands. Strand A (Social-Communicative Interactions) focuses on the child's use of words, phrases, and sentences to develop and enhance social interactions. Learning conversational roles and rules is essential to developing positive and meaningful interactions with peers and adults. Strand B (Production of Words, Phrases, and Sentences) addresses the proper grammatical structures children need for effective communication.

The pervasiveness of social-communicative behavior and its strong association with cognitive processes are strong arguments not to view these behaviors as independent of other behavioral domains. Examiners should observe the child's use of social-communicative behaviors across a range of settings and activities in order to determine if an impairment is related to or the result of other problems. For example, a child's ability to name colors is dependent on understanding questions such as, "Show me the

SC

191

green one," or "What color is this?" as well as being able to discriminate between colors, a cognitive skill. In addition, there are communicative behaviors that can be classified in more than one domain. For example, a smile directed to a familiar caregiver can be a social-communicative, cognitive, and social behavior.

The Social-Communicative Domain Curriculum is divided into four sections: 1) Intervention Considerations, 2) Suggested Activities, 3) Using Activity-Based Intervention, and 4) Domain Goals. Intervention Considerations addresses important factors an interventionist may wish to consider prior to and when working with children who are at risk for or who have disabilities. Suggested Activities provides a selected list of activities that may be particularly helpful when working on social-communication skills. This section also provides suggestions for additional materials that will increase the opportunities for children to practice targeted social-communication skills. The third section provides an illustration of how to target IEP/IFSP goals in the Social-Communication Domain using an activity-based intervention approach. The final section, Domain Goals, provides suggestions for concurrent goals, daily routines, environmental arrangements, and planned activities in the home and classroom for each goal identified in the Social-Communication Domain of the AEPS Test for Three to Six Years. This section also lists other commercially available curricula that provide intervention activities for each goal.

INTERVENTION CONSIDERATIONS

General considerations when working on social-communication goals are discussed below. (See Role of the Interventionist and Caregiver in Section III for strategies and techniques to use to facilitate social-communication goals with children.)

- The influence of cultural values on children's social-communication behavior should be considered when developing intervention goals and plans. For example, in some cultures establishing eye contact is not appropriate behavior. In other cultures, children may not be encouraged to communicate openly. Work closely with family members when targeting social-communication goals for the child.
- A hearing evaluation is a critical first step in assessing communication abilities and determining appropriate goals for children. If the child wears a hearing aid, the adult should make certain it is operating well. Consultation with a communication specialist is recommended for any child for whom a communication goal has been selected.
- The inability to communicate his or her wants, needs, and feelings can be an extremely frustrating and isolating experience for a child. In many cases, behavior problems in the classroom or at home can be attributed to inappropriate or unsuccessful attempts at communication (e.g., grabbing to get a toy, pushing down another child to get a turn). Adults should observe children with hearing/communication problems very closely to determine communicative intent, target communication skills that will effectively replace inappropriate behaviors, and develop appropriate intervention plans.
- It is important to create an environment in which a child needs to use communication to make his or her needs known during routine, child-initiated, and planned activities. For example, placing a juice pitcher within sight but out of the reach of a child may encourage the child to request "juice." Make sure the child's attempts to speak are consistently rewarded with things that are reinforcing to the child and are logical consequences to the child's language (e.g., If a child says, "Mo," the adult

SC

responds, "Oh, you want more juice" and hands the child juice). Model appropriate communication for the child, without sounding punitive.

- Provide opportunities for children to communicate but do not make repeated demands on children to respond that might intimidate them and actually stifle communication. If a child becomes frustrated or is unwilling to make any attempt to communicate, it is time to reevaluate programming strategies, taking into consideration individual children's learning styles.

- Positioning of a child with a hearing or communication impairment is critical for optimal use of sensory information. The adult should ensure that the child is facing a speaker and is in proper position to see lips, signs, or pictures, particularly during large group activities such as circle time or story time. The child may benefit from the addition of visual or kinesthetic cues (e.g., pictures, gestures, objects) to help him or her interpret information. During activities, seating children across from and next to each other (as opposed to facing an empty space or sitting alone) may facilitate communication.

- The adult/child ratio and the positioning of adults in the classroom may influence the frequency or types of child-to-child interactions. Be aware of the amount of "adult talk" in a classroom, as well as the number of adult–child interactions that occur, and whether these interactions stifle communicative attempts between peers.

- Some children may be very sensitive to noise or certain sounds. Sounds that seem normal to an adult may be uncomfortably loud to some children; certain frequencies may be painful; and combinations of sounds or too much noise may be uncomfortable or distracting. Be aware of how the environment affects children.

- Children with visual impairments may need additional encouragement to look at or orient to the direction of the person to whom they are speaking. Children may need to be taught what is appropriate personal space (e.g., there are times when it is okay to reach out and touch a friend and times when it is not).

Augmentative Communication

If a child is unable to produce intelligible speech, it may be necessary to choose an augmentative communication system. Continue to encourage the speech a child does have while pairing that speech with another system. Several systems such as picture communication symbols, language boards, computer-operated systems, or sign language are available. Consultation with parents and a communication specialist will assist in determining the best method for each child. Considerations include the following:

- Portability
- Cost
- Ease of use
- How understandable the system is to people in the child's environment (e.g., Do caregivers, siblings, and peers know the sign for water?)
- How much the system will interfere with the child's activities (e.g., Is it difficult to move from activity to activity with the system?)

After determining which communication system will work best for the child, rules for deciding what vocabulary to target should be considered. These decisions will also be important when considering what vocabulary to target with children with limited speech. Guidelines for choosing vocabulary items include 1) functionality, 2) frequency of use, and 3) ease or difficulty in pronouncing words. Examples of words/phrases to be included are 1) preferred words (e.g., a picture for "tickle me"); 2) questions or requests

SC

(e.g., "I want water"); 3) words used by peers (e.g., "awesome"); 4) funny words (e.g., "okeydokey"); and 5) feeling words (e.g., "sad").

SUGGESTED ACTIVITIES

The following list of activities and materials may be particularly helpful for eliciting skills within the Social-Communication Domain. For a complete list of activities, see Section V.

Dramatic Play Activities

Dramatic play centers provide excellent places for children to experiment with forms of communication they have been exposed to at home and in their community. Ideas for dramatic play are endless, and the children will enjoy providing suggestions for themes that are interesting to them. The following themes may be particularly helpful when embedding social-communication goals:

- House play
- Camping
- Spaceship
- Restaurant
- Veterinary Office

Other Activities

- Book Time
- Audiotape Recorder
- Singing/Chants
- Expressive Arts
- Books/Book Making

- Flannel board
- Construction toys (with figurines)
- Water table
- Zoos and barns
- Play-Doh

USING ACTIVITY-BASED INTERVENTION

An illustration of how an interventionist can incorporate activity-based strategies to enhance the development of a child's social-communication skills is provided below. The child's targeted IEP/IFSP objective is to use words to inform (e.g., describe objects, actions, and events).

- During free play at school, the interventionist notices that Joey is watching a bird through a window. The interventionist *follows the child's lead* and uses the strategy of *delay* (e.g., "Look, a ..."), providing an opportunity for Joey to say, "bird." If he is unable to verbalize "bird," the interventionist *models* "A bird. It's a bird," or encourages peers who have more advanced verbal skills to describe what they see.
- The interventionist uses *parallel talk*, commenting on what Joey is doing (e.g., "You're watching the bird"). Joey vocalizes, "Fly." The interventionist expands on his child's initiation with, "Yes, fly. Birds fly."
- The interventionist asks *open-ended questions* that are related to Joey's activity, such as, "What does the bird look like?" If Joey has difficulty answering, the interventionist provides him with a choice to encourage him to use words to describe the bird, asking, "Is the bird big or little?"

DOMAIN GOALS

This section provides suggestions for concurrent goals, daily routines, environmental arrangements, and planned activities for the social-communication goals listed in the AEPS Test for Three to Six Years. If an objective has been targeted, the interventionist can turn to the corresponding goal and determine which suggestions are relevant to address that objective. A standard format is used for each goal: 1) Strand, 2) Goal, 3) Objective(s), 4) Concurrent Goals, 5) Daily Routines, 6) Environmental Arrangements, 7) Planned Activities, and 8) Preschool Curricula with Similar Goals. Concurrent Goals list the AEPS goals that can often be addressed at the same time the child works on the target goal or associated objectives. Daily Routines present a list of routine activities that may provide opportunities to practice targeted skills. The Environmental Arrangements should be considered when designing children's programs around child-initiated, routine, and planned activities. The Planned Activities offer examples of how to embed targeted goals within the context of planned activities. Finally, Preschool Curricula with Similar Goals list other curricula that can be used to supplement the AEPS Curriculum for Three to Six Years. If a given program has one or more of these preschool curricula, the interventionist can refer to the referenced sections to find additional programming strategies for the targeted goal or objective. Additional information on daily routines, environmental arrangements, planned activities, and themes is provided in Section III.

Strand A   Social-Communicative Interactions

G1.0 Uses words, phrases, or sentences to inform, direct, ask questions, and express anticipation, imagination, affect, and emotions

    1.1 Uses words, phrases, or sentences to express anticipated outcomes

    1.2 Uses words, phrases, or sentences to describe pretend objects, events, or people

    1.3 Uses words, phrases, or sentences to label own or others' affect/emotions

    1.4 Uses words, phrases, or sentences to describe past events

    1.5 Uses words, phrases, or sentences to make commands to and requests of others

    1.6 Uses words, phrases, or sentences to obtain information

    1.7 Uses words, phrases, or sentences to inform

G2.0 Uses conversational rules

    2.1 Alternates between speaker/listener role

    2.2 Responds to topic changes initiated by others

    2.3 Asks questions for clarification

    2.4 Responds to contingent questions

    2.5 Initiates context-relevant topics

    2.6 Responds to others' topic initiations

G3.0 Establishes and varies social-communicative roles

    3.1 Varies voice to impart meaning

    3.2 Uses socially appropriate physical orientation

Strand B   Production of Words, Phrases, and Sentences

G1.0 Uses verbs

    1.1 Uses auxiliary verbs

    1.2 Uses copula verb "to be"

SC

          1.3   Uses third person singular verb forms

          1.4   Uses irregular past tense verbs

          1.5   Uses regular past tense verbs

          1.6   Uses present progressive "ing"

G2.0   Uses noun inflections

          2.1   Uses possessive "s"

          2.2   Uses irregular plural nouns

          2.3   Uses regular plural nouns

G3.0   Asks questions

          3.1   Asks yes/no questions

          3.2   Asks questions with inverted auxiliary

          3.3   Asks when questions

          3.4   Asks why, who, and how questions

          3.5   Asks what and where questions

          3.6   Asks questions using rising inflection

G4.0   Uses pronouns

          4.1   Uses subject pronouns

          4.2   Uses object pronouns

          4.3   Uses possessive pronouns

          4.4   Uses indefinite pronouns

          4.5   Uses demonstrative pronouns

G5.0   Uses descriptive words

          5.1   Uses adjectives

          5.2   Uses adjectives to make comparisons

          5.3   Uses adverbs

          5.4   Uses prepositions

          5.5   Uses conjunctions

          5.6   Uses articles

Strand A Social-Communicative Interactions

GOAL 1.0 Uses words, phrases, or sentences to inform, direct, ask questions, and express anticipation, imagination, affect, and emotions

Objective 1.1	Uses words, phrases, or sentences to express anticipated outcomes
Objective 1.2	Uses words, phrases, or sentences to describe pretend objects, events, or people
Objective 1.3	Uses words, phrases, or sentences to label own or others' affect/emotions
Objective 1.4	Uses words, phrases, or sentences to describe past events
Objective 1.5	Uses words, phrases, or sentences to make commands to and requests of others
Objective 1.6	Uses words, phrases, or sentences to obtain information
Objective 1.7	Uses words, phrases, or sentences to inform

CONCURRENT GOALS

Adap B:1.0	Carries out all toileting functions
Cog A	Participation (all goals)
Cog B	Demonstrates Understanding of Concepts (all goals)
Cog D:3.0	Retells event in sequence
Cog E	Recalling Events (all goals)
Cog F	Problem Solving (all goals)
Cog G:1.0	Engages in imaginary play
Cog I:1.0	Demonstrates prereading skills
Soc A:3.0	Resolves conflicts by selecting effective strategy
Soc B:1.0	Meets physical needs in socially appropriate ways
Soc C:2.0	Relates identifying information about self and others
Soc C:3.0	Accurately identifies affect/emotions in others and self consistent with demonstrated behaviors

SC A

DAILY ROUTINES

Routine events that provide opportunities for children to have an active role in conversations include the following:

Dressing	Snack time
Mealtime	Unstructured play time
Travel time	Transition time
Arrival and departure	Bathtime
Circle time at school	Bedtime

Example   During mealtime, family members provide opportunities for children to share what they did during the day. (*SC A:1.4*)

Example   Maria has a goal to point to a picture on her communication board to make commands to or requests of others. During circle time, the interventionist makes sure her communication board is accessible and includes pictures that represent a request to sing a song, listen to a story, or play a circle game. The interventionist provides an opportunity for Maria to use her communication board to make a request during circle time if necessary. The interventionist or a peer provides assistance. (*SC A:1.5, with adapted materials*)

Example   In closing circle, the interventionist provides opportunities for children to share what they will do when they leave school (e.g., go shopping, take a nap, ride the bus). (*SC A:1.1*)

Example   While driving on long trips, family members play the game "I see…" and children use words to inform by labeling what they see outside. (*SC A:1.7*)

ENVIRONMENTAL ARRANGEMENTS

■ Provide materials that promote communication and arrange the classroom into activity areas that include a dramatic play center (see Environmental Arrangements in Section III and Dramatic Play Activities in Section V). In the dramatic play center, roles can be varied so that children have opportunities to inform or direct (e.g., store clerk, police officer, forest ranger) or label their own or others' affects/emotions (e.g., doctor, nurse, patient).

   Example   While Joey is playing with a doll in the house play area, he says, "No cry. My baby." (*SC A:1.2*)

   Example   When using the play telephone at school, children practice using words, phrases, or sentences to obtain information. (*SC A:1.6*)

■ Include pictures in the classroom or books in the library of children displaying various emotions (e.g., happy, sad, angry) to provide opportunities for children to label others' affect/emotions.

   Example   After reading a story about people with different emotions, Maria touches "happy" on her communication board, and her friend says, "You happy, Maria?" Maria nods. (*SC A:1.3*)

■ Intervention strategies that involve environmental arrangements include the following:

Heterogeneous grouping	Piece by piece
Choices	Assistance
Forgetfulness	Sabotage
Visible but unreachable	Negotiation
Violation of expectations	

SC A

Example (Choices)   During transition to free play, the interventionist provides children with a choice of two or three activities. Children who are nonverbal indicate choices by touching a representative object (e.g., block, crayon, puppet, book), pointing to a picture on their communication board, or signing. (*SC A:1.7*)

Example (Negotiation)   In the art center, the interventionist provides children with only one bottle of glue. While sharing the glue, the children use words to request or obtain information. (*SC A:1.5, 1.6*)

PLANNED ACTIVITIES

Two examples of how to embed this goal and the associated objectives within activities are presented here. For a complete set of activities that address goals and objectives across domains, see Section V.

Growing Seeds

Children grow their own plants by planting seeds (e.g., corn, beans, marigolds) in paper cups filled with soil. Reading and talking about growing plants provide opportunities for children to ask questions and provide information necessary for children to express anticipated outcomes. Giving only one spoon or one bowl of soil for every two children gives the opportunity for children to make commands to or requests of others (e.g., "Ask Latifa for the spoon"). The interventionist should allow each child to water and care for his or her own plant and have children describe the process of planting seeds during group time.

Example   While planting seeds, the interventionist says, "I wonder what's going to happen when we plant these seeds?" and pauses to give time for children to respond. (*SC A:1.1*)

Garden Field Trip

The class takes a field trip to public gardens or a local plant nursery. Reading a book about flowers or springtime prior to the trip may help children prepare for the event. The interventionist should encourage children to ask questions on the field trip and to answer any questions directed at them. The interventionist can model appropriate questions or responses and provide opportunities for children to describe what they saw when the class returns. Children may enjoy drawing pictures of what they saw at the nursery, and the interventionist can use communication strategies to facilitate individual goals while looking at the pictures. Children can be encouraged to tell parents about their experiences, and a small report of the day's events can be sent home to aid communication. Drawing simple pictures to indicate the day's events is particularly helpful for nonverbal children so they can "tell" about their day while pointing to pictures.

PRESCHOOL CURRICULA WITH SIMILAR GOALS

The following preschool curricula provide information on this goal or similar goals. Interventionists whose programs have access to one or more of these curricula may refer to the referenced sections for additional programming strategies.

The Carolina Curriculum for Preschoolers with Special Needs

Conversational Skills

SC A

The Creative Curriculum
Blocks
House Corner
Table Toys
Art
Sand and Water
Library Corner
Outdoors

High Scope—Young Children in ACTION
Language
- Expressing feelings in words
- Talking with other children and adults about personally meaningful experiences
Classification
- Using and describing objects in different ways

Portage Guide to Early Education Activity Cards
Cognitive
- Predicts what happens next
Language
- Answers questions "What happens if…?"
Social
- Shows understanding of feelings by verbalizing love, anger, sadness, laughter, and so forth
- States feelings about self: mad, happy, love
- Joins in conversation at mealtime
- Contributes to adult conversation

GOAL 2.0   Uses conversational rules

Objective 2.1	Alternates between speaker/listener role
Objective 2.2	Responds to topic changes initiated by others
Objective 2.3	Asks questions for clarification
Objective 2.4	Responds to contingent questions
Objective 2.5	Initiates context-relevant topics
Objective 2.6	Responds to others' topic initiations

CONCURRENT GOALS

Cog A:2.0   Watches, listens, and participates during small group activities
Cog A:3.0   Watches, listens, and participates during large group activities
Cog D:3.0   Retells event in sequence

Cog E   Recalling Events (all goals)
Cog F:2.0   Makes statements and appropriately answers questions that require rea-
               soning about objects, situations, or people
Cog G:2.0   Engages in games with rules
Soc A:1.0   Has play partners
Soc A:2.0   Initiates cooperative activity

DAILY ROUTINES

Routine events that provide opportunities for children to use conversations include the
following:

Dressing	Snack time
Mealtime	Unstructured play time
Travel time	Transition time
Arrival and departure	Bathtime
Circle time at school	Bedtime

Example   At breakfast, Joey's father says, "We're going to the zoo today!" If Joey
does not respond, his father prompts him by saying, "We'll see tigers and elephants and
…" (*SC A:2.6*)

Example   Timmy has a goal to supply relevant information following another person's request for clarification, repetition, elaboration, or confirmation of his previous
statement using sign language. When Timmy wakes up, he signs, WANT. His mother
faces Timmy and speaks clearly: "What do you want?" Timmy responds, EAT. (*SC A:2.4,
with adapted materials*)

ENVIRONMENTAL ARRANGEMENTS

■ Provide materials that promote communication and arrange the classroom into
  activity areas that include a dramatic play/house play activity center (see Environmental Arrangements in Section III and Dramatic Play Activities in Section V).

  Example   While playing in the "beauty salon," children alternate between
  speaker and listener roles during conversations between stylists and clients. For
  example, one child asks another, "You want your hair cut?" and waits for a response.
  (*SC A:2.1*)

  Example   Latifa speaks on the "telephone" to her friend Joey and says, "Hi.
  Who's this?" The interventionist who is close by looks expectantly at Joey and nods,
  but, when Joey does not respond, the interventionist gives him a more direct prompt
  by modeling, "It's Joey." Joey responds, "Joey." (*SC A:2.4*)

■ Intervention strategies that involve environmental arrangements include the following:

Heterogeneous grouping	Piece by piece
Choices	Assistance
Forgetfulness	Sabotage
Visible but unreachable	Negotiation
Violation of expectations	

  Example (Choices)   During circle time, the interventionist lets children take turns
  choosing songs. For example, a child says, "I want duck song!" (*SC A: 2.5*)

SC A

Example (Violation of expectations)   During snack time, the interventionist serves "blocks" for the children to eat. A child laughs and asks, "Where snack?" *(SC A:2.3)*

PLANNED ACTIVITIES

Two examples of how to embed this goal and the associated objectives within activities are presented here. For a complete set of activities that address goals and objectives across domains, see Section V.

Family Puppets (see Puppets in Section V)

Children make puppets of their family members and put on a "show" (a stage can be created from an old refrigerator box or by turning a table on its side). The interventionist models appropriate conversational rules (e.g., turn taking) by communicating through puppets. Opportunities for children to use conversational rules (e.g., respond to topic changes, respond to contingent questions) occur when children "talk" to each other through their puppets or can be prompted by the interventionist if necessary. Encouraging children to play act an event they are familiar with, such as eating dinner, may help them focus on conversational rules.

Example   The interventionist plans an opportunity for children to converse by having two children at a time put on a show for the class. The interventionist may need to prompt the children (e.g., looking at them expectantly, modeling an exchange). *(SC A:2.0)*

Going to Grandma's

Children use conversational rules during a pretend visit to Grandma's house. They may dress up for their visit to play the role of "Grandma." The interventionist designs opportunities for a child to practice specific goals by playing the role of grandma and planning opportunities for targeted skills. For example, the interventionist questions the child during role play to provide opportunities for the child to supply relevant information when responding. The interventionist should be in close proximity when children are play acting to provide prompts if necessary. This activity can be modified for a wide range of events and places.

Example   Timmy's interventionist knows he enjoys making cookies with his grandmother, so when Timmy comes to "visit," his interventionist says, "I'm going to make cookies." The interventionist pauses to allow Timmy an opportunity to sign, ME HELP? *(SC A:2.6, with adaptation)*

PRESCHOOL CURRICULA WITH SIMILAR GOALS

The following preschool curricula provide information on this goal or similar goals. Interventionists whose programs have access to one or more of these curricula may refer to the referenced sections for additional programming strategies.

The Carolina Curriculum for Preschoolers with Special Needs
Conversational Skills

The Creative Curriculum
Blocks
House Corner

Table Toys
Art
Sand and Water
Library Corner
Outdoors

High Scope—Young Children in ACTION

Language
■ Expressing feelings in words
■ Talking with other children and adults about personally meaningful experiences

Classification
■ Using and describing objects in different ways

Portage Guide to Early Education Activity Cards

Language
■ Changes word order appropriately to ask questions

Social
■ Joins in conversation at mealtime
■ Contributes to adult conversation

GOAL 3.0   Establishes and varies social-communicative roles

Objective 3.1	Varies voice to impart meaning
Objective 3.2	Uses socially appropriate physical orientation

CONCURRENT GOALS

Cog A:2.0	Watches, listens, and participates during small group activities
Cog A:3.0	Watches, listens, and participates during large group activities
Cog G:1.0	Engages in imaginary play
Cog I:1.0	Demonstrates prereading skills
Soc A:1.0	Has play partners
Soc A:3.0	Resolves conflicts by selecting effective strategy

DAILY ROUTINES

Routine events that provide opportunities for children to establish and vary social-communication include the following:

Dressing	Snack time
Mealtime	Unstructured play time
Travel time	Transition time
Arrival and departure	Bathtime
Circle time at school	Bedtime

SC A

Example When Latifa comes inside from playing, her mother says, "Remember to whisper, Latifa. Your brother is sleeping." Latifa whispers, "Okay." (*SC A:3.1*)

Example Alice uses a wheelchair to get around at home and at school. During mealtime and unstructured play time at school, Alice uses an adapted chair or is positioned on the floor so she is at the same level as her peers and can look at her friends' faces when communicating. (*SC A:3.2*)

ENVIRONMENTAL ARRANGEMENTS

- Provide materials that promote communication and arrange the classroom into activity areas that include a dramatic play/house play activity center (see Environmental Arrangements in Section III and Dramatic Play Activities in Section V). Materials such as puppets, dollhouses, construction toys with miniature people or figurines, zoo and zoo animals, barn and barn animals, dolls, and class pets provide opportunities for children to take on different social-communicative roles.
- Take a field trip to a classroom of younger children. Have special days in your classroom for younger siblings to visit.

  Example As children speak to younger siblings, they have opportunities to use shorter and less complex sentences. (*SC A:3.0*)
- Intervention strategies that involve environmental arrangements include heterogeneous grouping.
- Children with visual impairments may need additional encouragement to look at or orient to the person to whom they are speaking. Children may need to be taught what is appropriate personal space (e.g., there are times when it is okay to reach out and touch a friend and times when it is not).

PLANNED ACTIVITIES

Two examples of how to embed this goal and the associated objectives within activities are presented here. For a complete set of activities that address goals and objectives across domains, see Section V.

Animal Puppets (see Puppets in Section V)

Children make puppets of animals or cartoon characters and have a puppet show. Puppet shows provide opportunities for children to vary their social-communicative roles as they interact with their puppets. The interventionist joins in the show by using a puppet, following the children's lead, and providing appropriate models of targeted skills.

Washing Babies

Children wash their baby dolls in small tubs of water with soap, shampoo, washcloths, soft hairbrushes, and towels. Provide fewer materials than the number of children to provide opportunities for children to share and use socially appropriate physical orientation to communicate need. As children take on the "caregiver" role, opportunities arise for them to alter their voices (e.g., speak softly and with a slightly higher pitch) as they talk to their babies.

SC A

PRESCHOOL CURRICULA WITH SIMILAR GOALS

The following preschool curricula provide information on this goal or similar goals. Interventionists whose programs have access to one or more of these curricula may refer to the referenced sections for additional programming strategies.

The Carolina Curriculum for Preschoolers with Special Needs
Conversational Skills

The Creative Curriculum
Blocks
House Corner
Table Toys
Art
Sand and Water
Library Corner
Outdoors

High Scope—Young Children in ACTION
Language
- Expressing feelings in words
- Talking with other children and adults about personally meaningful experiences

Classification
- Using and describing objects in different ways

Portage Guide to Early Education Activity Cards
Language
- Changes word order appropriately to ask questions

SC A

Strand B   Production of Words, Phrases, and Sentences

GOAL 1.0   Uses verbs

Objective 1.1	Uses auxiliary verbs
Objective 1.2	Uses copula verb "to be"
Objective 1.3	Uses third person singular verb forms
Objective 1.4	Uses irregular past tense verbs
Objective 1.5	Uses regular past tense verbs
Objective 1.6	Uses present progressive "ing"

CONCURRENT GOALS

FM A	Manipulation of Objects (all goals)
FM B	Prewriting (all goals)
GM A:1.0	Alternates feet walking up and down stairs
GM B	Play Skills (all goals)
Adap A	Dining (all goals)
Adap B	Personal Hygiene (all goals)
Adap C	Dressing and Undressing (all goals)
Cog C:1.0	Groups objects, people, or events on the basis of specified criteria
Cog D:3.0	Retells event in sequence
Cog E:1.0	Recalls events that occurred on same day, without contextual cues
Cog F:1.0	Evaluates solutions to problems
Cog G:1.0	Engages in imaginary play
Cog H:2.0	Counts 10 objects
Cog I:1.0	Demonstrates prereading skills
Soc A	Interaction with Others (all goals)
Soc B	Interaction with Environment (all goals)
Soc C	Knowledge of Self and Others (all goals)

DAILY ROUTINES

Routine events that provide natural opportunities for children to use verbs include the following:

Dressing	Snack time
Mealtime	Unstructured play time
Travel time	Transition time
Arrival and departure	Bathtime
Circle time at school	Bedtime

Example While traveling in the car, family members talk to their children about what they see people or animals doing (e.g., walk*ing*, play*ing*, runn*ing*), emphasizing the "ing" ending. (*SC B:1.6*)

Example During circle time, Manuel's interventionist says, "I *am* very happy to see you today!" emphasizing "am," and Manuel says, "I am too." (*SC B:1.2*)

ENVIRONMENTAL ARRANGEMENTS

■ Provide materials that provide communication and arrange the classroom into activity areas that include a dramatic play center (see Environmental Arrangements in Section III and Dramatic Play Activities in Section V). Provide a time for children to talk about what happened during the day and share their experiences.

Example While Manuel is playing in the "doctor's office," his interventionist follows his lead and gets involved in the play. The interventionist models an irregular third person singular verb form by saying, "Doctor, Joey *has* a broken leg. How is Timmy?" Manuel says, "Timmy has a cold." (*SC B:1.3*)

■ Sing songs, do finger plays, or tell nursery rhymes that use verbs.

Example Jack and Jill *went* up the hill to fetch a pail of water. Jack *fell* down and broke his crown and Jill *came* tumbling after. (*SC B:1.4*)

■ Intervention strategies that involve environmental arrangements include the following:

Heterogeneous grouping	Piece by piece
Choices	Assistance
Forgetfulness	Sabotage
Visible but unreachable	Negotiation
Violation of expectations	

Example (Forgetfulness) The interventionist pours juice during snack time but "forgets" to provide any snack items. A child says, "I'm hungry!" (*SC B:1.2*)

Example (Violation of Expectations) The interventionist serves the children blocks for snack, and children protest, "We can't eat blocks!" (*SC B:1.1*)

PLANNED ACTIVITIES

Two examples of how to embed this goal and the associated objectives within activities are presented here. For a complete set of activities that address goals and objectives across domains, see Section V.

Zoo Field Trip

The interventionist takes the class on a field trip to the zoo. Field trips are exciting for children and can be structured to provide opportunities for them to use verbs. Reading a book on the subject of the field trip ahead of time will help children anticipate events. Talking about what the animals are doing and how the child is feeling and providing models of verb forms throughout the field trip facilitates the use of verbs. Back in the classroom, the interventionist can set up a zoo in the dramatic play area, draw pictures of the trip, or write a story to further facilitate the child's use of verbs. The interventionist models the appropriate verb form if necessary.

   Example   After returning from the zoo, Latifa's interventionist writes a group story about what happened on the field trip. Latifa shares, "I went to zoo. Zebras ran around." (*SC B:1.4*)

Ants on a Log

Children make their own snacks by spreading peanut butter on a piece of celery (log) and placing raisins (ants) in a row on the peanut butter. The interventionist can talk about what he or she is doing (e.g., spreading, placing, eating) and encourage children to talk about what they are doing throughout the activity. Opportunities can be provided for children to explain how they made their snacks to facilitate the use of regular and irregular past tense verbs (e.g., opened, washed, spread, made, put).

   Example   While spreading peanut butter, the interventionist uses self-talk: "I'm spread*ing* and you are..." (providing an opportunity for a child to say, "spreading"). (*SC B:1.6*)

PRESCHOOL CURRICULA WITH SIMILAR GOALS

The following preschool curricula provide information on this goal or similar goals. Interventionists whose programs have access to one or more of these curricula may refer to the referenced sections for additional programming strategies.

The Carolina Curriculum for Preschoolers with Special Needs
Sentence Construction

Portage Guide to Early Education Activity Cards
Language
- Uses some irregular past tense forms consistently
- Uses regular past tense forms
- Uses "ing" verb form

GOAL 2.0   Uses noun inflections

Objective 2.1   Uses possessive "s"
Objective 2.2   Uses irregular plural nouns
Objective 2.3   Uses regular plural nouns

CONCURRENT GOALS

FM A:1.0   Manipulates two small objects at same time
FM B:2.0   Prints first name

Adap A:1.0	Eats and drinks a variety of foods using appropriate utensils with little or no spilling
Adap B:2.0	Washes and grooms self
Adap C:2.0	Selects appropriate clothing and dresses self at designated times
Adap C:3.0	Fastens fasteners on garments
Cog C:1.0	Groups objects, people, or events on the basis of specified criteria
Cog D:3.0	Retells event in sequence
Cog E:2.0	Recalls verbal sequences
Cog G:1.0	Engages in imaginary play
Cog H:2.0	Counts 10 objects
Cog I:1.0	Demonstrates prereading skills
Soc A:2.0	Initiates cooperative activity
Soc B:1.0	Meets physical needs in socially appropriate ways
Soc C:1.0	Communicates personal likes and dislikes

DAILY ROUTINES

Routine events that provide natural opportunities for children to use noun inflections include the following:

Dressing	Snack time
Mealtime	Unstructured play time
Travel time	Transition time
Arrival and departure	Bathtime
Circle time at school	Bedtime

Example At departure time, Manuel's teacher holds up Maria's coat and jokingly says, "Here's your coat, Manuel!" Manuel responds, "No, that's Maria's coat." (*SC B:2.1*)

Example While driving on long trips, family members play the game "I see…" and model appropriate regular and irregular plural nouns (e.g., horses, geese) for the child. (*SC B:2.2, 2.3*)

ENVIRONMENTAL ARRANGEMENTS

- Provide materials that promote communication and arrange the classroom into activity areas that include a dramatic play center (see Environmental Arrangements in Section III and Dramatic Play Activities in Section V). Provide objects as examples of regular plural nouns (e.g., blocks, cars, glasses, horses, cows, coats, hats) and objects as examples of irregular plural nouns (e.g., mice, geese, teeth, feet). Frequently model correct plural forms of both regular and irregular nouns during play with children.
- Place pictures around the classroom and books in the library area that show examples of regular plural nouns (e.g., bubbles, trees, birds) and irregular plural nouns (e.g., feet, geese, mice).
- Sing songs, read nursery rhymes, and do finger plays that involve both regular and irregular plural nouns, such as the following:

  - "If you're happy and you know it, clap your hands. If you're mad and you know it, stomp your feet…"
  - "The wheels on the bus go round and round…"
  - "Five little monkeys jumping on the bed…"

SC B

■ Intervention strategies that involve environmental arrangements include the following:

Heterogeneous grouping	Piece by piece
Choices	Assistance
Forgetfulness	Sabotage
Visible but unreachable	Negotiation
Violation of expectations	

Example (Forgetfulness)   The interventionist pretends to pour juice on the table, but a child reaches out to stop her. The interventionist asks, "Oh no. What do I need?" The child says, "Cups." (*SC B:2.3*)

Example (Violation of expectations)   The interventionist gives the children Popsicle sticks to draw with instead of crayons. Joey looks up and says, "No write." The interventionist asks, "What do you need?" Joey responds, "Crayons." (*SC B:2.3*)

Example (Sabotage)   Manuel has a goal to use nouns with "'s" to express possession. The interventionist hides Joey's coat, and Manuel says, "Joey's coat is gone!" (*SC B:2.1*)

Example (Negotiation)   The interventionist provides a few collage materials during a free-choice activity. A child comments, "I need more sticks." (*SC B:2.3*)

PLANNED ACTIVITIES

Two examples of how to embed this goal and the associated objectives within activities are presented here. For a complete set of activities that address goals and objectives across domains, see Section V.

Whose Shoes?

All children take off one shoe and put it in the middle of the circle. One child at a time picks a shoe (not his or her own) and guesses whose shoe it is by looking for the match. The interventionist lets each child have more than one turn and models or reinforces other children's appropriate use of "'s" to express possession (e.g., "That's right. It's Timmy's!"). Regular and irregular plural nouns are emphasized throughout the activity (e.g., socks, shoes, children, shoelaces, feet).

Example   The interventionist has Eric, who has a visual impairment, find the matching shoe by feeling the shoes on children's feet. Once he finds the match, the interventionist prompts him by saying, "You found the other shoe on Maria, so whose shoe do you have?" Eric replies, "Maria's."

Body Tracing

The interventionist or a friend traces around children while they lie on butcher paper. Children color their outlines with crayons or markers. The interventionist provides opportunities to use noun inflections throughout the activity by prompting the children to name different body parts that are plural (e.g., eyes, ears, toes, fingers, legs, arms, feet). During the close of the activity, a strategy that provides opportunities for children to use possessive "'s" is to "forget" whose picture is whose (e.g., "It's Lisa's").

SC B

PRESCHOOL CURRICULA WITH SIMILAR GOALS

The following preschool curricula provide information on this goal or similar goals. Interventionists whose programs have access to one or more of these curricula may refer to the referenced sections for additional programming strategies.

The Carolina Curriculum for Preschoolers with Special Needs

Sentence Construction

Portage Guide to Early Education Activity Cards

Language
- Uses possessive form of nouns
- Uses some common irregular plurals
- Uses regular plural forms

GOAL 3.0   Asks questions

Objective 3.1	Asks yes/no questions
Objective 3.2	Asks questions with inverted auxiliary
Objective 3.3	Asks when questions
Objective 3.4	Asks why, who, and how questions
Objective 3.5	Asks what and where questions
Objective 3.6	Asks questions using rising inflection

CONCURRENT GOALS

Adap A	Dining (all goals)
Cog A:2.0	Watches, listens, and participates during small group activities
Cog A:3.0	Watches, listens, and participates during large group activities
Cog B	Demonstrates Understanding of Concepts (all goals)
Cog C:1.0	Groups objects, people, or events on the basis of specified criteria
Cog D:2.0	Places objects in series according to length or size
Soc B:2.0	Follows context-specific rules outside home and classroom
Soc C:3.0	Accurately identifies affect/emotions in others and self consistent with demonstrated behaviors

DAILY ROUTINES

Routine events that provide natural opportunities for children to ask questions include the following:

SCB

Dressing	Snack time
Mealtime	Unstructured play time
Travel time	Transition time
Arrival and departure	Bathtime
Circle time at school	Bedtime

Example   After dinner, Manuel asks, "Can I have a cookie?" (*SC B:3.1*)

Example   During school, some of the children go outside while others do an art project inside. Manuel asks, "Why can't I go outside?" (*SC B:3.2*)

ENVIRONMENTAL ARRANGEMENTS

■ Provide materials that promote communication and arrange the classroom into activity areas that include a dramatic play center (see Environmental Arrangements in Section III and Dramatic Play Activities in Section V).

   Example   While talking on the "telephone" to her mother, Latifa asks, "When you come pick me up?" (*SC B:3.3*)

■ Intervention strategies that involve environmental arrangements include the following:

Heterogeneous grouping	Piece by piece
Choices	Assistance
Forgetfulness	Sabotage
Visible but unreachable	Negotiation
Violation of expectations	

   Example (Choices)   During free play, the children must ask permission to use the computer. A child asks, "I go to computer?" and the interventionist models, "May you go? Yes, you may." (*SC B:3.2*)

   Example (Forgetfulness)   During story time, the interventionist pretends to read from her hands, and a child comments, "Where book?" (*SC B:3.5*)

   Example (Negotiation)   During snack time, the interventionist provides more crackers at one table than another. When a child asks for more, the interventionist directs him to the other table. "Ask Joey for more crackers." (*SC B:3.1*)

   Example (Violation of expectations)   Serving the children blocks for "snack" may stimulate questions such as, "Where snack?" (*SC B:3.5*)

PLANNED ACTIVITIES

Two examples of how to embed this goal and the associated objectives within activities are presented here. For a complete set of activities that address goals and objectives across domains, see Section V.

Visit from the Vet

A veterinarian is invited to talk to the class about what he or she does at work and about care for pets. The interventionist informs the children about the visitor before the veterinarian arrives and provides opportunities for children to ask questions before, during, and after the visit. The interventionist provides appropriate models of questions or prompts the children to ask questions if necessary.

SCB

Example   When a veterinarian comes to visit, Latifa's interventionist prompts her during the question and answer time, "Latifa, would you like to ask a question like '*How* do you help animals?'" (emphasizing the words *why* or *how*). Latifa asks, "How you help animals?" (*SC B:3.4*)

Animal Charades

One child chooses a card with an animal (it is helpful to do this after talking about or reading a book about animals), and the other children ask questions about the animal. Children ask questions such as, "What do you eat?" or "Where do you live?" The interventionist provides prompts to facilitate the children asking and answering questions. The children may make animal cards by cutting out pictures of animals from magazines and gluing them on cardboard.

PRESCHOOL CURRICULA WITH SIMILAR GOALS

The following preschool curricula provide information on this goal or similar goals. Interventionists whose programs have access to one or more of these curricula may refer to the referenced sections for additional programming strategies.

The Carolina Curriculum for Preschoolers with Special Needs
Sentence Construction
Conversational Skills

Portage Guide to Early Education Activity Cards
Language
- Changes word order appropriately to ask questions
- Uses could and would in speech
- Says "is" at beginning of questions when appropriate
- Asks questions, "What's this (that)?"

GOAL 4.0   Uses pronouns

Objective 4.1	Uses subject pronouns
Objective 4.2	Uses object pronouns
Objective 4.3	Uses possessive pronouns
Objective 4.4	Uses indefinite pronouns
Objective 4.5	Uses demonstrative pronouns

SC B

CONCURRENT GOALS

FM A   Manipulation of Objects (all goals)
FM B   Prewriting (all goals)

GM A:1.0	Alternates feet walking up and down stairs
GM B	Play Skills (all goals)
Adap A	Dining (all goals)
Adap B	Personal Hygiene (all goals)
Adap C	Dressing and Undressing (all goals)
Cog A:2.0	Watches, listens, and participates during small group activities
Cog A:3.0	Watches, listens, and participates during large group activities
Cog B	Demonstrates Understanding of Concepts (all goals)
Cog C:1.0	Groups objects, people, or events on the basis of specified criteria
Cog E	Recalling Events (all goals)
Cog G:1.0	Engages in imaginary play
Cog I:1.0	Demonstrates prereading skills
Soc A	Interaction with Others (all goals)
Soc C	Knowledge of Self and Others (all goals)

DAILY ROUTINES

Routine events that provide natural opportunities for children to use pronouns include the following:

Dressing	Snack time
Mealtime	Unstructured play time
Travel time	Transition time
Arrival and departure	Bathtime
Circle time at school	Bedtime

Example   During mealtime, families wait for children to initiate requests for second helpings and model appropriate use of pronouns (e.g., "I want more potatoes, please"). (*SC B:4.1*)

Example   During outdoor play time, Manuel comes crying to the interventionist and says, "He hurt me." (*SC B:4.1*)

ENVIRONMENTAL ARRANGEMENTS

■ Provide materials that promote communication and arrange the classroom into activity areas that include a dramatic play/house play center (see Environmental Arrangements in Section III and Dramatic Play Activities in Section V).

Example   As a child sets the table in the house play center, she comments, "This is my cup and this is your cup." (*SC B:4.3*)

■ Intervention strategies that involve environmental arrangements include the following:

Heterogeneous grouping	Piece by piece
Choices	Assistance
Forgetfulness	Sabotage
Visible but unreachable	Negotiation

Example (Choices)   The interventionist asks, "Do you want to wash babies with *her* or play cars with *him*?" (*SC B:4.2*)

Example (Visible but unreachable)   At snack time, the interventionist puts the juice out of reach and pauses, waiting for children to initiate, "We want juice." (*SC B:4.1*)

Example (Piece by piece)   While building a fire station with Lego toys or Duplos, the interventionist gives blocks to the children a few at a time, waiting for the children to ask for more (e.g., Please give me more," "Give me all of them"). (*SC B:4.4*)

PLANNED ACTIVITIES

Two examples of how to embed this goal and the associated objectives within activities are presented here. For a complete set of activities that address goals and objectives across domains, see Section V.

Picture Day

Children bring in pictures of their family or use pictures taken at school to share during group time. The interventionist provides a time for other children to ask questions about family members (e.g., "How old is your sister?) to facilitate the children's use of pronouns.

Example   Manuel's interventionist prompts him, "*You* are with your brother in this picture; *he* looks really big." Manuel says, "That's José. He is big." (*SC B:4.1*)

ME Books (see Books/Book Making in Section V)

Children make a book by gluing pictures cut from magazines to represent their family members, tracing their hand prints, cutting out pictures of favorite toys or foods, and dictating stories about themselves to the interventionist. The interventionist arranges the environment, incorporating strategies such as negotiation to increase opportunities for children to communicate and use pronouns. If necessary, the interventionist models appropriate pronouns for the child.

Example   While dictating his ME Book, Joey says, "Mine brother." The interventionist models while writing "This *my* brother," and Joey repeats, "Ya, my brother." (*SC B:4.3*)

PRESCHOOL CURRICULA WITH SIMILAR GOALS

The following preschool curricula provide information on this goal or similar goals. Interventionists whose programs have access to one or more of these curricula may refer to the referenced sections for additional programming strategies.

The Carolina Curriculum for Preschoolers with Special Needs
Sentence Construction

Portage Guide to Early Education Activity Cards
Language
- Says "I, me, mine" rather than own name

GOAL 5.0   Uses descriptive words

Objective 5.1	Uses adjectives
Objective 5.2	Uses adjectives to make comparisons
Objective 5.3	Uses adverbs
Objective 5.4	Uses prepositions
Objective 5.5	Uses conjunctions
Objective 5.6	Uses articles

CONCURRENT GOALS

FM A	Manipulation of Objects (all goals)
GM B:3.0	Bounces, catches, kicks, and throws ball
GM B:5.0	Rides and steers two-wheel bicycle
Adap A:1.0	Eats and drinks a variety of foods using appropriate utensils with little or no spilling
Adap B	Personal Hygiene (all goals)
Cog A:2.0	Watches, listens, and participates during small group activities
Cog A:3.0	Watches, listens, and participates during large group activities
Cog B	Demonstrates Understanding of Concepts (all goals)
Cog C:1.0	Groups objects, people, or events on the basis of specified criteria
Cog D:2.0	Places objects in series according to length or size
Cog D:3.0	Retells event in sequence
Cog E	Recalling Events (all goals)
Cog F:2.0	Makes statements and appropriately answers questions that require reasoning about objects, situations, or people
Cog G:1.0	Engages in imaginary play
Cog I:1.0	Demonstrates prereading skills
Soc A:2.0	Initiates cooperative activity
Soc A:3.0	Resolves conflicts by selecting effective strategy
Soc C	Knowledge of Self and Others (all goals)

DAILY ROUTINES

Routine events that provide opportunities for children to use descriptive words include the following:

Dressing	Snack time
Mealtime	Unstructured play time
Travel time	Transition time
Arrival and departure	Bathtime
Circle time at school	Bedtime

Example   Parents encourage children to use adjectives to describe objects or events during bathtime by commenting on the temperature of the water, the "wet" washcloth, or the "slippery" soap. (*SC B:5.1*)

Example   While playing "dinosaurs" with a friend, a child says, "I have more dinosaurs than you." (*SC B:5.2*)

ENVIRONMENTAL ARRANGEMENTS

■ Provide toys that promote communication and arrange the classroom into activity areas that include a dramatic play/house play center (see Environmental Arrangements in Section III and Dramatic Play Activities in Section V).

   Example   While playing with blocks and cars, Manuel says to Joey, "I'm in front of you." (SC B:5.4)

   Example   While Latifa is "eating" in the kitchen of the housekeeping area, she says, "Umm. This tastes good." (SC B:5.3)

■ Intervention strategies that involve environmental arrangements include the following:

Heterogeneous grouping	Piece by piece
Choices	Assistance
Forgetfulness	Sabotage
Visible but unreachable	Negotiation
Violation of expectations	

   Example (Choices)   The interventionist serves animal crackers for snack and children choose the ones they want to eat. The interventionist models the use of articles by saying, "I want *a* horse. What do you want?" Latifa says, "I want *a* lion." (*SC B:5.6*)

   Example (Violation of expectations)   Serving children blocks for "snack" provides opportunities for them to use descriptive words (e.g., "Blocks taste icky.") (*SC B:5.3*)

   Example (Assistance)   When a child is working on a puzzle with shapes or colors, put pieces into a clear container with a lid. The child will have to request the item by describing it (e.g., "I need the blue square.") (*SC B:5.1*)

PLANNED ACTIVITIES

Two examples of how to embed this goal and the associated objectives within activities are presented here. For a complete set of activities that address goals and objectives across domains, see Section V.

Feely Bag

Children gather small objects from a nature walk (leaves, flowers, pebbles, pinecones, seeds) and put them in a paper bag or large sock. One at a time, children reach into the bag without looking and describe the object they are touching. While children gather objects, the interventionist can encourage opportunities to use prepositions to describe where they found objects (e.g., under a rock, on the stump). Children use adjectives to describe the objects (e.g., "the stone is cold") and to make comparisons (e.g., "the rock is heavier than the feather"), and they use adverbs to modify verbs (e.g., "the feather moves slowly").

SC B

Example   While describing a pinecone, Latifa says, "It feels hard." Her interventionist prompts her by saying, "It feels hard *and...*" Latifa continues, "It feels hard and prickly." (*SC B:5.5*)

How Fast Do They Grow?

Children plant seeds in small planters or paper cups and measure their growth over time. The interventionist can introduce the activity by showing pictures of full-grown plants or flowers, and provide opportunities for children to use adjectives to describe the pictures. Choose seeds for plants that grow quickly, such as grass, corn, or beans. While children plant seeds, the interventionist should encourage them to describe how the soil, water, and seeds feel, to compare the different seeds using descriptive words (e.g., "this one's bigger"), and to use prepositions to describe the process (e.g., "the soil goes in the cup"). To extend this activity over time, children can measure plant growth on a piece of paper taped to the wall behind the plants.

Example   The interventionist has children mark the growth of their plants on pieces of tape placed on a wall. The interventionist guides Eric's hands to feel the pieces of tape and says, "Feel this, Eric. This is your plant's height and this is Maria's. Her plant is bigger than yours. Now here is your plant and here is Manuel's. Your plant is..." Eric says, "Bigger than Manuel's." (*SC B:5.2*)

PRESCHOOL CURRICULA WITH SIMILAR GOALS

The following preschool curricula provide information on this goal or similar goals. Interventionists whose programs have access to one or more of these curricula may refer to the referenced sections for additional programming strategies.

The Carolina Curriculum for Preschoolers with Special Needs
Sentence Construction

Portage Guide to Early Education Activity Cards
Language
- Uses compound sentences
- Uses articles *the* and *a* in speech

REFERENCES
Bloom, L., & Lahey, M. (1978). *Language development and language disorders.* New York: John Wiley & Sons.

SCB

SOCIAL DOMAIN

As children interact with caregivers, siblings, and peers, their social behaviors are shaped by the reactions and guidance of these significant people. As children grow up, they will be expected to function in group settings, to interact in socially appropriate ways, and to follow rules. Adults in children's environments are responsible for teaching and encouraging the development of social skills that will provide the foundation for understanding and participating in increasingly complicated social exchanges.

Infants are born dependent on caregivers to meet all their essential needs. The relationship that begins as a physiological necessity develops into a social and emotional bond between caregiver and child. Within the context of these first relationships with familiar adults, the infant is introduced to the rules of social initiations and responses. For example, when an infant cries, the caregiver responds by feeding, comforting, or changing the child. When the infant laughs, the caregiver usually responds positively by laughing, smiling, or talking to the baby.

The socialization process entails a progressive movement away from the caregiver as a provider of social stimulation and regulation. The child begins to play independently for short periods of time and to play in the presence of peers. As children learn to care for themselves, they first master necessary skills (e.g., putting on clothing) and later become aware of the social implications for the activity (e.g., wearing a bathing suit when swimming). As children mature, their sensitivity to social expectations increases, and they become more responsive to subtle cues provided by other social agents.

Interaction with peers requires a group of skills that develop gradually during the first 3 years of life and are refined as the child's experiential base grows. Two babies may begin playing together by pulling and grabbing, but this behavior will evolve into social play as the babies get older and learn how to interact with each other. During the preschool years, children begin to learn to play together cooperatively. Play often originates with children engaging in parallel play. At this stage, children watch and imitate other children as they play, and they increase their overall rate of communication and social interaction. In time, children begin to share ideas or activities. For example, one child shows another how to build a tower or make a water wheel turn. Eventually children learn to maintain their communicative interchanges and engage in cooperative play by working together toward a common goal (e.g., building a house together).

It is important to view the Social Domain as interdependent with other behavioral domains. Social interactions generally have motor, communicative, and cognitive dimensions. When a child asks a peer to help move a large block, he or she is using motor skills (maintaining balance), communication skills (using words to direct others), and cognitive skills (problem solving). In addition, examiners should observe children's use of social behaviors across a range of settings and activities in order to determine if their social skills are related to other factors. For example, a child who

Soc

219

repeatedly quarrels with one child may actually have the ability to resolve conflicts with other children or with siblings. A child with a motor impairment may have difficulty maintaining participation in gross motor activities but not in art or manipulative activities.

The Social Domain is composed of three strands. Strand A (Interaction with Others) focuses on the child's ability to maintain a relationship with play partners, engage in cooperative activities, and resolve conflicts using effective strategies. Strand B (Interaction with Environment) examines the child's ability to meet physical needs in socially appropriate ways and follow rules in different environments. Strand C (Knowledge of Self and Others) focuses on the child's ability to communicate personal likes and dislikes, relate identifying information about self and others, and accurately identify affect/emotions in others.

The Social Domain curriculum is divided into four sections: 1) Intervention Considerations, 2) Suggested Activities, 3) Using Activity-Based Intervention, and 4) Domain Goals. Intervention Considerations addresses important factors an interventionist may wish to consider prior to and when working with children who are at risk for or who have disabilities. Suggested Activities provides a selected list of activities from Section V of this volume that may be particularly helpful when working on social skills. This section also provides suggestions for additional materials that will increase the opportunities for children to practice targeted social skills. The third section provides an illustration of how to target IEP/IFSP goals in the Social Domain using an activity-based intervention approach. The final section, Domain Goals, provides suggestions for concurrent goals, daily routines, environmental arrangements, and planned activities in the home and classroom for each goal identified in the Social Domain of the AEPS Test for Three to Six Years. This section also lists other commercially available curricula that provide intervention activities for each goal.

INTERVENTION CONSIDERATIONS

General considerations when working on social goals are discussed below. For additional information on integrating children into programs for children without disabilities and promoting social interactions, see The AEPS Curriculum and Children with Severe Disabilities in Section III.

■ The influence of cultural values on children's social behavior should be considered when developing intervention goals and plans. Understanding a child's social and ethnic environment can help prevent culturally inappropriate expectations; conflicting demands; and frustration and confusion for teachers, family members, and the child. For example, family-oriented cultures may place less importance on a child's ability to interact with peers than more peer-oriented cultures. The best way to understand a family's values is by talking to them and learning about their culture.
■ Identify primary adults who interact with the child and include them in the child's program. Young children tend to exhibit the most sophisticated social skills in the presence of familiar adults and peers and in familiar settings.
■ Routine events in the child's environment provide many opportunities for learning socially appropriate behaviors. Many of the accepted social conventions we share are grounded in the simple daily routines we learned as children (e.g., saying hello to friends).

- The range of social styles in young children is broad, and children should be allowed to develop interaction skills that match their temperament. Particular attention should be paid to how children communicate.
- Often a child's unacceptable behavior can be greatly reduced or eliminated by substituting a more socially acceptable behavior. For example, if children are grabbing toys from each other, instead of reprimanding them for their behavior (e.g., "don't grab"), provide them with an acceptable way of accomplishing the goal (e.g., "Ask Joe to share"). Especially when working with children with communicative impairments, it is important to provide frequent models of the language they are lacking, as well as the means to communicate their wants and needs (i.e., an augmentative communication system).

SUGGESTED ACTIVITIES

Activities that are child oriented are likely to elicit more social interactions between peers than those that are adult oriented. Activities that require sharing and cooperation among children to complete (as opposed to solitary activities such as puzzles or pegboards) will often encourage spontaneous social interactions among peers. The following list of activities and materials may be particularly helpful for eliciting skills within the Social Domain. For a complete list of activities, see Section V.

- Make-It-Move Painting
- Body Tracing
- Group Murals
- Shoe Store
- Birthday Party
- Post Office
- Hospital or Doctor's Office
- Grocery Store
- Blockhead
- Box Town
- Mud Play
- Group Outdoor Games
- Board Games
- Puppets
- Large Blocks
- Tents

USING ACTIVITY-BASED INTERVENTION

An illustration of how an interventionist can incorporate activity-based strategies to enhance the development of a child's social skills is provided below. The child's targeted IEP/IFSP objective is to establish and maintain proximity with peers during unstructured, child-directed activities.

- During a free choice time, the interventionist *observes* Manuel watching another child driving cars on "roads" in the sandbox. She has *arranged the environment* in a way to capitalize on his interests, knowing that Manuel really enjoys playing with cars and trucks.
- The interventionist *follows the child's lead,* noticing Manuel's interest in the cars, and decides to join in the activity, playing with the cars too. She *prompts* Manuel verbally to join in the activity (e.g., "Come play over here, Manuel!"). If he does not respond, the interventionist *provides additional guidance to facilitate his play* by taking Manuel by the hand to a spot that is in close proximity to the other child and handing him a car.
- The interventionist purposefully *includes interesting materials* in the sandbox, such as a dump truck and a fire truck, to encourage Manuel and his peers to be involved and close to each other. A *limited number* of toys provides an opportunity for children to

negotiate and share, and other children *model* for Manuel these more advanced social skills. The interventionist uses *self-talk and parallel talk* during the activity, commenting, "We're driving cars and sitting with our friends."

DOMAIN GOALS

This section provides suggestions for concurrent goals, daily routines, environmental arrangements, and planned activities for the social goals listed in the AEPS Test for Three to Six Years. If an objective has been targeted, the interventionist can turn to the corresponding goal and determine which suggestions are relevant to address that objective. A standard format is used for each goal: 1)Strand, 2) Goal, 3) Objective(s), 4) Concurrent Goals, 5) Daily Routines, 6) Environmental Arrangements, 7) Planned Activities, and 8) Preschool Curricula with Similar Goals. Concurrent Goals list AEPS goals that can often be addressed at the same time the child works on the target goal or associated objectives. Daily Routines present a list of routine activities that may provide opportunities to practice targeted skills. The Environmental Arrangements should be considered when designing children's programs around child-initiated, routine, and planned activities. The Planned Activities offer examples of how to embed targeted goals within the context of planned activities. Finally, Preschool Curricula with Similar Goals list other curricula that can be used to supplement the AEPS Curriculum for Three to Six Years. If a given program has one or more of these preschool curricula, the interventionist can refer to the referenced sections to find additional programming strategies for the targeted goal or objective. Additional information on daily routines, environmental arrangements, planned activities, and themes is provided in Section III.

Strand A   Interaction with Others

G1.0   Has play partners
    1.1   Responds to peers in distress or need
    1.2   Establishes and maintains proximity to peers
    1.3   Initiates greetings to familiar peers
    1.4   Responds to affective initiations from peers

G2.0   Initiates cooperative activity
    2.1   Joins others in cooperative activity
    2.2   Maintains cooperative participation with others
    2.3   Shares or exchanges objects

G3.0   Resolves conflicts by selecting effective strategy
    3.1   Negotiates to resolve conflicts
    3.2   Uses simple strategies to resolve conflicts
    3.3   Claims and defends possessions

Strand B   Interaction with Environment

G1.0   Meets physical needs in socially appropriate ways
    1.1   Meets physical needs when uncomfortable, sick, hurt, or tired
    1.2   Meets observable physical needs
    1.3   Meets physical needs of hunger and thirst

G2.0   Follows context-specific rules outside home and classroom
    2.1   Seeks adult permission
    2.2   Follows established rules at home and in classroom

Soc

Strand C   Knowledge of Self and Others
  G1.0   Communicates personal likes and dislikes
     1.1   Initiates preferred activities
     1.2   Selects activities and/or objects
  G2.0   Relates identifying information about self and others
     2.1   States address
     2.2   States telephone number
     2.3   Knows birthday
     2.4   Names siblings and gives full name of self
     2.5   Knows gender of self and others
     2.6   Knows name and age
  G3.0   Accurately identifies affect/emotions in others and self consistent
         with demonstrated behaviors
     3.1   Accurately identifies affect/emotions of others
     3.2   Accurately identifies own affect/emotions

Strand A   Interaction with Others

GOAL 1.0   Has play partners

Objective 1.1   Responds to peers in distress or need
Objective 1.2   Establishes and maintains proximity to peers
Objective 1.3   Initiates greetings to familiar peers
Objective 1.4   Responds to affective initiations from peers

CONCURRENT GOALS

GM B	Play Skills (all goals)
Cog A	Participation (all goals)
Cog G	Play (all goals)
SC A	Social-Communicative Interactions (all goals)
SC B	Production of Words, Phrases, and Sentences (all goals)

DAILY ROUTINES

Routine events that provide opportunities for children to interact with and respond to peers include the following:

Arrival and departure
Circle time at school
Snack time
Unstructured play time
Transition time

Example   At the park, Manuel's mother encourages him, "Why don't you see if that little boy would like to play catch with you?" (*Soc A:1.0*)

Example   When Latifa enters the classroom, the interventionist whispers to Latifa's friend Alice, "Latifa's here." Alice looks at Latifa. The interventionist models, "Hi, Latifa!" and Alice imitates, "Hi, Latifa!" (*Soc A:1.3*)

ENVIRONMENTAL ARRANGEMENTS

■ Arrange the classroom into activity areas that include a dramatic play center (see Environmental Arrangements in Section III and Dramatic Play Activities in Section V). Providing small, well-defined activity areas increases the frequency of interactions between peers. Cooperation often occurs during pretend play while plans are made, roles assigned, play ideas exchanged, and conflicts negotiated. Provide materials that promote cooperative play:

- Adult-size wheelbarrows
- Balls
- Wagons
- Oversize blocks
- Big boxes
- Seesaws
- Rocking boats
- Play sets with many pieces, such as a barn with animals
- Dramatic play props (e.g., wagon for ambulance, large sheet for tent)
- Games (e.g., board or card games, group games)
- Puppets

   Example   Maria clings to her interventionist during free play, while carefully watching the children make "cookies" with Play-Doh. The interventionist notices Maria's interest in this activity and brings Maria over to the table. The interventionist joins in the play and encourages Maria; as soon as Maria appears comfortable, the interventionist fades out of the activity. (*Soc A:1.2*)

■ Any activity in which a child is seated at a table or is playing with other children should be arranged so that the child is in a position to make eye contact and interact with peers. Having children face each other or sit next to each other (as opposed to facing an empty space, sitting alone, or sitting next to an adult) encourages social interactions. Children who have physical disabilities should be positioned (with adaptive equipment if necessary) at the same level as their peers. Consult a qualified motor specialist for individual positioning considerations.

■ Consider the adult/child ratio in the classroom and whether the number or proximity of adults is influencing the frequency or types of child-to-child interactions. Be aware of the amount of "adult talk" as well as the number of adult–child interactions that occur and whether these factors stifle social interactions between peers.

   Example   Manuel falls down while trying to catch a ball and starts to cry. A classroom assistant starts toward him but the interventionist stops her. "Wait a second. He's not hurt. Let's see what happens." Manuel's friend Joey runs over, helps him up, and asks, "You okay?" (*Soc A:1.1*)

■ Arrange for the child to participate in small group activities with peers whose social skills are slightly advanced. When grouping children, consider individual peer preferences and make attempts to group children who are compatible. When including children with severe disabilities, make a special effort to group them with children who are willing to include them in play activities. The interventionist may need to provide children with suggestions about how children with severe impairments can participate.

   Example   The interventionist pairs Eric, who has a visual impairment, with his friend Joey during a music activity. The children hold hands while marching around the room. (*Soc A:1.2*)

■ Provide a slightly inadequate amount of materials for routine and unstructured play periods. Children will need to "negotiate" with peers to get materials. For example, provide only one glue container at the art center or serve snack family style (i.e., crackers on one plate, fruit in one bowl) to encourage children to request, share, and maintain close proximity during activities.

PLANNED ACTIVITIES

Two examples of how to embed this goal and the associated objectives within activities are presented here. For a complete set of activities that address goals and objectives across domains, see Section V.

Farm Animals

This activity can be introduced by reading a book on farm animals, showing pictures, talking about different farm animals (e.g., cows, horses, pigs), and singing "Old Mac-Donald Had a Farm." Materials include a toy barn, small plastic farm animals (one for each child), fences, a pond cut of blue construction paper, and a food trough. Opportunities for children to establish and maintain proximity, greet one another, and respond to affective initiations and distress are facilitated as the children interact through the animals around the barn, pond, and food. If the group has more than four children, it may be necessary to provide two barns to avoid crowding.

  Example   Timmy sits at the edge of the rug holding his cow. The interventionist prompts him, "Look Timmy. Joey's horse is drinking. Does your cow need a drink of water?" If Timmy does not respond, the interventionist models taking an animal over to the pond and gestures to Timmy to bring his cow. "My chicken is thirsty. Bring your cow, Timmy." (*Soc A:1.2*)

Veterinary Office

A veterinarian's office is set up in the dramatic play center. This might be introduced by having a veterinarian come visit the classroom or by reading a book about what happens at the veterinarian's office. Opportunities for social interactions can be increased by having children dress up as cats, dogs, and bunnies instead of using stuffed pets. Ears are made of construction paper and secured with a long strip of paper that circles the child's head, tails are made of strips of fabric, and whiskers are painted on faces with makeup. The interventionist can include a small wagon for an ambulance (requiring cooperation among children to use), cots for beds, a white coat for the vet, a table and chair for the receptionist's office, bandages, and cotton. As children help each other, opportunities arise to interact and practice skills such as responding to peers in distress or need.

  Example   Maria, pretending to be a cat, comes crying to the veterinarian's office. Latifa says, "It's okay. I'll help you." (*Soc A:1.1*)

PRESCHOOL CURRICULA WITH SIMILAR GOALS

The following preschool curricula provide information on this goal or similar goals. Interventionists whose programs have access to one or more of these curricula may refer to the referenced sections for additional programming strategies.

The Carolina Curriculum for Preschoolers with Special Needs
Interpersonal Skills
■ Greets familiar people with word or sign

The Creative Curriculum
Blocks
House Corner

Table Toys
Art
Sand and Water
Library Corner
Outdoors

High Scope—Young Children in ACTION
Language
■ Talking with other children and adults about personally meaningful experiences

Portage Guide to Early Education Activity Cards
Social
■ Chooses own friends
■ Plays with two or three children for 20 minutes in cooperative activity
■ Comforts playmates in distress
■ Greets familiar adults without reminder
■ Greets peers and familiar adults when reminded

GOAL 2.0   Initiates cooperative activity

Objective 2.1	Joins others in cooperative activity
Objective 2.2	Maintains cooperative participation with others
Objective 2.3	Shares or exchanges objects

CONCURRENT GOALS

GM B:3.0	Bounces, catches, kicks, and throws ball
Cog A	Participation (all goals)
Cog G	Play (all goals)
SC A	Social-Communicative Interactions (all goals)
SC B	Production of Words, Phrases, and Sentences (all goals)

DAILY ROUTINES

Routine events that provide opportunities for children to initiate cooperative activities include the following:

Circle time at school
Snack time
Unstructured play time (indoors and outdoors)

Example   Manuel's mother invites a friend who has a child the same age as Manuel over for coffee. After a few minutes, Manuel's mother suggests, "Why don't you show Emilio your toys?" Manuel takes Emilio to his room and says, "Hey, do you want to make a fort?" Emilio says, "I guess so." (*Soc A:2.0*)

   Example   Children bring a toy from home to show to other children during circle time and share during free play. (*Soc A:2.3*)

ENVIRONMENTAL ARRANGEMENTS

■ Arrange the classroom into activity areas that include a dramatic play center (see Environmental Arrangements in Section III and Dramatic Play Activities in Section V). Providing small, well-defined activity areas may increase the frequency of interactions between peers. Cooperation often occurs during pretend play while plans are made, roles assigned, play ideas exchanged, and conflicts negotiated. Provide materials that promote cooperation:

   – Adult-size wheelbarrows
   – Balls
   – Wagons
   – Oversize blocks
   – Big boxes
   – Seesaws
   – Rocking boats
   – Play sets with many pieces, such as a barn and animals
   – Dramatic play props (e.g., wagon for ambulance, large sheet for tent)
   – Games (e.g., board or card games, group games)
   – Puppets

   Example   The interventionist models how to make balloons fly in the air while shaking a blanket held by two or more children. During free play, Joey says to Timmy, "Play balloons! Hold it." (*Soc A:2.0*)

   Example   Latifa runs over to the "doctor's office." "I'm gonna be the doctor. Alice, let me give you a shot." (*Soc A:2.2*)

■ Any activity in which a child is seated at a table or is playing with other children should be arranged so that the child is in a position to make eye contact and interact with peers. Having children face each other or sit next to each other (as opposed to facing an empty space or sitting alone or next to an adult) encourages social interactions. Children who have physical disabilities should be positioned (with adaptive equipment if necessary) at the same level as their peers. Consult a qualified motor specialist for individual positioning considerations.

■ Consider the adult/child ratio in the classroom and whether the number or proximity of adults is influencing the frequency or types of child-to-child interactions. Be aware of the amount of "adult talk" as well as the number of adult–child interactions that occur and whether these factors stifle social interactions between peers.

■ Arrange for the child to participate in small group activities with peers whose social skills are slightly advanced. When grouping children, consider individual peer preferences and make attempts to group children who are compatible. When including children with severe disabilities, make a special effort to group them with children who are willing to include them in play activities.

   Example   A small group of children make "cakes" in the sand. Eric stirs in the sand with a stick but is not involved in the other children's play. The interventionist helps Eric have access to the play by commenting, "Hmm, I wonder how Eric could help make a cake." One child hands Eric a spoon and says, "I know, you can stir. Here, Eric." (*Soc A:2.0*)

■ Provide an inadequate amount of materials for a given activity. Children will need to "negotiate" with peers to get materials. For example, provide only two rolling pins for four children at the Play-Doh table or serve snack family style (i.e., crackers on one plate, fruit in one bowl) to encourage children to request and share during snack time. Children may find it easier to share if they know they can first finish their play and then share. Using the phrase, "Can I use that when you're done?" usually gets positive results. The interventionist provides models of this language.

PLANNED ACTIVITIES

Two examples of how to embed this goal and the associated objectives within activities are presented here. For a complete set of activities that address goals and objectives across domains, see Section V.

Let's Go Fishing!

Small groups of children take a ride together on a boat and go "fishing." The boat can be a rocking boat that seats four children or a boat constructed of large boxes. Fishing poles are created from yardsticks or branches with a string attached and a small magnet for the "hook." Fish are made of construction paper, decorated, and then made catchable by securing a paper clip to them. This activity provides opportunities for children to play cooperatively by rowing together in the boat, sharing poles (provide fewer poles than there are children), sharing fish they catch, and trading roles (e.g., being captain of the boat).

Water Fun

This expansion of water play provides some new twists by introducing novel materials to explore in the water. The interventionist presents an egg beater and a small squeeze bottle of soap to the children and demonstrates how to use the egg beater and a few drops of soap to make bubbles in the water. These items can be given to two children to share (several "sets" of the items may be needed). There should still be some standard water play materials in the tub, such as spoons, cups, bowls, water wheels, and funnels.

Example The interventionist watches Eric and Latifa play and notices that Eric is using the beater and Latifa has not had a turn. The interventionist says to Eric, "I wonder if Latifa would like a turn with the beater?" When Eric does not respond, the interventionist says, "Ask Latifa, 'Want the beater?'" (*Soc A:2.3*)

PRESCHOOL CURRICULA WITH SIMILAR GOALS

The following preschool curricula provide information on this goal or similar goals. Interventionists whose programs have access to one or more of these curricula may refer to the referenced sections for additional programming strategies.

The Carolina Curriculum for Preschoolers with Special Needs
Interpersonal Skills

The Creative Curriculum
Blocks

House Corner
Table Toys
Art
Sand and Water
Library Corner
Outdoors

High Scope—Young Children in ACTION

Language
■ Talking with other children and adults about personally meaningful experiences

Portage Guide to Early Education Activity Cards

Social
■ Chooses own friends
■ Explains rules of game or activity to others
■ Plays with four or five children in cooperative activity without constant supervision
■ Plays with two or three children for 20 minutes in cooperative activity
■ Takes turns with eight or nine other children
■ Follows rules in group games led by an older child
■ Takes turns
■ Asks permission to use toy that peer is playing with
■ Follows rules in group games led by adult
■ Follows rules by imitating actions of other children

GOAL 3.0   Resolves conflicts by selecting effective strategy

---

Objective 3.1	Negotiates to resolve conflicts
Objective 3.2	Uses simple strategies to resolve conflicts
Objective 3.3	Claims and defends possessions

CONCURRENT GOALS

GM B	Play Skills (all goals)
Cog A	Participation (all goals)
Cog F	Problem Solving (all goals)
Cog G	Play (all goals)
SC A	Social-Communicative Interactions (all goals)
SC B	Production of Words, Phrases, and Sentences (all goals)

DAILY ROUTINES

Routine events that provide opportunities for children to resolve conflicts include the following:

Dressing and undressing	Snack time
Mealtime	Unstructured play time (indoors and outdoors)
Travel time in car	Transition time
Arrival and departure	Bathtime
Circle time at school	Bedtime

Try to be receptive to children's solutions to conflicts that arise if the solutions do not interfere with established rules.

   Example   Manuel's mother wants Manuel to wear his warm red shirt to school, but Manuel wants to wear his Ninja turtle T-shirt. Manuel asks, "How about if I put this on, too?", indicating a sweatshirt. His mother agrees to his solution. (*Soc A:3.1*)

   Example   On the way to school, Latifa quarrels with her sister about who will sit in the front seat of the car. Latifa's father comments, "I wonder how both of you can get a turn sitting up front." Latifa says, "I know, I'll sit in front now and you can on the way home." (*Soc A:3.1*)

ENVIRONMENTAL ARRANGEMENTS

■ Provide cubbies or lockers in the classroom where children hang their coats and store personal belongings. Labeling lockers with names and pictures of children helps define a child's private space and personal belongings.

   Example   Manuel goes to Timmy's cubby and takes out his coat. Timmy, who communicates through sign language, grabs it from him. The interventionist stoops down between the two boys and says, "Tell him it's your coat. Tell him 'mine' [modeling how to sign the word *mine*]." Timmy signs MINE and reaches for his coat. (*Soc A:3.3*)

■ Arrange for children to participate in small group activities with peers whose abilities to negotiate are slightly advanced. When grouping children, consider individual peer preferences and make attempts to group children who are compatible. This arrangement may provide children with effective models to resolve conflicts when peers offer different strategies and may cut down on the number of conflicts that arise.

■ Provide a safe environment where children know they can go to an adult for help if they are unable to resolve conflicts with peers.

   Example   A child comes crying to the interventionist, "Joey took my truck!" "What did you do?" asks the interventionist. "I told him to give it to me but he didn't so I hit him." The interventionist says, "It's not okay to hit people. What else can you do?" The child replies, "Tell you." (*Soc A:3.2*)

■ Provide an inadequate amount of materials for a given activity. The children will need to negotiate with peers to get materials.

   Example   In the outdoor play area, there are three tricycles for 10 children. The children must negotiate with peers to get turns on the tricycles. When Latifa comes crying to the interventionist, "José won't get off!", the interventionist goes with Latifa to talk to José. "Latifa would like a turn, too. In 5 minutes, it will be Latifa's turn." That afternoon the interventionist sees Latifa go to another child on a tricycle and say, "Five more minutes, okay?" (*Soc A:3.1*)

PLANNED ACTIVITIES

Two examples of how to embed this goal and the associated objectives within activities are presented here. For a complete set of activities that address goals and objectives across domains, see Section V.

Washing Babies

Children wash rubber baby dolls in tubs of water. The interventionist may want to introduce the activity by talking about the different things families do for us (e.g., feed us, keep us safe and clean). The number of washtubs can be limited so that children must share (two or three children to a tub) but are not overly crowded during the activity. The interventionist provides materials such as soap, shampoo, washcloths, soft brushes, towels, baby powder, and doll clothes. Each child is allowed to choose a baby doll of his or her own, but the soap, shampoo, and washcloths are limited to provide opportunities for negotiation among children. Conflicts may arise as children partici-pate in this activity.

Example   Joey lays his doll on a towel and turns to get the baby powder. Latifa picks up her doll, and Joey crys out, "No! Mine!" and the two pull on the baby. Latifa points to Joey's baby and says, "No, it's my baby. There's your baby, Joey." (*Soc A:3.2*)

House Play

This dramatic play theme is fun for children because they all have experience with what happens around a home. Children enjoy taking on new roles (e.g., mom, dad) and pretending to cook, clean, and play in their own "house." The house can be a com-mercial playhouse, a house constructed from a large appliance box, or simply a desig-nated area of the classroom. Props include miniature appliances, table and chairs, cups, plates, pretend food, a cot with blankets and a pillow, dress-up clothes, and so forth. The interventionist can limit the number of desirable materials (e.g., portable tele-phone, fancy dress, hat or jewelry, a play car a child can fit into) that are available and introduce the different roles children might play to provide opportunities for them to resolve conflicts while negotiating for different materials and roles.

PRESCHOOL CURRICULA WITH SIMILAR GOALS

The following preschool curricula provide information on this goal or similar goals. Interventionists whose programs have access to one or more of these curricula may refer to the referenced sections for additional programming strategies.

The Carolina Curriculum for Preschoolers with Special Needs
Interpersonal Skills

The Creative Curriculum
Blocks
House Corner
Table Toys
Art
Sand and Water
Library Corner
Outdoors

Soc A

Portage Guide to Early Education Activity Cards

Social

- Asks permission to use toy that peer is playing with

Strand B   Interaction with Environment

GOAL 1.0   Meets physical needs in socially appropriate ways

Objective 1.1   Meets physical needs when uncomfortable, sick, hurt, or tired

Objective 1.2   Meets observable physical needs

Objective 1.3   Meets physical needs of hunger and thirst

CONCURRENT GOALS

FM A:3.0	Ties string-type fastener
GM A:1.0	Alternates feet walking up and down stairs
Adap A	Dining (all goals)
Adap B	Personal Hygiene (all goals)
Adap C	Dressing and Undressing (all goals)
Cog B:4.0	Demonstrates understanding of 10 different qualitative concepts
Cog B:7.0	Demonstrates understanding of seven different temporal relations concepts
Cog D:1.0	Follows directions of three or more related steps that are not routinely given
Cog F	Problem Solving (all goals)
SC A	Social-Communicative Interactions (all goals)
SC B	Production of Words, Phrases, and Sentences (all goals)

DAILY ROUTINES

Routine events that provide natural opportunities for children to meet physical needs in socially appropriate ways include the following:

Arrival and departure	Transition time
Mealtime	Snack time
Travel time in car	Bathtime
Circle time at school	Bedtime
Unstructured play time	

Example   As he prepares to go outside, Joey goes to his cubby and gets his sweater. (*Soc B:1.1*)

Example   Timmy walks into the kitchen and reaches for the water. His mother models the sign, WATER. Timmy imitates her model, and his mother gets him a glass of water. (*Soc B:1.2*)

ENVIRONMENTAL ARRANGEMENTS

- Arrange the classroom into activity areas that include a quiet area and a dramatic play center (see Environmental Arrangements in Section III and Dramatic Play Activities in Section V). The quiet area should be cozy and comfortable, with carpeting and soft pillows where one or two children can go to relax and engage in quiet activities. In the dramatic play center, children practice meeting physical needs through role play (e.g., pretend to prepare and eat meals, go to bed, dress and undress, and mend injuries in the "doctor's office").
- Provide cubbies or lockers for children to store personal belongings such as sweaters, coats, and a change of clothing. Children with different impairments may need their spaces adapted to make them accessible (e.g., lower a coat hook for a child who uses a wheelchair, label the cubby of a child who has a visual impairment with a strip of wool).

    Example Manuel whispers, "I peed" to his interventionist. She reassures Manuel, "It's okay. That happens sometimes. Get your clothes from your cubby and change in the bathroom." (*Soc B:1.2*)
- Provide a child-size sink (with soap and paper towels) in the classroom and bathroom. Stepping stools make regular sinks accessible to children; plastic tubs of soapy water make good sink substitutes. Adaptations may be necessary to make sinks accessible to children with motor impairments. Consult a qualified specialist.
- Provide children independent access to food and water (e.g., a child-size drinking fountain, plastic or paper cups to get water from the sink, healthy snack foods within reach). Adaptations may be necessary for children who have visual or motor impairments. If independent access is not possible, provide the child a way to meet physical needs (e.g., ask an adult for help).
- Occasionally fail to provide necessary materials or overlook a familiar or important component of a routine or activity. For example, do not have food immediately available for snack time, "forget" to remind children to put on their coats before going outside, or "forget" to remind them to wash their hands before snack time. Observe how children respond to these situations. Provide the least level of assistance necessary for children to meet their physical needs; discontinue this strategy if children become upset or frustrated.
- Place snack items or clothing so that they are visible but out of reach. For example, place preferred foods or drinks in sight but out of reach, requiring children to request items. Do not overuse this technique, and provide children with skills necessary to meet their physical needs.

PLANNED ACTIVITIES

Two examples of how to embed this goal and the associated objectives within activities are presented here. For a complete set of activities that address goals and objectives across domains, see Section V.

Making Pancakes

Children make pancakes for breakfast or snack. Materials include measuring cups, pancake mix, spoons, spatula, water, butter, syrup, bowl, hot plate, and frying pan. Children help measure the pancake mix, stir in water, pour batter into the frying pan, and eat the pancakes when they are cooked. Opportunities to meet physical needs are facilitated by not giving children pancakes until they request them, placing milk or water in small pitchers that children can pour themselves (or can request help from an adult), and having children wash their hands before eating. Close supervision will ensure safety during cooking activities.

Field Trip to a Farm

Children enjoy taking field trips, and a trip to a farm provides information about the source of some foods (e.g., milk from cows, bread from wheat). Field trips also provide opportunities for children to meet their physical needs in socially appropriate ways. Interventionists discuss what children should do if they need to go to the bathroom, are hungry or thirsty, or are not feeling well during the field trip. Field trips often take half a day or longer, and children become hungry, thirsty, or tired during the day and may need assistance voicing their needs.

   Example   Before the trip, Maria's interventionist tells her, "If you get tired or need anything, tell me what you need, okay?" Occasionally during the trip, the interventionist asks her, "How are you doing? Do you need anything?" Maria's communication board includes pictures of food, water, a toilet, and a bed. (*Soc B:1.3*)

PRESCHOOL CURRICULA WITH SIMILAR GOALS

The following preschool curricula provide information on this goal or similar goals. Interventionists whose programs have access to one or more of these curricula may refer to the referenced sections for additional programming strategies.

The Carolina Curriculum for Preschoolers with Special Needs
Responsibility

High Scope—Young Children in ACTION
Active Learning
■ Taking care of one's own needs

GOAL 2.0   Follows context-specific rules outside home and classroom

---

Objective 2.1   Seeks adult permission
Objective 2.2   Follows established rules at home and in classroom

---

CONCURRENT GOALS

Adap A:3.0   Displays social dining skills
Adap B   Personal Hygiene (all goals)
Adap C:2.0   Selects appropriate clothing and dresses self at designated times
Cog A   Participation (all goals)

Cog D:1.0   Follows directions of three or more related steps that are not routinely
              given
Cog F   Problem Solving (all goals)
Cog G:2.0   Engages in games with rules

DAILY ROUTINES

Routine events that provide natural opportunities for children to follow rules include
the following:

Dressing	Unstructured play time
Mealtime	Appointments and errands (e.g., grocery shopping, doctor's
Travel time	office)
Arrival and departure	Transition time
Circle time at school	Bathtime
Snack time	Bedtime

■ The interventionist should try to avoid using negative language (e.g., instead of saying, "Don't run," say, "Remember to walk inside"). Children should be reinforced
whenever they follow rules (e.g., "You did such a nice job cleaning up your toys.
Let's make cookies now"). The interventionist should be positive whenever possible.
    Example Before they go shopping, Latifa's mother asks her, "Do you want to
ride in the cart or walk?" Latifa chooses to walk, and her mother reminds her,
"Remember to stay next to me in the store and touch only the things we are going to
buy. Okay?" Latifa's mother reinforces her while they shop, telling her what a good
job she is doing and letting her help push the cart or carry items. (*Soc B:2.0*)
    Example During circle time, the interventionist discusses different classroom
rules and why they exist. "Remember, raise your hand if you want to say something.
If everyone talks at the same time, we can't hear anything!" (*Soc B:2.2*)

ENVIRONMENTAL ARRANGEMENTS

■ Materials should be kept in predictable locations, and rules should be established as
to how to use them. Often a child combines materials from different activity centers
or uses materials in different ways than originally intended. Follow the child's lead
and encourage the child's creativity, unless the play becomes dangerous or disrup-
tive. If a particular use of materials is not okay, make sure the child understands why
it is not acceptable and encourage the child to think of acceptable alternatives.
    Example Manuel wants to bring some blocks up on the climber to make a tele-
vision set. The interventionist says, "That's a good idea, Manuel, but we don't play
with blocks on the climber. If one fell it might hurt someone. Can you think of
another place to build your TV set?" (*Soc B:2.2*)
■ Establish a predictable routine at home and in the classroom, and provide children
with warnings before making transitions to new activities. A warning such as, "In
5 minutes we're going to clean up and go outside," allows children to complete the
activity they are engaged in and prepare for the upcoming activity.
■ Arrange the schedule and classroom so that children have opportunities to make
choices. Providing children with acceptable choices that fall within established rules
often eliminates power struggles between children and adults.

Example   Joey does not want to come sit in circle. The interventionist gives him a choice: "Joey, would you like to bring a chair to circle or sit on the floor?" (*Soc B:2.2*)

■ Arrange for the child to participate in small group activities with peers whose ability to follow rules is slightly advanced.

Example   Manuel and Joey are eating a snack. Manuel finishes his snack, throws away his napkin, and asks (providing a model for Joey), "Can I go outside?" Joey gets up and asks, "Me too?" The interventionist responds, "Thanks for asking. You both can go outside." (*Soc B:2.1*)

PLANNED ACTIVITIES

Two examples of how to embed this goal and the associated objectives within activities are presented here. For a complete set of activities that address goals and objectives across domains, see Section V.

Bug Search

Children search outside for bugs to look at under a magnifying glass. The interventionist provides materials such as magnifying glasses and small plastic tubs with wire mesh lids or plastic lids with holes poked through for collecting the bugs. The interventionist outlines general classroom rules and any special rules before the activity begins. Before going outside, the interventionist might ask the children to line up and wait quietly for the rest of their friends. The interventionist might ask the children, "What do you do if you need to go to the bathroom when we're outside?" Rules specific to the activity should be few in number, and the children should be reinforced for remembering them. Examples of rules are 1) keep the magnifying glasses on the table so everyone can use them; and 2) let the bug loose after you have looked at it, so it does not get hurt.

Spiders

Children make spiders of black construction paper, cutting circles for the body and eight black strips for legs that are to be glued or taped to the body. Eyes can be made with glitter, markers, or small circles of a different colored paper. To provide opportunities for children to follow rules, they may need to be reminded of general rules and made aware of any rules specific to the activity. Examples of rules are 1) ask permission if you need to leave the group, and 2) stay at the table while using glue or glitter.

PRESCHOOL CURRICULA WITH SIMILAR GOALS

The following preschool curricula provide information on this goal or similar goals. Interventionists whose programs have access to one or more of these curricula may refer to the referenced sections for additional programming strategies.

The Carolina Curriculum for Preschoolers with Special Needs

Responsibility

The Creative Curriculum

Blocks
House Corner
Table Toys

Table Toys
Art
Sand and Water
Library Corner
Outdoors

Portage Guide to Early Education Activity Cards

Social
■ Stays in own yard area

Strand C   Knowledge of Self and Others

GOAL 1.0   Communicates personal likes and dislikes

Objective 1.1   Initiates preferred activities
Objective 1.2   Selects activities and/or objects

CONCURRENT GOALS

Adap A:1.0   Eats and drinks a variety of foods using appropriate utensils with little or no spilling
Adap C:2.0   Selects appropriate clothing and dresses self at designated times
Cog A:1.0   Initiates and completes age-appropriate activities
Cog B   Demonstrates Understanding of Concepts (all goals)
Cog F:2.0   Makes statements and appropriately answers questions that require reasoning about objects, situations, or people
Cog G   Play (all goals)
Cog I:1.0   Demonstrates prereading skills
SC A:1.0   Uses words, phrases, or sentences to inform, direct, ask questions, and express anticipation, imagination, affect, and emotions
SC B   Production of Words, Phrases, and Sentences (all goals)
Soc A:2.0   Initiates cooperative activity

DAILY ROUTINES

Routine events that provide natural opportunities for children to communicate their personal likes and dislikes include the following:

Dressing
Mealtime
Circle time at school
Snack time
Unstructured play time
Bathtime
Bedtime

   Example   Latifa's mother teases, "I have a chocolate cake in the kitchen, but I don't know anyone who likes cake." Latifa says, "I do!" (*Soc C:1.0*)
   Example   While reading a book about animals, the interventionist asks, "Who likes dogs?" Maria doesn't answer, so the interventionist asks her, "Do you like dogs, Maria?" and Maria shakes her head no. (*Soc C:1.0*)

Soc C

240

ENVIRONMENTAL ARRANGEMENTS

- Have materials available that are fun and interesting for children to play with during unstructured play periods and arrange the classroom into activity areas that include a dramatic play center (see Environmental Arrangements in Section III and Dramatic Play Activities in Section V). As often as possible, allow children to choose activities. Rotate theme centers and materials to keep centers exciting and interesting to children.

   Example   The interventionist shows Timmy a block, a ball of Play-Doh, and a crayon and asks, "Timmy, what do you want to do, play with blocks, play with Play-Doh, or draw a picture?" Timmy points to the Play-Doh. (*Soc C:1.2*)

   Example   Joey rushes to the "fire station" to put on one of the fire hats. (*Soc C:1.1*)

- Introduce new and unusual foods (e.g., pineapple, avocados, lemons, kiwis, mushrooms) during snack time along with familiar food items (e.g., crackers, cheese, fruit).

   Example   Eric grimaces after taking a bite of a lemon and states, "I don't like it." (*Soc C:1.0*)

PLANNED ACTIVITIES

Two examples of how to embed this goal and the associated objectives within activities are presented here. For a complete set of activities that address goals and objectives across domains, see Section V.

Tasting Party

This activity is particularly interesting when a classroom is composed of children from different cultural backgrounds. Children can indicate different foods they enjoy, and the interventionist can ask caregivers what foods the children eat in their households. Examples include salsas, curries, sweet rice, and spring rolls. Opportunities for children to communicate personal likes and dislikes occur as children get ready for the activity (e.g., choose who they would like to sit next to at the table), participate in the activity (e.g., select foods they would like to taste and communicate which foods they like or dislike), and complete the activity (e.g., choose which activity they would like to go to next).

Piñata Party

Piñatas are easy to make and even more fun to break. A large balloon is blown up, and children cover the balloon with thin strips (approximately 1 inch by 12 inches) of newspaper that have been soaked in diluted paste or glue. The balloon is allowed to dry for several days and then painted and decorated. After the paint dries, a small hole is cut in the piñata, the balloon is broken, and the piñata is filled with small bags of nutritious treats. Traditionally, a piñata is hung and children take turns hitting it with a stick until it breaks and the treats spill out. An alternative is to let children pass the piñata at snack time and take out a treat. Children communicate likes and dislikes throughout this process by discussing whether they like the feel of the paste, choosing the color to paint the piñata, and deciding what treats to put inside of the piñata.

PRESCHOOL CURRICULA WITH SIMILAR GOALS

The following preschool curricula provide information on this goal or similar goals. Interventionists whose programs have access to one or more of these curricula may refer to the referenced sections for additional programming strategies.

The Carolina Curriculum for Preschoolers with Special Needs
Responsibility

The Creative Curriculum
Blocks
House Corner
Table Toys
Art
Sand and Water
Library Corner
Outdoors

Portage Guide to Early Education Activity Cards
Social
■ Stays in own yard area

GOAL 2.0   Relates identifying information about self and others

---

Objective 2.1	States address
Objective 2.2	States telephone number
Objective 2.3	Knows birthday
Objective 2.4	Names siblings and gives full name of self
Objective 2.5	Knows gender of self and others
Objective 2.6	Knows name and age

CONCURRENT GOALS

FM B:2.0	Prints first name
Cog E:2.0	Recalls verbal sequences
SC A	Social-Communicative Interaction (all goals)
SC B	Production of Words, Phrases, and Sentences (all goals)

DAILY ROUTINES

Routine events that provide natural opportunities for children to relate identifying information about themselves and others include the following:

Soc C

Mealtime
Circle time at school
Snack time
Unstructured play time
Transition time

 Example   During dinner, Joey looks at his sister and says, "Milk." Joey's mother prompts him, modeling, "Lisa, milk please..." Joey says, "Lisa, milk." (*Soc C:2.4*)

 Example   When visitors such as parents and volunteers come to the classroom, the interventionist directs children to tell the guests their names and ages. Children communicate with a name sign, talk box with their name and age programmed into it, or other augmentative communication systems. (*Soc C:2.6*)

ENVIRONMENTAL ARRANGEMENTS

- In the large group area, provide a calendar with removable numbers and symbols to denote special days (e.g., cake symbol for birthdays). In addition to being highlighted on the calendar, birthdays can be an inspiration for classroom decoration. Colorful birthday balloons of construction paper both name a child and give the child's birthdate. Display balloons at child level, so that children can find their balloons and talk about their birthdays.

   Example   When the calendar is discussed in the morning, the interventionist points to the cake and says, "And whose birthday is this?" Alice says, "Mine. 'Cember..." The interventionist models, "December 10th," and Alice imitates, "December 10th." (*Soc C:2.3*)

- Display examples of children's names around the classroom. Label their cubbies, personal belongings, and artwork and include a "star helper" chart in the classroom. Write children's names on a piece of tagboard and place a moveable star next to the helper's name. The star helper for the day assists the staff in such tasks as setting the table for snack or being the leader in lines. (*Soc C:2.4*)

- Arrange the classroom into activity areas that include a dramatic play center and vary "themes" frequently (see Environmental Arrangements in Section III and Dramatic Play Activities in Section V). For example, during one week, create a "post office" where children are encouraged to identify their names and addresses as they write and mail letters. Another week, create a "doctor's office" where the "intake" process facilitates practice in giving identifying information like name, address, telephone number, age, birthdate, and gender. Many other themes also provide opportunities for children to relay identifying information.

- Include pictures of children and their families in the classroom. Children share their pictures with the class (perhaps during group time) and hang their pictures in the classroom. Adults provide children with opportunities to name their siblings and themselves by showing an interest in their pictures and asking them to talk about their families.

- Have a telephone(s) with readable numbers in the classroom. Post children's telephone numbers in big numbers on a telephone number list. Children pretend to call home and talk to family members or call their friends. Some caregivers may not want their telephone numbers disclosed, and permission should be obtained prior to this activity.

PLANNED ACTIVITIES

Two examples of how to embed this goal and the associated objectives within activities are presented here. For a complete set of activities that address goals and objectives across domains, see Section V.

ME Books (see Books/Book Making in Section V)

Children make books about themselves by stapling paper together or by making more elaborate creations with fancy covers (e.g., wallpaper sample books) and bindings made with yarn tied through punched holes. Children are asked to bring pictures of themselves, pictures of their families, and pictures of their homes. If no pictures are available, children can draw pictures with crayons or markers. Opportunities can be provided for children to relate identifying information by giving their names, ages, birthdays, siblings' names, addresses, and telephone numbers. The books might follow a format such as "My name is _____. I am _____ years old," and so forth. The interventionist will need to provide the least level of assistance necessary for children to complete their books, and children will have opportunities to practice this information as they "read" their books.

Example   Eric, who has a visual impairment, uses thin cardboard shapes (e.g., an outline of a child to represent himself, a number 4 for his age) in addition to written words to make his ME book. Eric reads his book by touching the outlined shapes and explaining what they represent. (*Soc C:2.6*)

Post Office

Children write a letter, put it in an envelope with a "stamp," and "mail" it in a mailbox (e.g., a shoebox with a slit cut in the lid). The interventionist can provide a variety of art materials, such as rubber stamps and stamp pads, stickers, markers, crayons, and pencils for children who cannot yet write letters but like to make pictures. Throughout this activity, the interventionist provides opportunities for children to relate identifying information about themselves and others. As children decide to whom they will write their letters, the interventionist might suggest their siblings and ask the siblings' names. The interventionist prompts children to "write" their names, ages, and telephone numbers (in case someone wants to call). When children address the envelopes, the interventionist asks them their own addresses.

Example   As the interventionist writes down a child's return address, she says, "And this letter is from…", pausing to allow the child a chance to say, "Alice Morris." (*Soc C:2.4*)

PRESCHOOL CURRICULA WITH SIMILAR GOALS

The following preschool curricula provide information on this goal or similar goals. Interventionists whose programs have access to one or more of these curricula may refer to the referenced sections for additional programming strategies.

The Carolina Curriculum for Preschoolers with Special Needs
Self-Concept

High Scope—Young Children in ACTION
Language
■ Expressing feelings in words
■ Talking with other children and adults about personally meaningful experiences

Portage Guide to Early Education Activity Cards

Language
- Tells address
- Tells telephone number
- Tells gender when asked
- Tells full name when requested

Cognitive
- Tells month and day of birthday

GOAL 3.0   Accurately identifies affect/emotions in others and self consistent with demonstrated behaviors

---

Objective 3.1   Accurately identifies affect/emotions of others

Objective 3.2   Accurately identifies own affect/emotions

CONCURRENT GOALS

Cog F:2.0	Makes statements and appropriately answers questions that require reasoning about objects, situations, or people
SC A:1.0	Uses words, phrases, and sentences to inform, direct, ask questions, and express anticipation, imagination, affect, and emotions
SC B:1.0	Uses verbs
SC B:3.0	Asks questions
SC B:4.0	Uses pronouns
SC B:5.0	Uses descriptive words
Soc A:1.0	Has play partners

DAILY ROUTINES

Routine events that provide opportunities for children to accurately identify affect/emotions in others and themselves that are consistent with demonstrated behaviors include the following:

Mealtime
Travel time
Arrival and departure
Circle time at school
Snack time
Unstructured play time
Transition time

Caregivers and interventionists facilitate the acquisition of this goal by labeling their own affect/emotions (e.g., "I like the picture you made for me. It makes me happy"). Often it is possible to read a child's affect and emotion and model for the child (e.g., "You didn't like it when Tom took your car. You must be angry").

Soc C

Example   During circle time, Manuel's interventionist has each child look at a "feelings" chart (the chart has pictures of children; e.g., one sad, one angry, one happy, one lonely) and point to or talk about how they feel that day. Manuel points to the angry picture, and his interventionist asks, "Why are you angry?" and Manuel responds, "Latifa won't share." (*Soc C:3.2*)

ENVIRONMENTAL ARRANGEMENTS

■ Arrange the classroom into activity areas that include a dramatic play center (see Environmental Arrangements in Section III and Dramatic Play Activities in Section V). Dramatic play centers provide opportunities for children to identify different affect/emotions during pretend play.

   Example   Maria and Latifa are playing in the "doctor's office." The interventionist asks Latifa how her "patient" is feeling. Latifa responds, "She's sad, but I'm fixing her." (*Soc C:3.1*)

■ Provide books and story audiotapes about affect and emotions in the library. Display pictures of children with different emotions in the classroom. Sing songs and do finger plays that explore affect and emotions (e.g., "If you're happy and you know it, clap your hands").

PLANNED ACTIVITIES

Two examples of how to embed this goal and the associated objectives within activities are presented here. For a complete set of activities that address goals and objectives across domains, see Section V.

Play-Doh Families

Children create little people out of Play-Doh to represent families. The interventionist provides big and little gingerbread men and women cookie cutters as well as cutters to represent children's pets, such as cats, dogs, and rabbits. While children share materials, the interventionist models for the children, labeling his or her own affect: "Thank you for sharing, Alice. That makes me feel good." If children get into conflicts during the activity, the interventionist asks for identification of other people's emotions: "How do you think Timmy must feel? He doesn't have any Play-Doh. Let's share some with him." As family members are created of Play-Doh, the interventionist prompts children to communicate how their "people" are feeling and to talk about their own affect and emotions.

House Cleaning

Children use sponges, water, paper towels, toy brooms, and a toy vacuum cleaner to clean the house play center. The interventionist prompts children to think about how family members feel when they help around the house and says, "I bet it makes your mom very happy when you help clean up" or "How does your mom feel when you help her at home?" Throughout the activity, as children share, trade, and exchange materials, the interventionist should be aware of opportunities for children to label affect and emotions in themselves or in others. (See Environmental Arrangements in Section III and Dramatic Play Activities in Section V for ideas on how to set up a house play center.)

PRESCHOOL CURRICULA WITH SIMILAR GOALS

The following preschool curricula provide information on this goal or similar goals. Interventionists whose programs have access to one or more of these curricula may refer to the referenced sections for additional programming strategies.

The Carolina Curriculum for Preschoolers with Special Needs
Self-Concept

High Scope—Young Children in ACTION
Language
- Expressing feelings in words
- Talking with other children and adults about personally meaningful experiences

Portage Guide to Early Education Activity Cards
Social
- States feelings about self: angry, happy, love
- Shows understanding of feelings by verbalizing love, anger, sadness, laughter, and so forth
- Comforts playmates in distress

Planned Activities

CONTENTS

INTRODUCTION

When working with teachers, interventionists, and support staff, we are often asked to suggest planned activities that meet two important criteria: 1) they provide appropriate and frequent opportunities for embedding children's IEP/IFSP goals and objectives, and 2) they are interesting and fun to children. During the 15 years that we have used activity-based intervention, we have tried hundreds of activities with infants and young children who are at risk for or who have disabilities. The activities described in this section of the curriculum are those we have found to be generally useful for children whose development ranges from 3 to 6 years .

We selected the activities that follow because they can generally be introduced throughout the child's day. Some of the suggested activities target specific skill areas (e.g., gross motor domain), whereas others may permit the embedding of children's goals from several domains. For example, a dress-up activity involves children developing peer relationships, manipulating objects, talking and listening, and engaging in pretend behaviors.

In addition to choosing appropriate activities for children, materials for the activity should be carefully chosen. Both activity and materials should be selected to help children practice their targeted goals and objectives. Materials used for multiple purposes are generally preferable to those with only one specific use. Commercial toys are often designed for one purpose, whereas materials such as sand, water, blocks, or paints invite involvement and use in a variety of ways. Materials should be selected that stimulate child initiations and actions; therefore, materials requiring constant adult intervention and guidance should be used sparingly. Finally, materials should be selected that are relevant and meaningful to children as they participate in daily and routine events at home and in the community.

When planning activities, it is important to remember that most children prosper when offered a consistent daily routine, either at home or at a center. The interventionist or caregiver should first devise a daily schedule. An example of a daily schedule for a center-based program is contained in Figure III.5 (see p. 32). It may be useful to plan activities for specific times of the day, with the understanding that child-initiated activities may supersede the interventionist's planned activity.

As shown in Table V.1., a variety of activities within and across domains can be planned, and children should be permitted to choose between activities or make choices within activities (e.g., "What color of paint would you like?") when appropriate. Activities and the interventionist's responses should focus on encouraging process rather than product. The focus should be on the learning that occurs during the activity, rather than the final product of the activity. For example, during an art activity, the interventionist supplies children with paper, scissors, glue, and crayons and asks how they might be used to create a butterfly. The goal is to stimulate child initiations, problem solving, and manipulation of objects, all process-oriented activities that possess a myriad of teaching and learning possibilities.

When guiding activities, the interventionist should follow the child's lead whenever possible and expand on child initiations. The interventionist should observe and wait until a child responds before offering help, and should provide the least support necessary for the child's successful completion of an activity. On occasion, unsuccessful completion of a task offers rich training opportunities. Adults tend to ask children many questions that only require one-word responses. Interventionists should ask questions sparingly and use open-ended questions that generally require children to use more

Table V.1.   Activities helpful for eliciting skills within a certain domain

Fine Motor	Gross Motor
Construction: Stringing, Weaving	Games: Obstacle Course; Follow the Leader; Duck, Duck, Goose
Literacy/Communication: The Writing Center	
Dramatic Play: Post Office	Dramatic Play: Police Officers
Art: Group Fingerpainting	Make it Move: Targets
Adaptive	**Cognitive**
Dramatic Play: Washing Babies, Restaurant	Literacy/Communication: Group Story
Make it Change: Cooking	Construction/Manipulation: Paper Chains; Blocks: Unit and Large
Construction/Manipulation: Dressing Babies	Dramatic Play: Hospital or Doctor's Office
Social-Communicative	Games: What's Missing?, Teddy Bear Counting Game
Literacy/Communication: Audiotape Recorder, Puppets, Acting Out Stories, Books/Book Making	**Social**
Art: Fall Colors	Dramatic Play: Birthday Party, House play, Circle Time (Group Time)
	Exploratory: Bubbles
	Art: Group Murals

language. Typically, open-ended questions begin with *what, how,* or *why* (e.g., "What will happen if you mix yellow with green?", "How do you do that?"). It is helpful for the caregiver or interventionist to describe actions, objects, and events while a child is participating in an activity. A running verbal account may enhance the child's learning during activities.

The activity descriptions that follow have been organized into the following categories: Art, Dramatic Play, Construction/Manipulation, Exploratory, Games, Literacy/Communication, Make-it-Change, Make-it-Move, and Nature Activities. Although most of the activities listed in this section incorporate skills across domains, some activities may be particularly helpful for eliciting skills within a specific domain. These activities are also described in the introductions to the domains in Section IV.

ART ACTIVITIES

Art activities provide children opportunities for self-expression. Creative activities involve all aspects of the child—cognitive, motor, and social/emotional. Interventionists should encourage children's imagination, and art is a useful vehicle. The interventionist should try not to make models for children but instead encourage children's ideas through self-expression. For example, if a child painting at the easel experiments with fingerprints or gets a leaf and paints it, both may be meaningful learning experiences. Children should be encouraged to write their names on completed art work (children can make a mark for their names if they are unable to print letters). The first word most children learn to write is their name.

Art centers can be set up with materials that provide a multitude of opportunities for children to engage in creative projects and develop fine motor skills. (For more information about setting up activity centers, see Environmental Arrangements in Section III.) Available materials can be rotated within the art center to maintain the child's interest and enhance learning opportunities. Materials used should be nontoxic and safe for children to use independently. Materials that might be included in the art center include the following:

- *Surfaces for drawing and writing:* easels, tabletops, walls covered with paper, chalk-boards, sidewalks
- *Paper materials for writing:* note pads, recycled paper, computer paper, butcher paper, origami paper, tissue paper, scraps from a local print shop, junk mail
- *Drawing/writing tools:* pencils, pens, crayons, chalk, Magic Markers, felt pens, colored pencils, fingerpaints, watercolors, tempera paints
- *Adhesive materials:* paste, glue, tape, sticky dots, Scotch tape (in a desktop dispenser), hole punches, staplers, stamps with stamp pads, templates
- *Scissors:* safety scissors, right- and left-handed scissors, training scissors, loop-handed scissors
- *Collage/construction items:* pinecones, leaves, seeds, buttons, yarn, fabrics, paper bags, paper plates, building materials (e.g., wood scraps, boxes, tiles, cardboard tubes, wall-paper, newspaper)

Body Tracing

Children lie down on pieces of butcher paper while a peer or the interventionist out-lines their bodies. The outlines are taped to the wall or floor and children are encour-aged to paint or draw in their faces and clothes. A mirror should be close by so children can look at themselves. The interventionist asks questions about such things as color of eyes and hair and points out body parts. This activity encourages cooperation, self-concept development, and creativity.

Collages

Children create collages out of scrap materials available in the home or classroom. Items that the children gather in nature make beautiful collages, as do paper scraps, material scraps, buttons, wood, macaroni, and pictures from magazines. Meat trays or paper plates work well for dividing collage materials so that children can see all avail-able materials. Collage material collections, small containers of glue, and 8- by 10-inch pieces of cardboard or heavy paper are placed around the table. The interventionist might put buttons and sequins in one tray, construction paper scraps and tissue paper in another, and yarn, string, wallpaper, and stick-on stars in another. Children walk around the table with a meat tray or piece of cardboard to collect materials to glue on wallpaper, a paper plate, meat tray, or heavy cardboard.

Dinosaur Eggs

Children make dinosaur eggs by cutting out oval shapes from paper and decorating them with crayons, markers, and glitter. Children have the opportunity to cut the eggs, cut out shapes with straight or curved lines as decorations for the eggs, and cut in half a piece of colored paper on which to glue their egg. Children may have many other ideas.

Fall Colors

This activity has many variations, all of which include painting with fall colors such as red, orange, and yellow. The children paint on any type of paper and may enjoy cutting out paper in the shapes of leaves to paint. The interventionist can cut out a large tree trunk to put on the wall of the classroom. After the leaves dry, the children can hang them on the tree. Children pick up leaves on a fall walk and paint them, make prints using the leaves, or spatter paint around the leaves by placing them on a piece of paper and using a toothbrush to spatter paint over them.

Feet Painting

Children take off their shoes and paint with their feet on a big piece of paper. This is a very messy project, and it helps to have tubs of warm water, soap, and towels to clean up. Children should be allowed to do as much for themselves as possible.

Group Fingerpainting

Children fingerpaint as a group on a large sheet of paper on the floor or table. Powdered tempera is placed in shaker bottles or small bowls, and children sprinkle paint and starch on paper and use their hands to mix and change colors. Fingerpainting can be done to music, as the interventionist models drawing shapes, letters, and names. The activity promotes cooperation, motor abilities, and practice in color concepts.

Group Murals

Group painting presents opportunities for cooperation and creativity because it encourages children to interact with peers, cooperate, and share. Children can discuss what they want to draw and how to arrange the elements on the paper, wall, or chalkboard. Children can choose what part they want to paint and can choose to work together.

Group Painting Projects

Children participate in creating the environmental theme in the dramatic play center or create other projects such as a river made of paper on the floor. Examples of group projects are painting large constructions such as a bus or fire engine made of a refrigerator box or painting the "river" in the "woods" dramatic play center.

Marble Painting

The class gathers shoe boxes or deep cooking tins, white paper cut to fit inside the boxes or tins, marbles of various sizes, several colors of tempera paint in shallow cups, spoons, smocks, tarps, and cleanup materials. Children first place a piece of paper in a box or tin. They then choose a marble, drop it in the paint, spoon it out, and drop it in the box or cooking tin. When the box is moved in different directions, the painted marble will make a design. Two or more children can move a box together.

Painting

Children enjoy fingerpainting, painting with their feet, easel painting, painting with watercolors, and painting large objects (e.g., making a playhouse by painting a refrigerator box and cutting out windows and doors, painting outdoor play structures or walls with paint or colored water). A variety of materials is used for painting activities, including brushes, toothbrushes, sponges, assorted shapes to print with, watercolors, and tempera paints and paintbrushes.

Paper Bag Animals

Children make animal puppets of small lunch sacks and glue on construction paper, fabric, buttons, and yarn. They make their puppets "talk" by putting one hand in the sack and moving the "mouth" up and down. Children can operate their puppets for a puppet show or play, stimulating creativity as well as motor and communication skills. This activity should be presented in a flexible manner, and children should be prompted to develop their own ideas.

Potato Prints

This activity requires a large potato for every two children, a cookie cutter, a sharp knife, a pie pan, liquid tempera, paper towels, and suitable paper. The interventionist cuts the potato in half, presses the cookie cutter into the potato, and cuts around it with a knife to make a shape. The children pour tempera on a pad of paper towels in the pie pan, dip the potato in, and print. This activity is useful for developing creativity, motor, and math skills.

Printing

Printing activities include 1) using objects dipped in paint to form a repeating pattern on paper and 2) pressing a blank piece of paper on a prepared surface, then removing the paper to lift the print from the surface. Materials needed for these activities include liquid tempera in a shallow pan; a variety of papers; and objects such as corks, cookie cutters, plastic blocks, thread spools, pieces of Styrofoam, sponges, leaves, or flowers.

DRAMATIC PLAY ACTIVITIES

The dramatic play center, whether a hospital or a dollhouse, provides children with the opportunity to use cognitive, social, social-communication, and motor skills. Children pretend to be various characters, and dramatic play centers provide excellent contexts for them to experiment with forms of communication they have been exposed to at home and in their community. Dramatic play facilitates cooperation with peers as children make plans, assign roles, exchange play ideas, and negotiate conflicts.

The most common role-play theme for promoting cooperation is house or family play, which can be extended to include baby washing and care, food identification and preparation, and literacy activities. The house play area may include a telephone, books, pads and pencils, newspapers, blackboards, and calculators. Children practice dining skills, personal hygiene, and dressing and undressing skills as they act out dramatic play scenarios. Children also work on gross motor goals in a naturally occurring context while engaging in dramatic play.

Ideas for dramatic play are endless, and children should be encouraged to provide suggestions for themes of interest to them. Theme areas and props will vary according to the different cultural and experiential backgrounds of children. Changing materials in the dramatic play area renews children's interest and creates new communication opportunities. Dramatic play is an excellent context for children to practice cognitive skills, and props should be selected that will provide opportunities for children to practice targeted goals. For example, if a child has a goal to sort objects on the basis of physical attributes, include materials such as socks, utensils, and coins that can be sorted by color, shape, or size.

In developing themes for the dramatic play center, the interventionist should use his or her imagination and follow children's initiation. One interventionist developed "Max's room" from the story, *Where the Wild Things Are* (Sendak, 1963), and later the "forest" of the Wild Things was developed. Another interventionist created the scene from *Mr. Gumpy's Outing* (Burningham, 1970) by helping children make animal costumes and construct a pretend boat. Children listened to the story and then acted it out over and over.

When developing a dramatic play center theme, start with a skeleton setup and add props as appropriate. Examples of theme areas with suggestions for props follow below.

House Theme

- Books to read to dolls or stuffed animals
- Dolls, doll clothes, dishes
- Empty food, toiletry, and cleaning containers
- Telephone books with children's names, addresses, and telephone numbers; cookbooks; newspapers
- Telephone, message pad, pencils
- Blankets and pillows
- Dishes, pans, plastic food, kitchen utensils
- Dress-up clothes with different kinds of fasteners, such as buttons, string-type fasteners, zippers, and Velcro fasteners; hats; mirrors
- Games and other props children want to add

Store Theme

- Carts, wagons
- Food, cans, boxes
- Pretend money
- Paper, pencil
- Dress-up clothing
- Purse, billfold

Farm Theme

- Small tools
- Dress-up clothing
- Stuffed animals
- Large boxes for barns
- Dishes to feed animals
- Plants, seeds
- Plastic fruit, veggies

Airplane

Props for this activity include paper and pencils for tickets, assortment of coins and play money, maps or an atlas, cash register, travel magazines, small trays with plastic food and utensils, suitcases with luggage tags, travel brochures, pilot and steward uniforms, several chairs in rows, and headphones. Children make an airplane out of a large box or blocks. Other props might include a control panel, tape deck, microphone, and old computer keyboard.

Beach

Props for this activity include sand in pools placed on tarps, towels, sunglasses, toy radios, magazines, stationery for writing letters, buckets, shovels, funnels, and animal figures. Other materials to include are fish shapes, fishing poles or nets, and posters of sea creatures.

Birthday Party

The class has a pretend birthday party at school. Children decorate a cake (whipped cream is fun), make birthday cards, sing "Happy Birthday," and wear party hats. When the children finish making their cards, the interventionist reminds them to write their names. Each child takes a turn saying his or her name, age, and birthdate.

Boat

In a variation on the other transportation themes, a boat is made of a box, blocks, or carpet squares. Inventive props include paddles made out of cardboard and binoculars made out of paper rolls; life jackets, picnic lunches, backpacks, books, and toy cameras can be included.

Bus

The class makes a bus from a large refrigerator box, including a steering wheel, money box, play money, telephone, bus schedules, and newspaper. This activity encourages cooperative play as well as language and math skills. Children use their imaginations to decide where to go on the bus. The interventionist facilitates this play by having the group go on the bus during circle time. Children act out riding on the bus, getting off the bus, and pretending to see people and animals on the street. Extensions include children painting the bus or painting a mural on the bus.

Camping

The interventionist can introduce camping by asking, "What do we need for our camping trip?" A campground drama corner includes props such as a tent (sheets make good tents), a campfire (stones in a ring with blocks), cooking pots, backpack, water bottles, old blankets or bed rolls, and pictures of the forest and animals. Other props include flannel shirts, raincoats, boots, binoculars, maps, fishing rods, and a pretend stream.

Firefighter Play

A large refrigerator box can be transformed into a wonderful make-believe fire truck; props include tricycles, hats, and hoses. Opportunities can be provided for children to solve problems by asking them questions such as, "Can anybody think of how we can make a fire truck out of this box?" The "truck" may be created by an adult cutting the long side of the box with scissors or knife, and the children painting it with red paint. The interventionist can use strategies to elicit children's imaginative skills and engage in pretend play. Extensions of this activity are a discussion of fire safety at home and a fire drill.

Forest

The interventionist provides a big piece of paper on the floor for the creek, lake, or river. Children can help make magnetic fish in different colors and sizes and fishing rods, animal masks, and a bridge or trail made of blocks or carpet squares. Other props include backpacks, rocks, lifejackets, and a boat (real or pretend). The children can draw or paint big trees and add birds and other forest animals to the panorama. Extensions include a hike to a forest, feeding the birds at school, looking at real fish, and eating fish crackers for snack.

Grocery Store

A grocery store includes props such as a cash register, shopping carts, bags of different sizes, pretend food on shelves, and cardboard food containers. This activity encourages classification, object labeling, and cooperative play.

Hospital or Doctor's Office

A medical dramatic play center uses dolls and children as patients. The office has a telephone, note pads, pencils, typewriter, and waiting area with books and magazines. The interventionist provides bandages, plastic gloves, blankets, medical kits, and books about hospitals and doctors. This activity encourages cooperative play and language (e.g.,"You be the doctor and I will be the mom"). Signs such as "Quiet, Please" or "No Smoking" can be incorporated into the play.

Let's Go Fishing!

The class makes poles of strong, short sticks and string with a magnet attached to the end. Fish are made of different sizes, shapes, and colors, with a paper clip attached. A big piece of butcher paper on the floor serves as the stream. This activity can address motor and cognitive skills.

Post Office

Props for the post office include paper, writing tools such as pencils and crayons, scissors to cut out "stamps," envelopes, blue or white shirts with buttons or zippers for postal workers, play money, caps for mail carriers, a mailbag, a mailbox, and boxes and tape for packages. Children each make their own mailbox as a planned activity and then children and the interventionist can write and deliver mail to each other. This activity is useful for enhancing social, prereading, and prewriting skills.

Restaurant

For the restaurant, include menus, magnetic board and letters to post specials, placemats (make by writing the name of the restaurant on construction paper), note pads and pencils for taking orders, play money, cash register, chef hat, and pretend and real food. As an extension, the interventionist can take children out to a real restaurant.

Shoe Store

Props for this activity include old shoes of different sizes and with different closures, pencil and paper to record sales, shoe boxes, chairs, mirror, play money, cash register, and shoe ruler. This activity encourages social skills and classification and number concepts.

Spaceship

Props include an old computer keyboard for the control panel, headphones, flashlights, and large foam pieces or pillows under a large sheet that is taped down as the planet on which children walk. This activity enhances gross motor and sensory skills. Photos of planets and art activities to create a sun and moon can be incorporated.

Teddy Bear Picnic

Children bring their teddy bears to a picnic or tea party. The interventionist provides a special picnic basket with a blanket to spread out on the ground, napkins, pretend or real food items, and a tea set with plastic cups, saucers, and a tea pot. Fine motor and adaptive skills are addressed as children dress themselves and their bears for the event, help prepare food and drinks, use social dining skills, and clean up after the activity.

Theater

A large curtain can be hung from a frame such as a swing set for the stage. Children use dress-up clothes and construct props such as animal ears, tails, and masks for the play. Props include water-soluble face makeup, scarves, a ticket office, a telephone, and small platforms. The interventionist begins with a play that uses stories familiar to children, or children create new scenarios. An extension includes shadow puppets that use light and shapes on a large screen covered with white paper or a sheet.

Train

The children place chairs, boxes, or large blocks in a long line to make a pretend train. This can be a group activity at circle or incorporated into the dramatic play center. Props include ticket-making supplies, hats for conductors, and objects to be carried on the train. An extension to this activity is singing train songs as children and adults hold onto a long scarf and weave around the room, in the hallway, or outdoors. Children take turns being the engine and the caboose.

Veterinary Office

The veterinary office includes stuffed animals, medical tools, note pads and pencils, charts of animals, examining table, telephone, leashes, and kennels. Children can bring their pets to the office and use communication skills to ask for help and explain their problems. Cooperative play can be encouraged also.

Washing Babies

Children wash their baby dolls in tubs of water with soap and washcloths, dry their "babies" with towels, and dress them in doll clothes with different fasteners. Children enjoy expanding on the activity by shampooing and brushing the baby's hair or pretending to brush the baby's teeth. To keep dry, children can wear smocks that fasten with zippers, buttons, ties, or Velcro fasteners and can learn body parts as they bathe their babies. The interventionist models reading baby a book, tucking baby in, or rocking baby to sleep. This activity can be incorporated into house play as well as doctor's office or hospital dramatic play.

CONSTRUCTION/MANIPULATION ACTIVITIES

Block play and construction activities enhance cognitive, motor, and social skills. As children play with blocks, they learn balance and construction skills. Cooperation is encouraged as they build with a friend and pretend by adding props such as animals, cars, or people. Encourage construction activities during free play or use as a planned activity.

Blocks: Unit and Large

Unit blocks facilitate cognitive skills as children compare size, shape, weight, and balance. Children can also use their imaginations as they "build" their ideas. They experiment with gravity as they build and knock down towers. Large blocks are used to build ramps, bridges, and boats that children can actually walk on and sit on. Cardboard blocks allow children to experiment with a lightweight block that does not hurt anyone if it falls down. Blocks can be used to construct roads and paths as well as upright structures.

Box Town

The children make a pretend city, town, or neighborhood with boxes of many sizes and shapes. They will need tape, boxes, and paper. The class can take a walk or bus ride around town to look at houses, buildings, schools, parks, and roads. Boxes can be used to build replicas of what children observe.

Dressing Babies

Children practice tying and fastening as they dress their dolls in different outfits. The interventionist should provide dolls of many ethnic origins, dolls with disabilities, and clothes with various fasteners.

Feely Bag

Children gather small objects from a nature walk, such as leaves, flowers, pebbles, pinecones, and seeds, and put them in a bag or a large sock. Each child takes a turn putting a hand in the bag. The child feels the object without looking, describes the object, and tries to guess what it is.

Group Block Building for Circle

Children cooperate at circle time and build a block structure together that is photographed or saved for a time. Extensions include writing a story about the structure and adding people and other props.

Lacing Cards

Children cut out simple pictures of familiar objects from magazines, glue the pictures onto sturdy cardboard, and cover them with clear contact paper. The interventionist punches several holes around the outside of the picture with a hole punch and ties a shoestring or heavy piece of yarn through one of the holes. The other end of the string should have tape wrapped around it to make a firm tip. The child sews in and out around the card.

Large Constructions

Large or medium-size boxes taped together are used to facilitate dramatic play. Children help develop props such as a city bus by planning what is needed and then helping to find or create the necessary objects. One box can be used for different purposes (e.g., building, train, telephone booth, bus).

Manipulatives

Provide materials that can be manipulated, such as Legos, Duplos, Tinkertoys, puzzles, pegs and pegboards, geoboards, vinyl picture stick-ons, 1-inch cube blocks, wind-up toys, Play-Doh with rolling pins or cylindrical blocks, cookie cutters, plastic knives, and objects that make impressions.

Paper Chains

The children cut construction paper into approximately 1- by 5-inch strips and make a link by gluing or taping the two ends of a strip together. A chain is created by inserting the next strip through the link.

Paper Strip Constructions

Children cut construction paper into strips of various lengths and widths. A base is provided for each child to construct a sculpture using strips and tape. In an extension of this activity, several children can construct one sculpture working cooperatively together.

Stringing Activities

The interventionist ties a large knot in the end of a piece of heavy yarn or string and wraps a short piece of tape around the other end to make a firm tip. Children string items such as Cheerios, Froot Loops, macaroni, cut-up pieces of drinking straws, and beads. This is an activity children can do repeatedly, or they can make a product by tying the string ends and painting the "beads."

Weaving

Children weave items such as pipe cleaners, straws, yarn, ribbons, or twine onto materials such as green plastic berry baskets, Styrofoam trays with holes punched in them, or a weaving mesh. A variation of this activity is to hang large weaving mesh between two structures or trees and have several children weave various materials onto the mesh as a cooperative activity.

EXPLORATORY ACTIVITIES

Children learn many useful skills and concepts as they explore materials such as water, sand, cornmeal, birdseed, rice, and beans, as well as combinations of these materials, such as water and dirt (mud play), water and soap (bubbles), and water and cornstarch (oobleck). Classrooms often have a designated table for these activities indoors or a wading pool for them outdoors. Additional materials include cups and pitchers of various sizes, scoops and spoons, buckets, funnels, egg beaters, water wheels, and water pumps. Children practice adaptive skills as they get ready for activities and clean up afterward (e.g., dressing and undressing, washing and drying hands).

Activities that explore materials such as shaving cream, lotions, pudding, and whipped cream facilitate many cognitive skills and can be designed to practice prereading skills by encouraging children to sound out letters and words written in the material. These activities can be conducted on any surface that is easy to clean (with pudding it is helpful to have individual plates or cookie sheets for each child). Expansions of these activities include adding food coloring or tempera paints, sand or cornmeal (to explore tactilely), or Popsicle sticks to draw or write.

Bubbles

This activity is fun to do outside! The recipe for bubbles is a capful of dishwashing liquid (Dawn works well) and water, which children mix until bubbles begin to form. Children hold about 1/3 cup of this mixture in small paper cups and blow bubbles through straws. Bubble wands of all sizes can he used to blow larger bubbles. It is important that children blow through the straws in order to prevent the consumption of this mixture.

Children should practice blowing through straws because some children suck through the straw by mistake.

Bubble Prints

Food coloring is added to soapy water in a margarine tub. When children have produced a froth of bubbles, they lay a piece of white paper over the top. When the paper is lifted off, a "print" of the bubbles will remain.

Mud Play

A place is selected to set an empty wading pool to make mud. Large shovels and buckets for children to dig and carry dirt and large pitchers for water are provided. Cooperation will occur as children work together digging, carrying dirt, and mixing water, as well as during cleanup time. The interventionist should have children wear old clothing and have a change of clothing for them afterward.

Play-Doh

Play-Doh is an excellent material for activities that embed cognitive, motor, and social goals. The interventionist can include a variety of materials and arrange the environment to provide children many opportunities to practice targeted goals. Materials such as cookie cutters of various colors, shapes, and sizes, rolling pins of different sizes, plastic utensils, and miniature figures can be provided. The interventionist should present the materials in creative ways. For example, half the Play-Doh can be put in the refrigerator and half in the microwave to vary the temperature of the material and facilitate understanding of qualitative concepts.

Pudding Painting

The interventionist makes instant pudding (food color can be added), puts it on individual paper plates, and invites children to fingerpaint with it. Children will be surprised when they realize they can lick their fingers and might discuss how the pudding feels, tastes, and smells. Children can be encouraged to draw letters and names in the pudding.

Shaving Cream Fun

This activity provides opportunities for children to experiment with their sense of touch while fingerpainting on a surface with shaving cream. The interventionist prompts children to copy shapes in the shaving cream and provides props such as sticks, animals, and sponges.

Tasting Party

This activity is particularly interesting when a classroom is composed of children from diverse cultural backgrounds. The interventionist asks children about different foods they enjoy and asks caregivers what foods the children eat at home. A variety of foods can be provided for children to try, such as salsas, curries, sweet rice, sticky rice, and sushi.

Washing Objects

Children select many items to wash, such as dolls, clothes, tricycles, and trucks. One interventionist brought his car for the children to wash, with sponges, soap, hoses, and towels for drying. Children like to wash walls and need only sponges, spray bottles, soapy water, and towels.

Water/Sand Play

Materials other than water and sand (e.g., cornmeal, flour, beans, macaroni) can be substituted. The interventionist can provide materials such as cups of different sizes, pitchers, spoons, scoops, funnels, water wheels, and plastic animals. The children are allowed to fill and empty the water/sand table with big buckets that require two children to carry. A wading pool makes an excellent water container in the summer, and water activities include washing rocks, pouring with different containers, dribbling (poke holes in the bottom of a margarine tub), basting, mixing colors in ice cube trays with eye droppers, making coffee filter blotches, and transferring water with an eye dropper to a dry sponge ("Where did it go?"). Children also enjoy filling small containers such as film canisters or jar lids, and squeeze bottles invite children to experiment with water. Bubbles come out of squeeze bottles under the water, and water dribbles as the bottles are held upside down. All these activities enhance motor skills.

GAMES

Games promote thinking and memory skills as well as cooperation. In the early childhood setting, games should be noncompetitive. Board games are set up in an activity center, and large group games are played outside or at circle time.

A Polar Bear Is Sleeping

This game can be adapted to use any animal. One child is in the middle of a circle of children who tiptoe around him or her singing, "A polar bear, a polar bear is sleeping in her cave" (Repeat once). "Speak very, very quietly in a whisper, because if you wake her, if you shake her, she'll get very mad!" (say the last part loudly.). Polar Bear wakes up and touches a child, who then becomes the next animal.

Blockhead

Two to four players play Blockhead with a variety of small blocks of different shapes. Each player has a turn to place a block on top of other blocks until the blocks fall over. As the blocks fall over, the players shout, "Blockhead!"

Board Games

Board games provide opportunities for children to participate in games with rules and provide practice in cognitive skills such as counting colors and shapes. Games such as Color or Shape Bingo, Candyland, and Chutes and Ladders and card games such as Go Fish and Old Maid can be included.

Duck, Duck, Goose

This is a favorite circle game of young children. Children sit in a circle as one child walks around the outside gently tapping heads and saying "Duck, duck, goose." When the child says "goose," the tapped child gets up and runs around the circle while being chased by the first child. The child who got up to run takes the next turn walking around the circle tapping heads.

Follow the Leader

One child or the interventionist is the leader, and the other children follow behind in a line, copying any movement the leader makes.

Group Outdoor Games

Ball games such as basketball, soccer, kickball, and baseball can be modified so that young children can participate. Small basketball and soccer balls are available, as are mini hoops and goals. Children enjoy practicing bouncing, catching, kicking, and throwing skills even though they may not be playing by the rules of the game.

Simon Says

Leader "Simon" gives directions to the other children. The leader calls out a command (e.g., "Simon says jump on one foot"), and the group follows Simon's direction and model. The instructions can be expanded to make this activity more cognitively challenging. If the leader does not precede a command with "Simon says," the children should not follow the direction. For example, if the leader calls out, "Put your hands on your head," the children do not follow the direction until the leader restates the command as, "Simon says put your hands on your head."

Teddy Bear Counting Game

This game requires two large wooden dice or homemade wooden dice. Teddy bear counters or other objects such as farm animals, plastic chips, or rocks are placed into a large basket. The dice are rolled and the numbers added up. Then that number of bears (or other counters) is removed from the large container and placed in front of the children. Children also roll the dice to count the bears and put them back into the basket.

What Time Is It, Mrs. Monster?

Mrs. Monster is a game played outside with a group of children. One child (the monster) faces the larger group as the children ask, "What time is it, Mrs. Monster?" The monster answers with a time such as three o'clock. Children take three steps toward the monster. When the monster says, "Dinner time," the children scatter so they will not be eaten! Whoever is caught becomes the monster.

What's Missing?

This game can be played with any assortment of objects. It is best to start with a small number of objects and increase the number as children become more competent. Children look at and identify objects. One child hides his or her eyes while another child removes an object, and then the first child guesses which item is missing.

LITERACY/COMMUNICATION ACTIVITIES

Literacy/communication involves the child as listener, speaker, writer, and reader. Children need many opportunities to experience oral and written language. Most children are interested in communicating and enjoy printing when activities are available that encourage experimenting with writing tools. Literacy props can be added to dramatic play centers, signs posted at activity centers, names written on artwork, and lists made of what children saw on a walk. Literacy/communication activities should be integrated into all aspects of the child's day. Activities especially designed to enhance the child's social-communication, motor, and cognitive skills follow.

Acting Out Stories

Children learn about the beginning, middle, and end of a story as they act out familiar stories such as *Caps for Sale, Mr. Gumpy's Outing* (Burningham, 1979), and *The Gunniwolf.* You can change characters or endings to eliminate stereotypes and violence.

Audiotape Recorder

This activity promotes communication and fine motor skills as the child operates the machine and controls the tape. An audiotape recorder is used to record the group when they sing or talk, and later the group can play it back, listen, and discuss what they heard.

Book Time

Book time is an integral part of any home or classroom. Books can be integrated into daily activities and presented at special times. The interventionist can model reading for children and encourage them to read on their own or with peers or to read a story to a puppet or stuffed animal. The interventionist should create an atmosphere of love for books.

Books/Book Making

Children enjoy drawing and writing in their own books. Plan books around a theme or create them during unstructured play time. Ideas for books include forest book, leaf book, "anything" journal, animal book, group story book, photo album, and a book about an experience or field trip. Books are made of paper of any size or quality. Children use markers and crayons to create their own illustrations and practice drawing or writing. The completed book can be stapled, taped, or sewn together by punching holes and threading them with yarn.

Group Story

A story can be written about almost anything, from a shared experience to, "I feel frightened when...." When children see their words become print, magic happens. They become excited about writing and reading when they realize there is a message to be discovered and transmitted.

Group Time

This activity is successful when children's voices can be heard in both song and speaking. Questions are used to facilitate children's expression of their feelings, thoughts, and ideas. Children like to choose a song, story, or game for the group. Interventionists should monitor children's behavior as group time proceeds and, when children get restless, the form or pace should be changed.

Making Lists

Writing down children's thoughts and ideas helps in developing literacy/communication skills. The interventionist can make a list of the animals seen at the farm, what children saw on the bus ride, and names of fruits or favorite foods.

Music

Children experiment with instruments and listen to and sing songs, chants, and play circle games. Music and movement contribute to learning self-esteem, language, and cooperation. The interventionist and children can sing about cleaning up, who is here today, and moving to another activity. Children can sing to their "babies" as they rock them.

Photo Albums

Children form attachments with parents, caregivers, and peers. Children practice language skills as they look at and talk about pictures of themselves and their family and friends at home and school.

Puppets

Puppets are used to enhance language, concepts, discussion about feelings, or problem solving. Puppets are "alive" for children, and they often talk to puppets about anything. Interventionists use puppets to facilitate social problem solving with children. Children can be allowed to operate the puppets, and access to puppets can be provided during any activity. Puppets can be created out of a variety of materials, such as paper bags, socks, sticks, construction paper, toilet paper rolls, or faces drawn on fingers.

Singing/Chants

Children's language skills are enhanced through repetition and rhythm. Chants and songs can be sung about anything at any time. For example, songs can be incorporated into routines such as transitions and group time. Chants and songs are found in many books and audiotapes, and instruments can be added to enhance the activity. Interventionists facilitate the children's exploration through modeling soft, loud, fast, and slow. Play instruments to tunes such as, "Play your instruments and make a pretty sound, play them fast, play them slow. Play the drums, stick, tone block,...." Children play along with a chant or music on tape and will make up their own songs if encouraged.

Specific Theme Books

Theme books include ME Book, My Animal Book, Our Trip to the Pumpkin Patch, I Feel, My Book of Fruit Prints, or others of interest to children.

The Writing Center

This activity invites children to regularly experiment with writing tools. They learn to hold a pencil correctly through practice and gain confidence when they can write or draw their own messages. This center can be located near the library or book area, integrated into the drama corner, or placed in a separate area.

Videotape

Most children are fascinated with seeing themselves on television. The interventionist can videotape the children giving a special presentation such as a puppet show or during regular play activities. The tape is shown to the group to stimulate language and discussion.

Water Music

Children experiment with tones by tapping jars filled with water. Glass jars provide the clearest tones, but safety should be considered when choosing containers. The interventionist should provide several sizes of containers for water and several items for tapping, such as blocks, spoons, or chopsticks. Children vary the amount of water in the jars and tap the jars to produce different sounds. Opportunities to demonstrate understanding of size concepts occur as the children use different sizes of containers, different levels of water, and different objects for tapping. This activity promotes listening, experimenting, and following directions.

MAKE-IT-CHANGE ACTIVITIES

Transformation of materials fascinates young children and helps them understand their world. Examples include flour when water is added or crayons when they are melted. Make-it-Change activities enhance math, science, problem-solving, and language skills.

Applesauce

The interventionist reads the story *Rain Makes Applesauce*. Children cut up apples to make applesauce and need only plastic knives, a cutting board, and a large bowl. Children add sugar and a small amount of cinnamon to the apples and transfer them to a cooking pot. The interventionist places the pot on the burner, adds a little water, and stirs occasionally, and the children watch the apples change!

Flour and Water Mixing

Children are given small bowls and spoons (tasting spoons from Baskin-Robbins work well). The interventionist places flour in small bowls or shaker bottles and provides water, eye droppers, and small pitchers. Children mix small amounts of water and flour and watch it change.

Fruit Salad

Children cut soft fruits such as bananas, watermelon, pears, and strawberries into chunks with plastic knives. They put the fruit in a bowl, stir in yogurt, sprinkle granola over the top, and eat their creations for snack. Children have opportunities to manipulate objects as they get ready, participate, and clean up.

Ivory Snow and Water

Ivory Snow and water are mixed into a heap of lather. This activity can be done at a sensory table, on a flat table, or in containers.

Making Bread

The interventionist chooses a favorite quick bread recipe such as zucchini bread. The children gather all necessary ingredients and utensils and measure the ingredients, stir the batter, butter the pan, and help clean up.

Melted Crayon Art

This activity invites children to observe the properties of color mixing and solids turning to liquids. Materials needed are a warming tray, unquilted aluminum foil, crayon stubs, a variety of paper, paper towels, and a pencil with an eraser. The tray is covered with smooth, heavy-duty foil or two sheets of regular foil, folding over the edges and pressing so the foil does not slip off. When the tray is warm, the children draw on the foil with crayon stubs. The crayon markings will melt on the foil. When the children are satisfied with their designs, they place a piece of paper over the top of the foil and the drawing. The paper is pressed firmly using the eraser end of a pencil and then lifted to remove the design. The designs can be lovely. The excess wax should be wiped from the foil with a paper towel before using the tray again. Adults must supervise activity with the warming tray, but children can do the artwork independently.

Smoothies

Smoothies are a nutritious shake made by blending together different fruits (e.g., bananas, strawberries), juices, and anything else that tastes good and blends well (e.g., yogurt, milk, wheat germ). Children choose what they want in their smoothies and must be sure to include enough liquid to blend easily. Children count how many seconds it takes to blend their smoothies.

Super Soup/Stone Soup

After reading the story *Stone Soup*, the interventionist invites the children to participate in making soup by washing and cutting vegetables and combining vegetables, broth, and spices. Opportunities can be provided for children to sample foods of different textures (e.g., cooked meat, raw and cooked vegetables).

Toilet Paper and Water

Toilet paper and water can be mixed together and then molded into interesting sculptures and dried. Large pans of water are used to allow children to wet the paper and watch it change.

MAKE-IT-MOVE ACTIVITIES

Children learn about their physical world in part through interacting with objects, as when a baby accidentally bats a ball and it rolls. Children need to understand the physical attributes of their world to advance cognitively. The following activities may enhance a child's knowledge of the physical world.

Fun with Straws

In this activity, children use straws to blow objects (e.g., Ping-Pong balls, feathers, blocks) across different surfaces such as tabletops and water. Children can be encouraged to experiment with blowing objects and to compare and contrast attributes of the objects they are blowing (e.g., "Is the feather harder or easier to blow than the Ping-Pong ball", "What do you think would happen if you used two straws?"). The interventionist should allow time for reflection. "What happened when you blew on the block? Why didn't it move?"

Make-it-Move Painting

This activity promotes cooperation, motor skills, and creativity. One child puts paper on a lazy Susan or old record player and draws as the wheel turns. The interventionist provides markers or paint and paper cut to the size and shape of a turntable on a record player, with a hole poked in the middle. Children work together by having one friend spin the turntable while the other draws. This activity requires adult supervision.

Ramps

Ramps are made from wooden planks or from cardboard or Plexiglas tubes of varying lengths that are supported at an angle by a chair, crate, or block. The interventionist should offer materials such as balls of various sizes and weight, marbles, and cars or trucks of various sizes, as well as objects that slide rather than roll. Children experiment with how the height of the plank affects speed and the distance the objects move. Opportunities for children to participate in activities, learn new concepts, categorize, sequence, solve problems, and demonstrate premath skills can be embedded within this activity.

Targets

Children love to throw objects at a target, such as bags into movable containers. Children can also set up plastic bowling pins or roll balls at large, soft cardboard blocks. Mini targets can be developed using blocks and small rolling objects on a table with sides or a container. These activities promote problem solving and knowledge of the physical world.

NATURE ACTIVITIES

The natural world is a wonderful tool to help children understand themselves in relation to their environment. Children learn about animals through observation, touch, and experience. Children can learn much about nature and their environment through hands-on experiences. For example, during an outdoor walk in the fall, children collect leaves, find seeds, observe squirrels scurrying about, and feel the temperature getting cooler. Through learning respect for the natural world that includes bugs, birds, animals, and plants, children's curiosity is stimulated and they learn to appreciate beauty.

Bird Binoculars

Children make binoculars with toilet paper rolls and colored or clear cellophane. Children decorate the rolls with markers, tape or staple them together, cover the ends with colored cellophane, and attach a string. When the binoculars are completed, it is time to take a bird walk!

Bug Search

This activity can help alleviate children's fear of bugs. Children become involved in looking for insects on the playground or surrounding area and collect them to observe for a short time. To prepare for this activity, children can look around the classroom for containers that might be usable. The interventionist can ask questions about what is needed (e.g., "Do we need a lid?", "Does it need holes?"). To find bugs, children theorize about where bugs live (in eggs, under rocks, under the ground). *Note:* Make sure this activity is safe and that the bugs found are not poisonous. Children should treat the living creatures with respect and return them to their home. Children can also observe the bugs in their natural habitats, such as a spider on its web.

Collections Walk

Children love collecting pieces of nature. The class can take a walk in any season and pick up items found on the ground. Fall is particularly interesting, with colorful leaves, nuts, seeds, and flowers. These objects can be placed on a sensory table to examine or made into individual or group collages.

Exploratory Table

The interventionist fills a table with nuts, leaves, shells, moss, flower petals, sand, and shells and allows the children to examine or use the materials in a variety of ways.

Expressive Arts

The class can dramatize stories such as *The Three Bears* or *The Gunniwolf*, or pantomime, "We're going on a lion hunt. We're not afraid. What's that up ahead? Big, tall grass (or a mountain or a river). We can't go over it, we can't go around it, we can't go under it. I guess we'll have to go through it." Children make movements (arms moving forward and back) and sounds (swish, swish) as if they are moving through tall grass, over a great big mountain, or across a river. The interventionist can elicit children's ideas about how they will get across the river or up the mountain. "When you find the lion, take a picture of it and run, run, run back the way you came." Many children love this activity and may ask for it daily. The interventionist should listen to the children for ideas and adapt and make up the story as they go along. Puppets can also be used.

Feed the Birds

The interventionist can instill respect for the world's living creatures in the children by inviting birds to the playground with sunflower seeds, suet, and water. This activity provides an opportunity for children to practice a variety of language skills.

Leaf Prints

Leaves of all shapes and sizes are placed on a table. Children dip leaves in paint and print with them on paper.

Leaf Rubbings

The children take a walk and gather leaves in small bags. Leaf rubbings are made by placing a piece of lightweight paper over a leaf and rubbing a crayon over the top of the paper.

Litter Walk

Children and the interventionist take a litter walk to identify litter that should be in garbage cans. Children wear plastic gloves to put litter in garbage bags.

Pinecone Birdfeeders

In small groups, children spread peanut butter on large or medium-size pinecones and then roll the pinecones in birdseed to make birdfeeders. The interventionist can enhance children's problem solving by posing questions such as, "I wonder how we can put the peanut butter on the cone?", "Where should we put the feeders so the birds can get them?", or " How can we put them on the high branches?" The interventionist should listen to and attempt to use the children's ideas even if they will not work.

Planting a Garden

Planting a garden can be a rewarding project for children. Because this activity involves several steps (e.g., hoeing the ground, planting the seeds, watering the ground, weeding), it provides opportunities for children to retell events in sequence. Reading a story about growing things (e.g., *The Carrot Seed*) gives children information about the sequence of events. Children and the interventionist keep a record of planting, sprouting, and so forth and retell the sequence of events.

Seedy Faces or Seedy Collage

A face is carved in a pumpkin or other vegetable. Later, children use dried pumpkin seeds or birdseed to make faces on paper (gluing the seeds down). The class can take a walk in fall to collect seeds and grasses to make a collage.

REFERENCES

Brown, M. (1986). *Stone soup*. New York: Macmillan.

Burningham, J. (1970). *Mr. Gumpy's outing*. New York: Holt, Rinehart & Winston.

Evans, J. (1979). *The three bears*. Allen, TX: Developmental Learning Materials.

Harper, W. (1967). *The Gunniwolf*. New York: Dutton.

Hoff, S. (1985). *Danny & the dinosaur*. Scranton, PA: HarperCollins.

Kraus, R. (1989). *The carrot seed*. Scranton, PA: HarperCollins.

Scheer, J. (1964). *Rain makes applesauce*. New York: Holiday House.

Sendak, M. (1963). *Where the wild things are*. New York: Scholastic.

Slobodkina, E. (1968). *Caps for sale*. Scranton, PA: HarperCollins.

Preschool Curricula with Similar Goals

The following preschool curricula provide additional programming strategies for many of the goals and objectives in the AEPS Curriculum for Three to Six Years. The Domain Goals sections of the curriculum specify the areas of particular relevance to the various target goals.

The Carolina Curriculum
for Preschoolers with Special Needs

Paul H. Brookes Publishing Co.
Post Office Box 10624
Baltimore, MD 21285-0624
(800) 683-3775 Telephone
(410) 337-8539 Fax

The Creative Curriculum

Teaching Strategies
Post Office Box 42243
Washington, DC 20015
(202) 362-7543 Telephone
(800) 637-3652 Telephone
(202) 364-7273 Fax

High Scope—Young Children in ACTION

The High/Scope Press
High/Scope Educational Research Foundation
600 North River Street
Ypsilanti, MI 48198
(313) 485-2000 Telephone
(313) 485-0704 Fax

Peabody Developmental Motor Scales Activity Cards

Riverside Publishing Co.
Attn: Clinical
8420 Bryn Mawr Avenue
Chicago, IL 60631
(800) 767-8378 ext. 360 or 361

Portage Guide to Early Education Activity Cards

The Portage Project
CESA #5
Post Office Box 564
Portage, WI 53901
(608) 742-8811 ext. 264

INDEX

Page numbers followed by *t* or *f* indicate tables or figures, respectively.